# Modernism, Periodicals, and Cultural Poetics

# Modernism, Periodicals, and Cultural Poetics

Matthew Chambers

MODERNISM, PERIODICALS, AND CULTURAL POETICS
Copyright © Matthew Chambers, 2015.

Permissions

The text of Chapter 2 was in part originally published as an article in *Language and Literary Studies of Warsaw* 3 (2013).

The text of Chapter 4 was in part originally published as an article in the *Journal of British and Irish Innovative Poetry* 5:2 (2013).

All rights reserved.

First published in 2015 by PALGRAVE MACMILLAN® in the United States—a division of St. Martin's Press LLC, 175 Fifth Avenue, New York, NY 10010.

Where this book is distributed in the UK, Europe and the rest of the world, this is by Palgrave Macmillan, a division of Macmillan Publishers Limited, registered in England, company number 785998, of Houndmills, Basingstoke, Hampshire RG21 6XS.

Palgrave Macmillan is the global academic imprint of the above companies and has companies and representatives throughout the world.

Palgrave® and Macmillan® are registered trademarks in the United States, the United Kingdom, Europe and other countries.

ISBN: 978-1-137-54135-2

Library of Congress Cataloging-in-Publication Data

Chambers, Matthew, 1978–
   Modernism, periodicals, and cultural poetics / Matthew Chambers.
      pages cm
   Includes bibliographical references and index.
   ISBN 978-1-137-54135-2 (hardback)  1. English poetry—20th century—History and criticism.  2. Modernism (Literature)—Great Britain.  3. Literature and society—Great Britain—History—20th century.  4. Periodicals—Publishing—Great Britain—History—20th century.  I. Title.
   PR478.M6C467 2015
   821'.912—dc23
                                                            2015005020

A catalogue record of the book is available from the British Library.

Design by Amnet.

First edition: July 2015

10   7 6 5 4 3 2 1

For Karolina Krasuska

# Contents

| | |
|---|---|
| Acknowledgments | ix |
| Introduction | 1 |
| 1  Standards of Criticism | 21 |
| 2  The English in English Surrealism | 55 |
| 3  Popular Poetry and Mass-Observation | 77 |
| 4  The Politics of Reception | 109 |
| Conclusion: Periodical Formations, Anthologies, and Canons | 137 |
| Notes | 147 |
| Bibliography | 181 |
| Index | 197 |

# Acknowledgments

The seeds for the idea of this book can be found in the Buffalo literary community at large with all the years of readings, performances, chapbooks, and magazines. In particular, Craig Reynolds and Leah Rico for Murder the Word, Big Orbit Gallery, and Soundlab, the staff at Rust Belt Books for the venue, Second Reader Bookshop for the friendship, and Jonathon Welch and the staff at Talking Leaves for the community and the belief.

I thank my colleagues and friends at SUNY Buffalo for their energy, time, insight, and company; I would like to specifically acknowledge Richard Owens, Margaret Konkol, Justin Parks, Divya Victor, Stephanie Farrar, Sarah Hogan, Matt Garite, Alex Porco, Jonathan Skinner, Linda Russo, Chris Alexander, Michael Kelleher, Kyle Schlesinger, and Barbara Cole. Among my friends and vital members of the Buffalo literary community, who gave me more than I can repay, I would like to thank John and Dana Rigney, Kevin Thurston, Ric Royer, Jessica Smith, Aaron Lowinger, Chris Fritton, Robin Brox, John Long, Paul and Karma Martone, Matthew Bottiglieri, and Jen Lees. Additional thanks to the Sparts community, especially Ron Kittle for all the cheer, as well as Jimy Chambers, Kevin Corbett, Michael Bouquard, and Brandon Delmont for the time with Odiorne. Additional thanks to Neil Pattison, Sean Bonney, Frances Kruk, Keston Sutherland, Sophie Robinson, Andrea Brady, Matt ffytche, Emily Critchley, Andrew Frayn, Eric White, Tony Lopez, and Larry Lynch.

I would like to thank David Schmid for guiding me through my writing and thinking. I hope this book in some way reflects his insight, feedback, and investment in me. I thank Cristanne Miller for improving my writing and for underlining the value of textual criticism and Damien Keane for always asking challenging questions. I would additionally like to thank Keith Tuma for his valuable insight from afar and for his ongoing promotion of British poetry to an American audience. Charles Bernstein, Robert Creeley, Susan Howe, Rachel Blau DuPlessis, Peter Quartermain, Steve McCaffery, and Karen MacCormack all profoundly influenced my thinking on poetry and the inherent value of poetry communities. Also, thanks to Jason Harding and Sean Latham for graciously responding to my out-of-the-blue requests. Finally, special thanks to Wiesław and Elżbieta Oleksy for giving me a home at the Transatlantic and Media Studies Center, University of Łódź.

This book owes much to the holdings and staff at libraries in the United States and the United Kingdom. My greatest debt is to the Poetry Rare Books Room at SUNY Buffalo. James Maynard and the entire staff were as great a resource as the archive itself. In particular, my thanks to the curator, Michael Basinski, for his endless amount of time and help. I owe much to Mike's friendship over the years. I am also indebted to Richard Price and the staff at the British Library for making available material difficult to find in the United States. Furthermore, the staff and collection at the Cambridge University Library aided some key moments in this writing.

All my love and thanks to the Chambers, Fischer, and Rico families, especially my mother, brother, and sister, who have been through so much with me. None of this would have been possible without you. A special thank you to my mother-in-law for making the time and the commitment to me. And finally, to my wife Karolina and our daughters, everything.

# INTRODUCTION

In the September 20, 1923, issue of the *Times Literary Supplement*, an unsigned review of T. S. Eliot's *The Waste Land* appeared. The review, later attributed to Edgell Rickword, opens by asserting that "between the emotion from which a poem rises and the reader there is always a cultural layer of more or less density from which the images or characters in which it is expressed may be drawn" (178). The "cultural layer," also referred to as the "middle ground" between the poem and the reader, is judged to be obscured by "this refractory haze of allusion," and as a result "there is in general in [Eliot's] work a disinclination to awake in us a direct emotional response" (178). The review establishes a schema for a poem's reception: a transit from the poem through the cultural layer to the reader. Rickword does not clarify what this layer consists of, or is bounded by, but in his critique of *The Waste Land*'s "refractory haze of allusion," it can be surmised that uniformity, consistency, and transparency are desirable aspects. What is striking, then, about this review is Rickword's culturalist emphasis, and, in turn, his opinion that there can be a certain degree of appropriate structuring of this layer—in other words, that there exists a more or less correct level of mediation (or "middle ground") between the poem and the reader, and furthermore, that that level can be identified and assessed. Ultimately, if the requirement is that the poem elicits a "direct emotional response," then there must be a singular readership similarly bound by a shared culture.

*Modernism, Periodicals, and Cultural Poetics* addresses how late modernist poetry in Britain tended precisely toward a culturalist expression that shaped the perception of poetry's role in solidifying an ethnolinguistic English identity. Importantly, it demonstrates how this process occurred within the pages of literary periodicals and was shaped by their specific modes of functioning within the sphere of cultural production. I use the term "periodical formations" to describe networks of exchange within and between different literary periodicals that condition the types of poetry published and the kinds of poetic discourse that come to cohere and predominate. Recent publications have clearly signaled how active, widespread, and absolutely central literary magazines were to modernist literary production: for example, Richard Price and David Miller's *British Literary Magazines, 1914–2000: A History and Bibliography of "Little Magazines"* (2006); Peter Brooker and Andrew Thacker's *The Oxford Critical and Cultural History of Modernist Magazines* (2009); and the recently established *Journal of Modern Periodical Studies* all indicate a resurgent interest in modernist literary magazines. A reemphasis on periodical production following the publication of Eliot's *The Waste Land* and culminating with a transitional set of magazines in the 1940s illustrates a complex and diverse series of debates and negotiations about not only the tradition of English poetry and its role in contemporaneous form, but also how poetry of the period related to the avant-garde trends prominent on the European continent and in America.

Periodicals have been source material for modernist studies and in some cases have been utilized to make overarching structural claims. For example, Michael Levenson argues in *The Genealogy of Modernism* that T. S. Eliot's *The Waste Land* was the provocation of English modernism directed at and against traditional forms, but the magazine it first appeared in—Eliot's *Criterion* (1922–39)—was its consolidation (167). The poem was originally published in *Criterion*, and Levenson characterizes the site of its publication as a study in contrasts: "If the poem threatened to outrage, the intellectual pedigree of the adjacent essays provided reassurance . . . [as they were] reputable, restrained, even staid" (213). The longevity and respectability of *Criterion*'s run resulted in the legitimization of Eliot's experiment. *Criterion* was a site where a unified vision of literature could be articulated, defended, and propagated over time and in response to competing articulations. Jason Harding insists that "consideration of the institutional role of *Criterion* in the cultural and intellectual debates of the interwar period necessitates constant attention to the periodical *qua* periodical" (1). Harding counters Levenson's generalization with a call for a rigorous review of the details of *Criterion*'s publishing history, especially in relation to other literary magazines, as "literary journalism is not a private speculation in a vacuum, rather an intervention in an ongoing cultural conversation, most immediately a dialogue with a shifting set of interlocking periodical structures and networks" (1). Most importantly, centering periodicals as the site where poetic claims were presented and contested fleshes out a literary period too often reviewed under the terms and production of its most canonical figures.

This work utilizes Jason Harding's work on periodicals as one possible way to think beyond the canon by reemphasizing periodical production following the publication of Eliot's *The Waste Land*. For Harding, treating Eliot's periodical within its social and historical context provides a more nuanced understanding not only of the periodical itself but also of the period in which it was published. More complex than a straightforward illustration of Eliot's intellectual development, the periodical networks *Criterion* was engaged in demonstrate the "centrality of print journalism" for the interwar period, which requires "the modern reader to develop an awareness of the complexity of the reception of these commonly hotly contested debates by multiple interpretative communities" (2). Harding, in treating *Criterion* as centrally involved in a specific set of periodical networks, prioritizes the literary journal as the core genre of literary development in the interwar period. Harding's periodization is one common to studies of early twentieth-century British literature, which treat 1939 as an *annus horribilis* for British society as a whole, and indeed for much of the world, and it thus delimits a literary period with a military event. Indeed, there is much evidence that is used within a narrow literary frame to suggest that 1939 was the end of a period: even more strictly within the scope of literary magazines, not only *Criterion* but other influential journals such as *New Verse* and the *Left Review* had ceased publication by that year. Paper rationing and a prohibition against beginning new magazine titles in the early part of the war additionally meant that there were few titles whose runs extended into the 1940s. However, certain literary debates that had thrived in the 1930s—Romanticism vs. Classicism, poetry and belief, as well as the influence (or rejection) of Auden's poetry—persisted into the 1940s, most notably in the pages of *Poetry (London)*, a journal widely considered then and now as the central location of poetry publishing in Britain in the 1940s.[1] Vitally, many of these debates express a culturalist dimension that is not always tethered to Eliot and *Criterion*. Instead, they reflect what Jed Esty terms the "romance of retrenchment," or "to reclaim territorial and cultural integrity for English culture was to disavow the history of British expansionism while assimilating the anthropological (and colonial) notion of solidarity back to the core" (39). Read in the context of the shift from high to late modernism in the 1930s in Britain, this means that "if high modernism offered a *cosmopolitan-aesthetic* mediation of universal perspectives and their local antithesis, then late modernism represents a new *national-cultural* mediation of the universal and the local" (Esty 36). In this work, this diagnosis is applied to the study of literary periodicals where the claims for poetry and a sense of Englishness productively overlap.

## Reapproaching Late Modernism in England

Writing on post–*Waste Land* British modernism tends to present literary production in terms of this increasing cultural insularity. Krishan Kumar argues that such policing of English identity in the interwar period did not result in strong nationalist claims, partly as a result of the ramifications of the nationalist ideological drive of the First World War, and instead English nationalism "saw itself in a quieter, more introspective mode" (232–33). Jed Esty also refers to this shift as "demetropolitanization," or the retrenchment of a nationalist perception from a metropolitan one. Esty argues that "contraction was both a material predicate and an available metaphor for the revival of cultural integrity in midcentury England . . . [and] if expansion had exacerbated . . . the fundamental unknowability of

English society as a totality, then contraction mitigated . . . that unknowability" (47). Indeed, how Eliot envisions his place, and the place of *Criterion*, was symbolic of a broader structural trend within English modernist poetry from the late 1920s to the late 1940s: validating projects in an English poetic tradition, as well as claiming the cultural centrality of the work.[2]

I refer to this period as "late modernist" against the popular reading of the term as a post–World War II phenomenon. This book works partially from Tyrus Miller's framing of the term. He argues that "the late modernist response to modernism is inseparable from its emergence as a *historically* codified phenomenon . . . [as modernism] had to have become in a way 'historical'" (22–23). For Miller, late modernism is necessarily tied to high modernism as an "allegory" of the latter's demise. Late modernist work more readily engaged with the cultural and political context it was writing from, reflecting the increasingly fraught international political situation in the 1930s, and additionally it challenged the "relatively strong symbolic forms still evident in high modernist texts" (20). And yet, it is important to underline that it is an Anglo-American shift from high to late modernism that Miller outlines. For example, Peter Nicholls, in his *Modernisms*, identifies James Joyce's *Ulysses* as the seminal text of high modernism and links a group of contemporaries of Joyce—T. S. Eliot, Ezra Pound, Wyndham Lewis, and Virginia Woolf—to declare that their "family resemblances" could be characterized by an emphasis on the "self's unoriginality, its embeddedness in a complex tradition." For Nicholls, high modernism describes a "polemical thrust given . . . to an antimimetic art . . . directed against the imitative tendencies associated with the mass politics of a democratic age" (251). High modernism, in short, is best described as a literary tendency in a small group of Anglo-American writers that emphasized aesthetic formalism over subjective or political expression.

Miller's perspective on late modernism, diagnosing its strengthened cultural and political emphasis, fits into newer and larger trends in modernist studies focusing on its embeddedness in historicity and its cultural conditioning. In fact, the field of work has become so expansive, it would be difficult to name enough representative examples, but sticking to those that foreground periodicals as an object of study, Suzanne W. Churchill, Eric White, Adam McKible, Mark Morrison, and Faith Binckes, among many, many others, have all presented approaches of how we need to think about modernisms in their immediate context.[3] Recently, in calling for the consideration of a "planetary aesthetics of modernism," Susan Stanford Friedman argues that we need to rethink the aesthetic requirements for considering modernist form, as they have historically been conditioned by terms set in a European core. Friedman argues that we need to "provincialize" such modernisms "as ONE articulation of a particularly situated modernism—an important modernism but not the measure by which all others are judged and to which all others must be compared" (487). Despite Nicholls's careful attention to a multiplicity of modernisms, he leaves his European-centered construction unproblematized, and more relevant to this writing, he commits the same oversight with high modernism—i.e., at no point does he interrogate the Anglo-American dimension of high modernism. What is most significant about Friedman's treatment of high modernism is that she relativizes high modernism among a geographical plurality of equally significant modernisms. What this book argues is that this "relativization" is indeed actually part of the rhetorical logic of late modernist poetry in Britain, and thus Friedman's argument that we need to focus on other modernisms globally can effectively be used to claim closer attention to the retrenchment of English identity.

## Periodical Formations

Claims about movements, periods, and trends are overdetermined by the dominant form of media from which they are disseminated. Jason Harding proposes looking at this conditioning when framing the development of modernism in his essay "Modernist Poetry and the Canon":

> It involves tracing the emergence of the new poetic in the avant-garde "little magazines" established just before or during the

First World War; the subsequent discussion of this poetry in the critical reviews of the interwar period; culminating in the institutional consolidation of a revolutionary poetic moment in university textbooks and syllabuses after the Second World War. (225)

Following Harding's claim about the developing modernism "in the critical reviews of the interwar period," this book focuses on periodicals that temporally coincide with the disciplinary interest in canon formation. For example, Hugh Kenner identifies F. R. Leavis's *New Bearings* (1932), a book we will return to in the first chapter, as "an intelligent start at canon-defining" (365). In other words, to rephrase E. P. Thompson's famous phrase that opens *The Making of the English Working Class*, "The English literary canon was present at its own making."[4] By analyzing periodicals, the nature of the rise and solidification of those canonical structures can be laid bare. There are clearly many more magazines contemporary with the ones reviewed here, and this puts real constraints on the kinds of claims that can be made about the period in which they are produced. In taking a few of the better-known magazines, such as *Scrutiny* and *New Verse*, and setting them next to some more obscure ones, such as *The Calendar of Modern Letters* and *Contemporary Poetry and Prose*, connections to trends and debates among other books and magazines can be brought into focus.[5]

One core issue at stake is how do we think about, for example, *Scrutiny*, which primarily functioned as a literary review, in relation to *New Verse*, which is best known for publishing poetry and could be better classified as a "little magazine," when both were centrally engaged in the shaping of poetic production in 1930s Britain. In 2006, Sean Latham and Robert Scholes argued in "The Rise of Periodical Studies" that "as digital archives become increasingly available, we must continue to insist on the autonomy and distinctiveness of periodicals as cultural objects (as opposed to 'literary' or 'journalistic' ones) while attempting to develop the language and tools necessary to examine, describe, and contextualize them" (519–20). Robert Scholes and Clifford Wulfman, in *Modernism in the Magazines*, propose that "instead of assigning a single signifier to a magazine (*little* versus *mass*, for example), we need to identify a set of characteristics that contribute to our understanding of the magazines and then cluster them in different ways . . . a *language of magazines*" (70). In other words, periodical studies have recognized a broad range of styles, formats, and even economies of scale, and this both justifies the analysis of periodicals as objects of study and raises the issue of classification, framing, and naming.

I use the term "periodical" over "little" or "literary" magazine to emphasize the regularity and rootedness these publications projected (as opposed to the purposeful immediacy and kinetic irruption attempted by Wyndham Lewis's *Blast* and *Tyro*). Scholes and Wulfman address the historical development and construction of such terminology. "Periodical," they argue, expresses a general category that includes any publication "issued at regular or irregular intervals" (45). A "magazine," which originally meant a storehouse for items, by the early twentieth century also included the meaning of periodicals that "collected and published a miscellany of textual objects" (46). "Journal" or "review," they explain, is often used distinctly from magazine.

> There is still . . . a connotation of seriousness attached to the word *review* and of frivolity attached to *magazine*. No learned journal would call itself a magazine. The word *journal* itself is derived from *diurnal*, or daily, but it lost that specificity very early in both English and French and is now just a synonym for *periodical*. (46)

Many of the periodicals in this writing, with these definitions, would be considered "magazines," with the possible exception of *Scrutiny* (more rightly thought of as a "review"). The idea of the "little magazine" further complicates matters, as Scholes and Wulfman point out: "The *lit* in *little* suggests literariness in the context of magazines, and the notion of a 'little magazine' connotes cuteness as well" (56). In other words, "literary," in their estimation, "combines a generic and a qualitative signification," and words like "little" or "mass" "are in fact modernist notions, designed to make an invidious division into versions of 'high' and 'low'" (61).[6] As "periodical" most broadly describes the varying types of publications analyzed without also prescribing a set of assumptions of their content, I use this term throughout.

Harding uses the concept of "networks" to foreground the flow of the exchange between Eliot, *Criterion*, and certain corresponding periodicals. I prefer the term "formations" to "networks" to emphasize how exchanges and interactions between publications and authors can sediment. Hence, I use the term "formations" and not "networks" to characterize the interrelationships of periodicals in the 1920s, 1930s, and 1940s, to emphasize how these exchanges were not free floating and were indeed engaged in rhetorical power struggles. I take my cue from Peter Brooker and Andrew Thacker's walk through Raymond Williams's thinking on "cultural formations" in their introduction to *The Oxford Critical and Cultural History of Modernist Magazines*, where they highlight the complex space periodicals inhabit in modernist discourse. As Brooker and Thacker paraphrase Williams, a cultural formation is "a formal or informal association of individuals engaged in some nature of cultural production which in turn sets them in different relations with broader trends in society" (18). Williams develops a tripartite structure for both the "internal organization" and "external relations" of a formation.[7] The second form of "internal organization" is most relevant to our discussion here: "those [organizations] not based on formal membership, but organized around some *collective public manifestation*, such as an exhibition, a group press or periodical, or an explicit manifesto" (68). Williams's listing of a "group press or periodical" as a "collective public manifestation" points to the value of analyzing magazines in their historical context, as the manner in which literary periods rise, cohere, and are memorialized is seldom the result of isolated actors or publications. Brooker and Thacker's take on this assertion by Williams emphasizes the way it "reveals how formations change over time: encompassing the often characteristic relations between magazines of imitation, rivalry, and competition or of their amalgamation, evolution, and decline" (20). Thinking of periodicals as cultural formations entails an approach that is sensitive to the hegemonic structure that produces certain aspects of their production as well as the individualistic or local conditions that take shape briefly, intermittently, or even in ways that do not suit master narratives of the period in which they are found.

Andrew Thacker with David Peters Corbett, in discussing "cultural formations," argue that the "point of the term 'formation' rather than 'group' is that it expresses its relation to the general social history, and its extension into the specific forms and practices of the group, aesthetic or otherwise" (91). Citing Williams's "The Uses of Cultural Theory," they establish why treating artistic developments as "formations" is most useful. They point to Williams's argument that cultural activity is "extending and interpenetrating," and thus it is "the *congruence* of discourses—the intersection of, say, the aesthetic and the economic—that creates the character of the formation" (97). To treat literary periodicals as "formations" is to foreground their own complex social character as the character of the groups they are traditionally associated with. Several of the literary magazines analyzed in this writing have been commonly associated with well-defined literary historical groups—*Scrutiny* with the Cambridge School, *New Verse* with Auden and his peers, *Contemporary Poetry and Prose* with Surrealism, and *Poetry (London)* with the New Apocalypse. Yet none of these magazines can be reduced completely to these associations, and to do so papers over the complex nature of the multiple discourses in which they participated. Brooker and Thacker mildly criticize Williams's term "cultural formations" as a "broad concept . . . need[ing] a vocabulary for the embryonic, modest, or limited examples as well as the 'simple' and 'complex' formation Williams identifies" (20). They leave, in their capacity as editors, the refinement of this term to their contributors, and in this writing, one solution is offered that combines Harding's claim for the networked nature of periodical publication and Brooker and Thacker's articulation (via Williams) of periodicals as cultural formations—namely, periodical formations. In this way, the culturalist emphasis functions here both as a method and a diagnosis—as a method because it utilizes key approaches of Cultural Studies, centrally following Raymond Williams, Paul Gilroy, and Jahan Ramazani, among others, to foreground various processual modes of production of (literary) value. But, in reference to earlier work, such as Tyrus Miller's discussed above, it constitutes an essential part of the thesis in the change of emphasis in British late modernist poetry and poetics. What may seem at first a theoretical and methodological conflation is disentangled in the analysis in Chapter 1 zeroing in on the periodical formation cohering around *The Calendar of Modern Letters* and *Scrutiny* that both shaped late modernist poetics and served as an early foundation for British Cultural Studies.

## THE LONG SHADOW OF I. A. RICHARDS

One clear and present figure in periodical formations in the late 1920s and 1930s is, of course, T. S. Eliot. However, there is another powerfully felt influence who arguably had an even broader, if not as explicitly stated, impact on poetic development in the 1920s and 1930s: I. A. Richards. The "long shadow of I. A. Richards" is cast simultaneously with Eliot's but is often overlooked, as it is so embedded in the discourse that it often appears as common sense. His emphasis on the psychological aspects of reading, his faith in poetry as central to lived experience, and his expression of a universal "reader" that was entirely coded as "English"—all of these ideas greatly impacted the various culturalist expressions of poetry in late modernist Britain. Richards's influence on literary criticism is much better understood, but his immediate impact on the discourse surrounding the kinds of poetic production prevalent from the early 1920s to the end of the 1940s has not been fully appreciated.

In the 1920s, in his teachings and publications (*The Principles of Literary Criticism* [1924], *Science and Poetry* [1926], and *Practical Criticism* [1929]), I. A. Richards constructed a taxonomy for poetry: a system for assessing meaning and value in poems; he further argued that the proper reading of poetry could teach the readers as much about themselves and society as the meaning of the poem itself: "There is no gap between our everyday emotional life and the material of poetry" (*Practical Criticism* 300). Indeed, he insisted that encountering rhythm and meter in the poem was an act of "becoming patterned ourselves."[8] For Richards, experiencing rhythm and meter entails an internalization of commonly perceived patterns that assumes the reader is a universal particular: that is, that he or she inhabits a culturally undifferentiated space.[9] Most importantly, Richards's proclamations resonated as an ideological approach to thinking about English culture and society.

*Scrutiny* was the classic example of how poetry could be used to appeal to a specific tradition in order to legitimate specific culturalist claims. Francis Mulhern, in his study of *Scrutiny*, opens with a consideration of the Leavis circle's intellectual influences and situates Matthew Arnold—by way of Richards—as central to the magazine's defense first of the poet and then of the literary critic as the gatekeeper of a minority culture that represented the "best" of the English tradition. While discussing Richards's *Science and Poetry*, Mulhern foregrounds Richards's debt to Arnold's claim that poetry is most vital for English society.

> The sciences would henceforth rule alone in the domain of knowledge [after the dismissal of the now "redundant" old philosophies and religions], but in order to maintain the psychological coherence of existence, men and women "would be thrown back, as Matthew Arnold foresaw, upon poetry. It is capable of saving us; it is a perfectly possible means of overcoming chaos." (Richards qtd. in Mulhern 26–27)

As Mulhern indicates, this epigraph for *Science and Poetry* is the same one Arnold used for *The Study of Poetry*.[10] In that work, Arnold famously claimed that "religion has attached its emotion to the fact, and now the fact is failing." Alternatively, the "future of poetry is immense . . . [as] poetry attaches its emotion to the idea; the idea *is* the fact . . . The strongest part of our religion today is its unconscious poetry" (340). Arnold's use of "fact vs. idea" contrasts the ossification of religion to the dynamism of poetry, but more powerfully, Arnold secularizes a universalist vision for English society. He cites Aristotle's claim that "poetry is something more philosophic and of graver import than history since its statements are of the nature rather of universals, whereas those of history are singulars" to argue that the "superiority of poetry over history consists in its possessing a higher truth and a higher seriousness" (Aristotle qtd. in Arnold 473 fn. 16; Arnold 349). The extent to which one should seriously accept Arnold's, and later Richards's, defense of poetry as "capable of saving us" can be debated.[11] However, the effect of these statements on subsequent poets and critics in Britain was powerful. This is especially true following the publication of the lament for modern disintegration—*The Waste Land*—and the central position that poem took not only in debates over poetry and poetic form but in English society as a whole. Moreover, the fact that these debates primarily occurred within the pages of literary periodicals ultimately argues for a more extensive and careful consideration of these periodicals and the cultural formations they participated in shaping.

In the period between the publication of *The Waste Land* and the *New Lines* anthology that institutionalized the Movement and a particularist vision of a modernist-free English literary tradition, a series of formations arose that incorporated an idea of an insular Englishness that mediated their various claims for poetic form and value. While each chapter in this book focuses on a unique formation—the rise of the literary critic as cultural gatekeeper, the advent of English Surrealism, the origins of Mass-Observation as poetic experiment, and the phenomena of Tambimuttu—they collectively speak to a growing insistence within Britain, from the early 1920s to the late 1940s, to relativize English culture and use poetry as a means to articulate the singularity of Englishness through a poetic tradition. Each formation coheres around, but was by no means limited to, a few periodicals in dialogue. Moreover, some individuals find themselves at the heart of multiple formations (e.g., Edgell Rickword, Humphrey Jennings, and Geoffrey Grigson). Ultimately, despite the distinct issues that each periodical formation was invested in, all four conflate poetic production with various culturalist claims.

The first chapter—"Standards of Criticism"—introduces how the discourse of tradition, standards, and culture cohered in the pages of literary review magazines such as *The Calendar of Modern Letters* (1926–29) and, with more immediate and lasting impact, *Scrutiny* (1932–53). The former arose out of a skepticism toward Eliot's *The Waste Land* and his own journal *Criterion*; the editors of *The Calendar* argued that literary criticism should be pursued by establishing "standards of criticism" that could be universally applied. This chapter further explores the previously unaddressed influence of I. A. Richards's ideas on the editors of *The Calendar* by analyzing Edgell Rickword's review of *Principles of Literary Criticism*. Key terms defined by Richards and picked up by Rickword in the review—such as "rhythm," "meter," and "tradition"—become central to the magazine's rhetoric in its reviewing and assessment. Ultimately, these key terms are used to articulate a notion of "standards" for literature. The ability to apply these standards requires constructing the notion of a singular audience, and thus *The Calendar*'s use of the term "reader" becomes culturally coded to mean an English one. The editors never explicitly articulate a culturally essentialist or insular vision, but in their conception of literary practice and tradition, they demonstrate a reductive universalism that assumes the particular in claiming the whole.

*The Calendar*'s legacy survived in the form of perhaps the most influential critical review in literature studies in the twentieth century—*Scrutiny*. Helmed primarily by F. R. Leavis, who espoused a vision for the literary critic as the protector of an English tradition, it looked to a past constructed out of "great" works of literature to resituate a present he felt had been lost or corrupted. Instead, Leavis constructed a vision of Englishness rooted in the contained and knowable world of literary texts. *Scrutiny* developed its own attitudes toward poetry, culture, and literary criticism from the previous work of T. S. Eliot, I. A. Richards, and the reviewing found in *The Calendar of Modern Letters*. This meeting of influences, while commonly acknowledged as the initial set of inspirations for the magazine's editorial agenda, has not led to much scholarship emphasizing a key feature of *Scrutiny*, i.e., that it was a production that initially valued poetry above all other literary forms and only later, when the general disenchantment of the editors with contemporary poetic output was established, turned to literary criticism as the privileged site of cultural stewardship.

The second chapter—"The English in English Surrealism"— addresses Surrealism in Britain and argues against the prevailing perception that its manifestation in Britain in the late 1930s was never more than a brief flirtation with continental modernism. Rather, given the widespread and well-informed attention it received in British literary magazines—most particularly, between 1935 and 1938—I read English Surrealism as a unique manifestation of the French incarnation, which took on board some of the founders' poetic and aesthetic claims but then fused them with an already developing structural trend that I have previously identified as a shift away from high modernist aesthetics to late modernist culturalism.

This was, in part, due to Surrealism's belatedness in Britain. David Gascoyne's *A Short Survey of Surrealism* (1935) brought attention and a frame to the movement that had originated in France in the early 1920s but was underrepresented and underreported in Britain until the mid-1930s. The major effect of this belatedness was that Surrealism's reception and influence in Britain involved all of its proclamations. No longer simply the aesthetic revolution proclaimed in Breton's "First Manifesto" (1924) but also the namechecking of Freud and Marx in the "Second Manifesto" (1930), it was theorized as a psychological and cultural revolution as well. In his 1936 essay "What Is Surrealism?," Andre Breton sums up the development of Surrealism as from linguistic experimentation to cultural action (131). Breton's attraction to the Communist Party and leftist politics was mainly fueled by the perceived compatibility of Surrealism's textual revolution with Communism's political and cultural revolution (140). It is this latter culturally and politically invested phase of Surrealism that was primarily imported to Britain in the mid-1930s and was greeted with some sympathy as another face of the British Popular Front, which incorporated a broad range of leftist discourses to combat the rise of Fascist sentiment in Britain and on the European continent.

In other words, Surrealism's textual innovations were muted in favor of cultural claims that could be made not only in service of anti-Fascist sentiment but also in terms of an English literary tradition. For example, *New Verse* (1932–39), which published French and British Surrealists, as well as reviewed their work, viewed Surrealism as necessarily developing out of national literary traditions and thus favored cultural framings over aesthetic ones. *Contemporary Poetry and Prose* (1936–37), commonly described as the only Surrealist magazine to appear in Britain in the 1930s, did indeed publish a wide variety of Surrealist work. However, the magazine, much like *New Verse*, was prone to nationalizing the traditions in which it engaged. *Left Review* (1934–38) approached Surrealism strictly within the terms of class struggle, and its charge of Surrealism's "bourgeois" form stressed cultural politics over aesthetics. In addressing the competing discourses over Surrealism's role in Britain, a picture develops of a periodical formation that carried out a vibrant exchange, but that sacrificed poetic production in favor of cultural claims.

The third chapter—"Popular Poetry and Mass-Observation"—focuses on Mass-Observation (formed in 1937), which was a movement that envisioned a project that would collect everyday observations of the British people, in the hope of identifying a "collective image" of the state of the nation from the mass of contributions. Mass-Observation has been characterized variously as "autoethnography," "ethnographic surrealism," and a "science of everyday life," and as a result of this emphasis on its more obvious scientific claims and methods, scholars have missed the literary antecedents and implications that Mass-Observation presents in its initial formation. Mass-Observation, originally named "Popular Poetry," from the very beginning was a mixture of poetry, anthropology, psychology, and sociology. Mass-Observation's publications in periodicals are well documented, but never as a part of a periodical formation in the midst of other poetic formations (such as the attention paid to Auden in *New Verse*, or the widespread formation around T. S. Eliot's *Criterion*).

The first 18 months of the movement's life are mainly found in the pages of periodicals. The founders advertised, and later debated, in *New Statesman* (1913–); promoted M-O's poetic potential in *New Verse* (1932–39) and its cultural and mythical potential in *Left Review* (1934–38); and published extracts in *New Writing* (1936–46) and *Life and Letters To-day* (1928–50).[12] It was only with the publication of *First Year's Work* in 1938, which contained a critique by Bronisław Malinowski, who chastised the movement for not pursuing more orthodox anthropological practices, combined with the ascendancy of Tom Harrisson, who combated any suggestion of M-O's literary pretensions, that M-O ceased to be a literary movement of any sort as well as ceased to be published in any literary or cultural periodicals. Thinking of M-O as a periodical formation, therefore, requires understanding the political potential for poetry. Drew Milne argues, in the context of discussing M-O, that the "uncertain social function of poetry, its purposeful lack of purpose, remains the site of conflicts in which the idea of poetry is almost more potent than the continuity of poetry as a practical and aesthetic orientation of social being" ("Charles Madge" 68). As Surrealism's particular impact in Britain in the late 1930s demonstrates, the uneasy relationship between poetry and politics lies in the differing modes each operates under; Surrealism's inability to gain a foothold in British leftist politics can thus be best understood as a result of its attempting to change the pragmatically driven limits of political discourse through its individualized aesthetic. As for Mass-Observation, rehabilitating its literary origins more accurately explains its project as a literary movement invested in a culturalist vision that eventually transformed into a social science.

The final chapter—"The Politics of Reception"—focuses on *Poetry (London)* (1939–51) and its editor, the Ceylonese-born Meary James Tambimuttu. As the preeminent poetry periodical of 1940s Britain, *Poetry (London)* serves in this project as a counterpoint to the periodical formations addressed in the previous chapters, primarily for its direct assault on those periodicals reviewed. Yet, Tambimuttu's marginalization in the English literary canon is not simply attributable to his Ceylonese birth. He has been long perceived as a lead publisher and advocate of the New Apocalypse poets of the 1940s, themselves claiming Dylan Thomas as their prime figure of influence. Their heavily metaphorical poetry was directly at odds with the reportage form of many of the politically minded poets of the 1930s, and later, the Movement singled them out as being particularly worthy of rebuke. In short, Tambimuttu has been twice marginalized, both for his cultural identity and his perceived poetic affiliation.

In readdressing Tambimuttu, and *Poetry (London)*, his centrality within the metropolitan scene can be reclaimed, but more importantly, his editorial proclamations and choices illustrate a far more focused and organized approach than has been commonly assumed by his peers and subsequent critics. Furthermore, his association with Thomas too often marginalizes Tambimuttu's investment in Welsh writers in English, themselves cohering into a sort of regional movement following the opening of the publications *Wales* and *Welsh Review*. This chapter firstly deals with a series of "Letters" that Tambimuttu published in the magazine that repeatedly focused on the state of poetry in 1940s Britain. Tambimuttu used the Geoffrey Grigson–edited *New Verse* as a synecdoche for what he termed the "objective reporter" poetry of the 1930s, and in his critique of socially and politically motivated poetry, he declared the need for an alternate tradition stemming from English Romanticism. He found that alternative, partly, in the Welsh poets he published. In other words, "objective reporter" meant for Tambimuttu an insular culturalist poetry that implicitly cordoned off its practitioners and audience as English. Tambimuttu's publishing of Welsh, Scottish, and Irish poets problematized such assumptions. Furthermore, his tendency to draw attention to the Welsh poets he published may have been in part due to his relationship with Dylan Thomas, but it was more importantly a reflection of how he read his own hybrid identity. In other words, far from advocating an adversarial literary tradition, Tambimuttu sought to expand what was perceived to be a highly restricted notion of the English literary tradition, and the periodical formation that featured *Poetry (London)* reflected a briefly claimed advocacy for a more radical inclusivity.

"Periodical formations," then, offers a more precise term to reflect the actual nature of the development not only of the culturalist turn in late modernist poetry in Britain but also of the central role poetry played in voicing an essential Englishness at a time when Britain's imperial influence was becoming greatly attenuated. Periodical formations do not operate as master narratives for a period; instead, they reflect a network of relations in flux that at times endorse those narratives but in other moments conflict greatly with the received wisdom of the canon.

CHAPTER 1

STANDARDS OF CRITICISM

In order to contextualize *The Calendar of Modern Letters*, the ground it attempted to stake out needs to be considered, as well as how the process of articulating a "standards of criticism" came to influence F. R. Leavis and *Scrutiny*. Despite the editors' catholicity in publishing creative work, *The Calendar*'s critical literary reviewing was its central and most influential feature. The best-known reviews from *The Calendar* were a series entitled "Scrutinies"—after which F. R. Leavis would name his magazine—that took a cold look at what were judged to be inflated literary reputations of the time.[1] The essays and reviews in *The Calendar* articulate a restricted, and culturally essentialist, vision of "standards" rooted in a shared experience of the English literary tradition. This aspect of *The Calendar* comes into focus if we think of the magazine as influenced not only by Eliot's *The Waste Land* and *Criterion* but also by the literary theory published by I. A. Richards in the 1920s. The combination of Eliot's challenge to subsequent poetic development and Richards's centralizing poetry as the cultural form par excellence resulted in *The Calendar* simultaneously criticizing the poetic orthodoxy while declaring the need for "standards of criticism." In the end, *The Calendar* anticipates the broader poetic trend in late modern Britain: that is, from an aesthetic to a culturalist emphasis.

Yet, *The Calendar* should not be reduced simply to either the junior competitor of the *Criterion* or the "prequel" to *Scrutiny*.

*The Calendar* was invested in the difficult work of staking out new ground, and in the words of Edgell Rickword, this required looking for "revolutions of technique and so on . . . are an advancing, a making of language, whatever medium it may be in . . . making more wide and deep an understanding possible" ("Conversation"). As will be addressed, references to audience and readers in *The Calendar* fall under the frame of a singularly understood, nationally identified group. Jed Esty reads such a conception as a "second-order universalism," which unlike first-order universalism is "based not on the unmediated human *subject* as a universal type but on the national *culture* as a universal type" (191). The editors' and contributors' tendency toward identifying their agenda within a unitary vision of Englishness thus needs to be understood as an aftereffect, but a powerful and instructive one, as it partook in a broader trend of prioritizing literature, and specifically poetry, as the site where a national identity could be articulated, analyzed, and defended.

*The Calendar*'s posturing about reviewing the "literature which reflects the spirit of the present day" was a view maintained from strictly within an English perspective. The faith in Richardsian empiricism in performing criticism and the appeal to the reformation of a literary tradition active in the present were core characteristics of *The Calendar of Modern Letters* that *Scrutiny* chose to inherit. *Scrutiny* never shared the *The Calendar*'s promotion of more experimental writing (such as work by James Joyce or Wyndham Lewis) and did not attempt to publish nearly as much creative work; however, it embraced *The Calendar*'s claim of literary crisis while moving away from the former magazine's more inclusive approach and toward a restricted vision of gatekeepers of an English literary tradition. When *The Calendar* signed off in 1927, it laid the groundwork for Leavis and his coeditors, who would develop Rickword's initial questioning of the cultural value of the contemporary literary field. *Scrutiny* would move in a direction that would equate literary criticism's ability to decide what was important about poetry to an assessment of the lived experience of being English.

First, the particular influence of *The Calendar of Modern Letters* on the editorial format of *Scrutiny* needs to be unpacked. Second, the role of poetry in society as it was conceived by I. A. Richards and T. S. Eliot will be outlined, with a particular emphasis on how their theorization of poetry stressed it as a *part* of English culture. Third, Leavis's own early statements on poetry and literary criticism will be reviewed—particularly his book publications *Mass Civilization and Minority Culture*, *New Bearings in English Poetry*, and *Revaluation*—as they provide a more complete picture of how poetry and literary criticism came to be understood in the pages of *Scrutiny*. Finally, the poetry reviewing from the 1930s in *Scrutiny* itself presents a trajectory of ideas that moved initially from celebration and hope to the utter dismissal of contemporary production and in turn sheds new light on how what we now take as axiomatic in Leavis and *Scrutiny* really was the result of a development of thought over time.

## THE CALENDAR OF MODERN LETTERS[2]

*The Calendar* published its first issue in March 1925, and as Rickword explained in an interview in 1973, "We were a sort of discontented club, discontented with all the established novelists and the literary cliques" ("Conversation").[3] *The Calendar* has been primarily remembered, as has been noted, for its cautious enthusiasm for T. S. Eliot and the scathing nature of its reviews.

As Rickword would later characterize the magazine's focus, "I think literature is basically communication, and I think you can't communicate what isn't in some sense common" ("Conversation"). What is at stake for the editors is not the "old vs. new," the "modern vs. traditional," or attacking established writers for the sake of those debates themselves, but rather using such rhetoric to reconnect literature back to a kind of common expression or understanding. This, in turn, fuels a perspective on literature as a form of cultural production that can guarantee a singularly imagined community. For example, in Edgell Rickword's review of I. A. Richards's *Principles of Literary*

*Criticism*, there is a set of terms or themes that come to predominate through many of the contributions, which reinforce a vision of literature (and literary criticism) as acts of production from within a culture.

I. A. Richards's *Principles of Literary Criticism* is listed at the end of the "Among New Books" section of the first issue of *The Calendar of Modern Letters* (March 1925). The editors note that the book "will be referred to again" but in this particular review assert that it is "a remarkable synthetic effort; Mr. Richards dissociates all the familiar ideas of aesthetic values" and "lays down a track which he thinks will lead to a firmer basis for the appraisement of values" (88). The full review appears in the next issue, written by Edgell Rickword, and is largely favorable. Rickword characterizes the book in terms of its value in offering new tools for the critic, in contrast to what the editors of *The Calendar* identify in pre–World War I criticism as a "herd of literary worshippers" (March 1925 70).[4]

> Its analysis of current methods of evaluating works of art is delicate, destructive, and final; the mechanism with which it replaces them may not have the same quality of finality, but its adaptation to the needs of our time is so nearly complete that we cannot imagine its essential modification. (April 1925 162)

This description emphasizes the single importance of Richards's book (it is "final"), which provides us with a clue as to how seriously the editors themselves received the book when shaping their own ideas about how literary criticism ought to be pursued. Rickword, then, emphasizes Richards's treatment of poetry as a subset of all forms of communication.

> He does not differentiate between the kind of stimulus which we receive from raw life and the kind which we receive from the representation of life in the arrangements recognized as artistic forms. He shows, in fact, that there is no basic difference, though there is a difference of degree in the quality of response, which we receive from certain arrangements and not from others; it is this difference of degree which determines his scale of values. (162)

Richards clearly articulates that while poetry "may have also an ulterior value as a means to culture or region . . . [it cannot] directly determine its poetic worth as a satisfying imaginative experience; and this is to be judged entirely from within" (*Principles* 67). Rickword blurs the line between poetic meaning and general communication to a greater extent than Richards does in his own book, perhaps as a result of Rickword's own efforts to argue for the necessity of a socially viable literary production.[5] Richards is careful to categorize poetry as a type of experience, differentiated from the nonpoetic, which can reflect on, and be related to, other forms of experience, but can only be judged within its own terms.

For Rickword, following Richards, poetry's value lies in the fact that it communicates meaning, and its unique way of doing so entails a specific approach to its form and content, which in turn gives readers a more complex, if not fuller, understanding of themselves.

> This existence of poetry *in* the audience is the crucial point in Mr. Richards' theory of value . . . [as in Richards's view] poetry [is] the supreme social attitude, and similarly, his reasoning tends to diminish the importance of the solitary illuminant who is the natural outcome of a metaphysical theory of criticism. (163)

It is important to note here the idea of the legitimating emphasis of poetry operating through universal channels. Rickword underlines Richards's own stress on the poet and poetry as engaged in everyday life, and it is important to emphasize this, as it results in an argument for the special role of poetic meaning ("supreme social attitude") as well as normalizing poetry *as* communication.[6]

It is also important to addresss the two paragraphs Rickword spends discussing Richards's definition of "meter," especially as the terms "rhythm" and "meter" not only become central for *The Calendar*'s reviewers in their imagining of an ideal reader, but would also be picked up by Leavis and other *Scrutiny* contributors. In the chapter "Rhyme and Meter," Richards's coverage of these terms can be seen to influence the writers in *The*

*Calendar*, as these terms become a thematic refrain throughout the course of the magazine. The two longer passages from this chapter articulate the heart of the project *The Calendar* pursued. In this chapter, Richards firstly addresses his definition of rhythm.

> Grammatical regularities, the necessity for completing the thought, the reader's state of conjecture as to what is being said, his apprehension in dramatic literature of the action, of the intention, situation, state of mind generally, of the speaker, all these and many other things intervene. The way the sound is taken is much less determined by the sound itself than by the conditions into which it enters . . . This texture of expectations, satisfactions, disappointments, surprisals, which the sequence of syllables brings about, is rhythm. (125)

Rhythm, in this accounting, consists of a complex of factors, but the key element is the social encounter of speaker and reader—it is the tension generated by the relationship between the above-described forces that produces rhythm. With this understanding of rhythm, Richards can treat the term both formally as a feature found in all poems and culturally as a condition that arises out of the interaction between author and audience.[7] Meter, on the other hand, regulates the anticipation brought about by a reading of the poem (i.e., it is not innate or static prior to, or after, the moment of interaction).

> As with rhythm with meter, we must not think of it as in the words themselves or in the thumping of the drum. It is not in the stimulation, it is in our response. Meter adds to all the variously fated expectancies which make up rhythm a definite temporal pattern and its effect is not due to our perceiving a pattern in something outside us, but to our *becoming patterned ourselves* [my emphasis]. With every beat of the meter a tide of anticipation in us turns and swings, setting up as it does so extraordinarily extensive sympathetic reverberations. (127)

Meter, in this sense, is the measurement of the effect of a kind of conditioning that a reading of the poem, any poem, produces.

A "pattern" is not a neutral site here but rather a shared experience. "Becoming patterned ourselves" entails a repetition of form that can be identified among individuals. In some sense, it is akin to Louis Althusser's notion of "interpellation," where we are joined to a community when we are called out in the street.[8] Meter identifies the moment when we join in a common experience, and that experience conditions us both as readers of the poem and as subjects in a community of readers.

The implication here is significant. Richards is not simply articulating "principles of literary criticism" for their own sake but is staking out space for using the reading of poetry as a means by which we can understand broad cultural conditions. While Richards is always vague when he speaks of the "reader" or the "audience" for poetry, it is illuminating that these terms can be singularly conceived. In other words, Richards treats "audience" as a universal particular, and thus he co-opts an uncomplicated, or at least undifferentiated, sense of community and identity. The act of reading poetry socializes the reader in a pattern that can be anticipated (i.e., preconditioned) but also in production (we build our identity in relation to its effects).

Rickword argues that Richards's discussion of meter "is an example of the heightened understanding which is reached by his way of approach to the subject" (163). For Rickword, the close attention required to write and read poetry provides tools for reading society as a whole, in that poetry is simply read here as an elevated form of experience. The practical implications this would have on future reviewing in *The Calendar* may be measured by how Rickword closes the review: "It may, perhaps, stand as a sort of colophon to an appreciation which is far from exhaustive" (164). It is my contention that we can regard this as an assertion that the application of Richards's ideas as expressed in *Principles of Literary Criticism* would resonate in future issues of the magazine. Richards and his ideas on literary criticism, perhaps even more so than the commonly acknowledged debt to T. S. Eliot, serve as the template for the criticism developed in *The Calendar of Modern Letters*, and subsequently with Leavis and his contributors in *Scrutiny*. This fact alone will not only better explain the tone of the content but also more helpfully address the legacy of influence that followed after the end of the former's run.

## Tradition, Standards, and the "Spirit of the Age"

Perhaps the most significant influence *The Calendar*'s reviewing had on Leavis was its foregrounding of ideas on "tradition" and "standards" when it came to assessing value in poetry. Discussions of "tradition" or "standards" so often went hand in hand with the articles and reviews in *The Calendar* that, with perhaps two exceptions, nearly all the issues contain at least one reference to at least one of these two words.[9] The closest the editors come to naming an editorial agenda is declaring that their reviewing will tend "towards standards of criticism," which will be built out of a comparative analysis of examples of contemporary literary production. Thus, the emphasis in much of the reviewing was whether or not the piece under review simply reproduced what were judged to be worn out modes of writing or advanced the reader's conception of their lived experience.

In Rickword's essay "The Returning Hero" (August 1925), which discusses the role of the concept of the hero in past literary production, he examines how different ages demand different forms of writing. He uses the example of T. S. Eliot's influence to illustrate this point.

> No doubt, too, all young men of poetic ambition have their version of *The Waste Land* in their wash-stand drawer. If this is not quite the same thing as popularity it means at least that Mr. Eliot's inspiration was not merely personal; in its coarser manifestations, if not in its ultimate delicacy, it tuned in with an emotion common to the best spirit of the age, a fastidious and anguished rejection of the various forms of satisfaction offered by the Spirit of Historical Culture. (473)

What Rickword here values in Eliot is *The Waste Land*'s ability to read the contemporary scene and reflect it in an imaginative way. In other words, Eliot is not writing occasional poetry, but rather, in readdressing the course of history regarding the modern condition, he has presented a poem that offers readers something new about what they commonly share. For Rickword, Eliot's influence is not simply fashionable but innovative, precisely because he does not reproduce the status quo of received forms or wisdom, and he thus qualifies as an extension of the "living tradition."

Rickword was not alone in *The Calendar*'s reviewing in articulating the central importance of a living tradition. Edwin Muir, one of the magazine's most regular contributors, in two of his essays—"The Zeit Geist" (*sic*) (October 1925)[10] and "The Present State of Poetry" (January 1926)—stresses the historical specificity of literary production, with the stated assumption that literary production needs to be judged by modern standards and not a received tradition. In "The Zeit Geist" (*sic*), he defines the German word as the "spirit of the age" and uses this term to perform an assessment of what features should be present in contemporary writers. He then develops a contrast between "weak" and "good," arguing that "the good writer is not concerned with the things which in literature have been proved permanent, but rather with the things in his age and his experience which have not been so proved, to which by his realizing and objectifying them he may give permanence" (114). In this understanding, the tradition as a static institution can only work against the full effect of contemporary poetic production. Similarly, in "The Present State of Poetry," Muir stresses that he and his readers live in "an age of poetic debility" (322). After arguing that English poetry has become the "poetry of the city," he concludes that the result is that "the individual has been substituted [by] the mass, and to the mass the order of feelings which expressed his relations towards his circle of acquaintances is no longer relevant" (324). The effect seen in poetic production is that "poetry is colder, more intellectualized, more skeptical, than it used to be" (325). The poet's response should not be pessimism, "for pessimism is a reasonable and traditional thing . . . [and] the poet is not concerned because ideals do not correspond to realities" (326). Despite his stressing the contrary, Muir expresses a kind of despair for the contemporary conditions for poetry, rooted in the rapidly changing nature of modern society. For him, the poet's work is invested in social conditions, as these are the very contributing factors to any literature.

> Modern thought and modern life present the poet with a number of possible worlds, but not with the one which he needs if he is to feel, as well as to speculate upon, reality. His temptation in this quandary is to accept these possible worlds provisionally, and build fanciful hypotheses round them. (327)

It is this quandary that results in the kind of poetry Muir rejects. What is interesting here is that the agency is displaced away from the poet and onto the society from within which he or she writes. If, as Muir argues, the task for the poet "is not so much to treat the universe of life as to evoke it," then the kind of poetry that ought to be written is one that produces new objects. As evidenced from this particular way of stating "the present state of poetry," Muir becomes mired in abstractions and offers no practical poetics that might be enacted by his audience. However, this essay again expresses an attitude frequently found in *The Calendar*. The poet is placed in the role of the advance guard, as one who innovates how a culture sees itself, and it is the job of the critic to confirm or deny the accuracy of these contributions. The traditional forms not in service to the "spirit of the age" will be discarded by the poet, and the standards that determine what kind of poetry will be of value are determined by the critic in an assessment of that work in relation to contemporary production.

An example of this attitude can be found again in the October 1926 issue when Rickword, writing under the pseudonym Jasper Bildje, publishes "Some Aspects of Yahoo Religion." In a transparent reference to Jonathan Swift's subarticulate humanoids in *Gulliver's Travels*, Rickword finishes the essay by breaking down how the system of literary reviewing operates, implicitly critiquing it in the process.

> A literary editor is usually a yahoo with remarkable social gifts, an easily-excitable volubility, and some knowledge of the

broader principles of literary production. He is assisted in his task of encouraging literature by a number of reviewers who . . . form certain ritualistic anecdotes illustrative of their personal proclivities . . . These two orders are largely responsible for the taste of the reading public. (242)

Such a form of literary production is antithetical to Rickword's desire that the critic judge works based on objective standards and not simply reproduce a small network of institutionalized names. At stake is the cultural vibrancy and relevancy of new literary production for the audience, who are seen as passive agents and thus need the critic to responsibly inform them of what usefully contributes to their lived experience. Such a conception displaces the role of literature away from the notion of individual expression and toward a collective act of shared meaning. "Standards of criticism" becomes another way of treating literature as a social obligation and, in the process, mutes literature's aesthetic function in favor of its cultural role.

## "Comments and Reviews"

Aside from the opening manifesto-like statement in the first issue, there are only two editorial statements in *The Calendar*—in the first and last issues.[11] The first is notable both because the reader does not encounter it until page 70 in the "Comments and Reviews" section and because it does not prescribe an attitude toward literature.[12] This piece, which runs for two pages, carefully breaks down the editors' attitude toward the role of criticism.

> The reader we have in mind, the ideal reader, is not one with whom we share any particular set of admirations and beliefs. The age of idols is past, for an idol implies a herd—to each literary idol a herd of literary worshippers—and for the modern mind the age of herds is past. For some time after the breakdown of the Victorian religion of great men, disconsolate worshippers sought refuge from the rigor of solitary conviction in a succession of literary chapels, each of which claimed its patron as most efficacious to salvation . . . This view of society means the death of dogma. Parson may roar in the pulpit (and the lay preacher

is trying hard just now to snatch a share of the old prestige) but the congregation turn round amicably in the pews to discuss the text with their neighbors.[13] (70–71)

The attempt to identify the "ideal reader" seems to be in line with the notion of the "reader" that Richards presents: namely, as a kind of abstract and theoretical concept. The distinction from Richards may be that the reader presented by these editors seems like one who does not exist prior to, but maybe in collaboration with, the production of the magazine.[14] In other words, *The Calendar*'s "ideal reader" is any reader who arrives at judgments in the manner that the magazine propounds—the content of that judgment is less significant than the fact that it was arrived at individually.[15] Yet, in a magazine that clearly situates itself as a product from England ("it will publish articles on . . . foreign writers who are being discussed in England" [ii]) and runs an advertisement in its front matter for its first eight issues asking for donations to the National Institute for the Blind to buy braille books, there is clearly a cultural and political positioning assumed beforehand, however hesitantly articulated.[16] In ways never properly schematized or advocated over the course of its run, the editors reproduce in every issue an image of nationally based literatures (they would also publish Russian, French, and American authors, but would clearly signal them as such), and thus proclamations about audience, readership, criticism, or even periodicity (how when work was published affects its reception) are all subsumed under an umbrella of what Eliot would term "organic wholes" ("Function" 68).

*The Calendar* ended its final issue in July 1927 with a statement entitled "A Valediction Forbidding Mourning." In it the editors assert that the "cessation of a literary review is not an event to ruffle the surface of national life; to expect it to do so, would expose a misunderstanding of values" (175). To its last, *The Calendar* claims to speak to and for a national audience, implicitly English, and further, that the service it provided was one that contributed not only to the reviewing of literature but also to a more abstract and general concept of "values." As they demonstrated over and over again in their essays and reviewing,

*The Calendar* envisioned itself as a cultural agent, and this was based on an idea of literary criticism as that which evaluates literature in terms of its contribution to cultural production. Through this linkage, they portrayed literature as the base for a singularly conceived culture and, as a result, established the ground on which future literary reviews would come to articulate their own mission as cultural gatekeepers. Understanding *The Calendar*'s run in terms of its cultural essentialism is not to diminish its accomplishment but rather to fully and responsibly explain its appeal to the editors of *Scrutiny*. *Scrutiny* not only adopted its name from *The Calendar*'s review series, but many contributors built upon these shared attitudes an argument in defense of a "minority culture" of literary critics protecting the most vital aspects of English culture.

## "Living Traditions": Out from *The Calendar of Modern Letters*

In 1933, Leavis published an edited version of selections from *The Calendar* entitled *Towards Standards of Criticism*. In the introduction to this collection, Leavis claims that *The Calendar*'s original contribution lay in its lament of the current institutional climate for poetry and the arts, as well as its ongoing call for a change in the way poetry was produced and consumed that was more reflective of a "living tradition." Rickword's assertion in the aforementioned "Valediction" at the close of *The Calendar* that "the value of a review must be judged by its attitude to the living literature of the time" leads Leavis to posit his own sympathetic addendum that "where there is a 'living literature of the time' there is also a 'contemporary sensibility,' and it is always the business of criticism . . . to define—that is, help to form—and organize this, and to make conscious the 'standards' implicit in it" (395). Leavis, in ways he would pursue more systematically shortly after the publication of *Towards Standards of Criticism*, builds on *The Calendar*'s claim for literary criticism's social role as an arbiter of standards by positing more forcefully the role of the critic as the center of gravity in this cultural exchange. In other words, in the network of author-critic-reader, the critic has been given pride of place, whereas previously in *The Calendar* less emphasis was placed on the critic's product and more on the value of the literature itself. This shift in emphasis leads Leavis to emphasize one particular aspect of *The Calendar*'s rhetoric: namely, the idea that the modern world was experiencing a cultural "disintegration."

> Disintegration, it is plain involves more than "splitting," and where it has gone so far that the "contemporary sensibility" depends on a negligible few—negligible, that is, in influence on the contemporary world, then the assertion of "standards," now indeed a matter of assertion, becomes "dogmatism." (396)

Leavis's concern lies in the ability of literature and criticism to actually shape the "contemporary sensibility." Disintegration involves both fracturing and degeneration, with the result that, contrary to how Leavis's emphatic proclamations are popularly remembered today, here he laments the idea of "standards" and "dogmatism" becoming synonymous. In other words, cultural disintegration undermines the ability for a "common understanding" among the readership.

> There may be a good deal of room for difference about particular valuations, but there is enough common understanding of what value is to make differences discussible, and enough agreement to make the question whether there has been a cultural decline in the past two centuries, say, a real and urgent one, and to make the effort towards standards fruitful in further and more conscious agreement. (396)

This statement may get us closer to how Leavis thinks about how culture operates and, in turn, the critic's role in deliberating over the function of literature as a guarantor of that culture's form. The "Leavisite method" can be most simply expressed through the five-word question "this is so, isn't it?" As we see above, Leavis's approach to criticism is based on consensus building. The question is not really a question at all but rather an insistent emphasis: you see what I see, as you understand what I understand. In this question, he closes the gap between author-critic-reader, and as a result this culture is envisioned as unitary and whole. His method is grounded in the idea that modern culture, through technological development and industrialization, has lost touch with the standards of the past, and that it is the role of the critic, as a representative member of an enlightened minority, to educate society about its "living tradition" and thus reclaim the "organic community" that thrived before.

> The fact that the other traditional continuities have . . . so completely disintegrated, makes the literary tradition correspondingly more important, since the continuity of consciousness, the conservation of the collective experience, is the more dependent on it: if the literary tradition is allowed to lapse, the gap is complete . . . Literary criticism provides the test for life and concreteness; where it degenerates, the instruments of thought degenerate too, and thinking, released from the testing and energizing contact from the full living consciousness, is debilitated, and betrayed to the academic, the abstract, and the verbal. It is of little use to discuss values if the sense for value in the concrete—the experience and perception of the value—is absent. ("Standards" 397)

On the one hand, in a neat trick, Leavis has claimed *The Calendar*'s concern as his own and equated the magazine's cessation with the problem facing the literary tradition in Leavis's present. He has claimed the "continuity of consciousness" from *The Calendar* for *Scrutiny* itself, as it is literary criticism that is the guarantor of the tradition in his formulation. On the other hand, Leavis's emphasis that "literary criticism provides the test for life" presents us with a claim never found in *The Calendar*. What Leavis has meant by "test for life," or even simply "life," is not readily clear, but given the close association he grants between how we read and understand literature, he has taken *The Calendar*'s focus on the role of literature as an act of communication and built upon it an understanding of literature as the sole means by which one can read and understand how a culture operates. Additionally, as David Gervais stresses, Leavis does not use "life" as a philosophical concept (i.e., in the abstract), but what "gives [it] meaning is [its] context in some specifically *English* 'human nature,' apprehended at some particular moment of English history" (147). In short, Leavis never uses such abstract words wholly untethered from a specific historical context that can condition their meaning. As we see above, "test for life" has everything to do with how he reads the modern condition of literary production. Against the "disintegration" he posits something generative: life.

Finally, poetry is significant in this context because it offers all the formal complexity to truly test the literary values of the period: "If one is not intelligent about poetry one is unlikely to be intelligent about fiction, and the connoisseur of fiction who disclaims an interest in poetry is probably not interested in literature" (404). This comes out of a conversation on *The Calendar*'s frequent use of the concept of "rhythm" and its debt to I. A. Richards's definition of the term. Leavis quotes Richards's sense of rhythm as a "texture of expectations" and in the process aligns formal poetic complexity with human emotional complexity. Criticism of poetry, in this understanding, as a "test for life," bridges the gap between the metaphorical and physical performances of living. As we will see below, Leavis's early vision of poetry's role for the literary critic in supplying this "test for life" was vital to the groundwork of his entire project, which attempted to shore up an organic conception of Englishness against the growth of mass culture and modernization.

## I. A. Richards and T. S. Eliot: The Role of Poetry in Culture and Criticism

In the publication *Practical Criticism*, which was the fruit of a course Leavis often attended, I. A. Richards contended that "there is no gap between our everyday emotional life and the material of poetry" (300).[17] In the course, Richards would issue poems to his students, ask them to write freely on the poems, and then analyze and lecture on their responses.[18] *Practical*

*Criticism* overwhelms the reader with close readings of poems, close readings of his students' close readings, and exhaustive theoretical extrapolation. Richards, in the "Introductory," refers to the role of criticism as an "exercise in navigation" showing "what [poetry] communicates and how it does so and the worth of what is communicated" (10). Poetry is especially important for Richards as it acts as a "test for reality."

> For a comparison of the feelings active in a poem with some personal feeling still present in the reader's lively recollection does give a standard a test for reality . . . [The poem] exists perhaps to *control and order* such feelings and to bring them into relation with other things, not merely to arouse them. But a touchstone for reality is so valuable, and factitious or conventional feelings so common, that these dangers are worth risking. (227)

Richards's empiricism values testability, measurement, and verifiability, and in poetry he argues that he has a way to measure human emotion and consciousness. We can find two direct influences of this theorization in Leavis's thinking: first, Leavis adopts Richards's "test for reality" reconfigured as a "test for life," with the changed word seemingly muting the psychological discourse found in Richards in favor of a more generally applicable term free of methodological association; and second, the idea that literature (and here, specifically poetry) offers "control and order," the very tools needed to mitigate the "disintegration" Leavis was concerned about above.

Richards would also have something to do with Leavis's initial reception of T. S. Eliot: Leavis's first contact with T. S. Eliot was during the latter's Clark Lectures at Cambridge in 1926, but Leavis, as a student of Richards, would have read *Principles of Literary Criticism*, which was republished that same year with a new appendix attached reviewing Eliot's poetry. Richards's claim that Eliot's poetry can be summed up in three words—as the "music of ideas"—echoes his own emphasis on the importance of rhythm shaping the poem and the reader (*Principles* 276). In that appendix, Leavis biographer Ian MacKillop finds that two aspects of Richards's discussion were "basic for

Leavis": namely, "the emotive logic of poetry and the desiderated 'right reader'" (83).[19] As a poet, T. S. Eliot offers Leavis evidence for his theory of cultural disintegration, as evidenced especially in *The Waste Land*. MacKillop characterizes Leavis's attitude toward *The Waste Land* as "uneasy" but ultimately claims that Leavis valued it because the poem "exactly fitted Leavis' conviction that modernity meant alienation from an older, unified world, 'the civilization in touch with the rhythms, sanctioned by nature and time, of rural culture'" (137). He goes on to state that Leavis felt that the "[old] world implied a structure or rationale that could be 'anthropologically' accounted for" and that "the new world *appeared* to be fragmentary, but it had to have a rationale, if obscure" (137). If, as Leavis stresses in *New Bearings in English Poetry*, Eliot was "too conscious . . . of the break-up of forms" (80), then *The Waste Land* operated as a limiting case of modern society's ability to understand the poem.[20] Leavis's critique lay partially in the poem itself, but as he respected Eliot's technical performance, the "new world's" fragmentation was to blame as well. In essence, Eliot's "anthropological gaze" demonstrated the knowability of the past and perhaps could be useful in understanding the present.[21] However, as we have seen, Leavis's characterization of modernity's cultural disintegration means that an anthropological approach is locked in an irrecoverable pastness. Eliot's poem, although not explicitly thus characterized by Leavis, heralded the end of poetry's ability to usefully participate as the most sensitive measure of society.

If poetry reflects the disintegration of cultural traditions, then it was the role of the literary critic to salvage those aspects worth maintaining. This brings us to Leavis's attitude toward Eliot as a literary critic. Leavis shared with Rickword a sort of cautious respect toward Eliot's proclamations on the role of the critic and the function of "tradition" in relation to literary production. Eliot's emphasis on the critic's "disinterestedness" (in particular, in his essay "The Function of Criticism") provided Leavis with a useful way to theorize the special role of literary criticism in maintaining an English tradition in contemporary life. However, Leavis was at odds with Eliot's notion that present-day life could be treated as an "organic whole"—a characterization Leavis reserved for the past.[22] Francis Mulhern reads the difference thusly: that Eliot defined "tradition" (especially in his early essays in *The Sacred Wood*) from a "purely literary order," and that Leavis in contrast treated tradition as nationally constructed, historically situated, and developmental, and literature was thus the resulting remnant of these processes (116). The critic thus provided "an eligible past that could guide poetic practice in a detraditionalized society" (Mulhern 117).[23] Leavis always remained at odds with Eliot's faith in orthodoxy. In the former's "Restatement for Critics" (*Scrutiny* March 1933), a response to a *New English Weekly* article disparaging *Scrutiny* in part for bowing to the altar of Eliot and his *Criterion*, he takes pains to parse out what he inherits and rejects from Eliot.[24] Leavis dissociates himself from Eliot's "rejection of life implicit in [his] attitude towards sex" (as it is informed by his "orthodox Christianity") (318) but earlier approvingly quotes Eliot's definition of tradition as something that "cannot be inherited . . . [as] you must obtain it by great labor" (316). For Leavis, criticism as a "test for life" must not rest on cultural assumptions: "When it performs its function, not merely expresses and defines the 'contemporary sensibility'; it helps to form it" (319). Eliot, in "The Function of Criticism," had carefully differentiated the poet and the critic: the former was engaged in creatively producing new forms, whereas the critic objectively, and disinterestedly, weighed, evaluated, and judged the quality of these forms. Leavis, no poet himself, reserves for criticism the ability to create forms, not simply out of a vain desire to "be creative" but rather as the root explanation as to how "literary criticism" can operate as the "center of real consensus" (319). Leavis superannuates Eliot's identification of the critic with the ability to create, and in the process he claims literary criticism's special educative role in the cultural sphere. His justification for doing so can be found in his formative writing on culture collected in *For Continuity* (1933), and most especially in his essay *Mass Civilization and Minority Culture* (1930, reprinted in *For Continuity*).

## Minority Culture, Literary Criticism, and Poetry: Some Ideological Backgrounds for *Scrutiny*

Leavis theorized that the literary critic belonged to a special "minority." In his 1930 monograph *Mass Civilization and Minority Culture*, Leavis laments that "modern [man] is exposed to a concourse of signals so bewildering in their variety and number that, unless he is especially gifted . . . [then] he can hardly begin to discriminate," and further that "the distinctions and dividing lines have blurred away, the boundaries are gone, and the arts and literatures of different countries and periods have flowed together" (31). Moreover, the challenge, according to Leavis, to be faced is the relative paucity of literary reviews active in the early 1930s.

> We ought not, then, to be surprised that now, when a strong current of criticism is needed as never before, there should hardly be in England a cultivated public large enough to support a serious critical organ. The *Criterion* carries on almost alone . . . For the short-lived *Calendar of Modern Letters*, as intelligent and lively a review as ever appeared in English, died for lack of support . . . The critically adult public, then, is very small indeed: they are a very small minority who are capable of fending for themselves amid the smother of new books.[25] (31–32)

The "minority" are those "especially gifted" who can protect the boundaries and dividing lines: "Upon them depend the implicit standards that order the finer living of an age, the sense that this is worth more than that, this rather than that is the direction in which to go, that the centre is here rather than there" (15). Leavis has manufactured a special role for the literary critic: steward of the "living tradition" of English literature, and by extension, English culture.

The literary critic could especially appreciate the "finest human experience of the past," which for Leavis meant "Dante, Shakespeare, Donne . . . [and their] latest successors" (15). Gervais reads Leavis's exclusion of science and philosophy from the minority for their "inhumanity . . . leaving them outside the human sense accessible to the literary critic" (165). For the critic, in Leavis's understanding, is suited best to deal with language as such, as "in their keeping, to use a metaphor that is metonymy also and will bear a good deal of pondering, is the language, the changing idiom, upon which fine living depends, and without which distinction of spirit is thwarted and incoherent." He adds that "by 'culture' I mean the use of such a language" (15). Returning to Gervais's gloss on this passage, he finds notable "the attribution to the minority of readers and critics of qualities originally identified by Richards (and by Ezra Pound) with the peculiar qualities of the poet" (165). We can add to this that culture is understood by Leavis to be constructed by language, and it is in the "finest" uses of language that culture can be understood in its historical and present manifestations. Metaphor and metonymy, poetic forms that point to the likeness and seriality of images, are used as terms by Leavis to point to the connectedness of literary forms to cultural traditions. In other words, metaphor considered as an image used to represent another and metonymy considered as a part representing the whole both provide a sense of culture and tradition as an interlocked and interchangeable set of symbols, whose relations can be collectively understood. That is, metaphor and metonymy "work" most powerfully when the relations they create are recognized by the reader. Poetry thus operates in ways that carry real-world applications: it can, following Richards (and by way of example, Eliot), provide an understanding of the culture from within which it is produced, and it thus provides the raw data of the "test for life" so valued by Leavis.

## NEW BEARINGS AND OLD POETS: POETRY AS THE EXPRESSION OF THE TRADITION IN ENGLISH CULTURE

Leavis had yet to flesh out how he specifically saw poetry's role in culture. He approached this problem in his 1932 publication *New Bearings in English Poetry*, where, with a nod toward *The Calendar*, he demanded the consideration of poetry's situation in the "modern world." After positing that the poet is "the most conscious point of the race in his time" (19), he walks through a series of poets—a collection of "First World War poets," T. S. Eliot, Ezra Pound, Gerard Manley Hopkins, and finally, in reference to the future for poetic production, W. H. Auden, William Empson, and Ronald Bottrall—and uses their work to make claims about the situation of contemporary culture and the role of poetry in reflecting that world.

> The potentialities of human experience in any age are realized only by a tiny minority, and the important poet is important because he belongs to this (and has also, of course, the power of communication). Indeed, his capacity for experiencing and his power of communicating are indistinguishable; not merely because we should not know of the one without the other, but because his power of making words express what he feels is indistinguishable from his awareness of what he feels. (19)

Leavis built on Richards's insistence on the full complexity of properly processing what poetry provides and theorized that only a "minority" of the population, of which the poet is only one member, is capable of processing poetry adequately. The value of these poets' work lies not in the advancement of poetry alone but rather in the poems' ability to "communicate the actual quality of experience with a subtlety and precision unapproachable by any other means" (20). Poetry, in this articulation, serves as an acute form of communication and organization and in turn operates primarily in service to how a culture imagines itself. In short, Leavis developed from Richards a concept of English culture articulated as a universal humanism, and literature as the means by which the morals of English culture are best expressed.

If *New Bearings in English Poetry* outlined the poet's social function as the arbiter of experience, then by 1936 with the publication of *Revaluation* that outline had been fleshed out and rerooted in a timeline beginning with the Elizabethans. In *Revaluation*, Leavis claims that this book was planned at the same time as *New Bearings*, with the focus in this newer work being "to complete the account of the present of English poetry with the correlated account of the past" (1). The main goal of the book is to offer perspective for the critic and the reader when judging the present, as contemporary poetic production is "continuation and development . . . as the decisive, the most significant, contemporary life of tradition" (2). He characterizes the discussion as one of definition: "to define, and to order in terms of its own implicit organization, a kind of ideal and impersonal living memory" (2). Leavis constructs a poetic canon to which the "continuation and development" of present-day poetry needs to work directly in relation. Beginning with a discussion of "wit" in which he covers names such as Robert Herrick, he moves on to John Milton, Alexander Pope, the "Augustan Tradition" (Thomas Gray, among others), William Wordsworth, Percy Shelley, and John Keats.[26] If the historical optic in the first book was the mid-nineteenth century to the early 1930s, which would stress more the inheritance and the "living" of the "living tradition," then the optic in the second book roots the vitality of poetry firmly in the pastness of the past. This shift, from our contemporary perspective, appears to be inevitable, as the bulk of Leavis's writing invests itself in mapping out his conception of the "great tradition" of English literature. However, too little attention has been paid to the mechanics of that shift, and how, in the transition from a dialogue with high modernist poetry to a trenchant disapproval of any and all contemporaneous poetic production, Leavis articulated a specific Englishness rooted in a historically selective textuality. Through the reviewing process in *Scrutiny*, Leavis attempted to police a mode of Englishness mediated strictly through literary texts and thus circumscribe a field for "a morally and culturally unified audience" (Anderson 99).

Now that the methodology had been established by Leavis, it required a vehicle to implement and maintain it. While the idea of publishing a literary review was not Leavis's, he came to embrace this forum as the mode to which literary criticism was best suited. The literary review, published with some regularity and focused on contemporary publications with an eye on how it fit into the "living tradition," would be that vehicle for Leavis and his circle.

## "This Is So, Isn't It?": The Early Purpose of *Scrutiny*

In 1940, the editors of *Scrutiny* looked back across the previous decade and declared it a "very barren" one for poetry. The reception of the magazine has since adopted this claim as the one and only attitude ever posed by the editors toward contemporary poetry, and not one arrived at after years of increasingly frustrated and virulent reviewing. This accepted perspective clouds one key aspect of the magazine's development: namely, that even though its initial editorial proclamations and attitude created a set of conditions that result in the general abnegation of modern poetry, the editors, and F. R. Leavis in particular, read contemporary poetry as a vital part of cultural production. As Francis Mulhern notes, Leavis in *New Bearings* "had already provided *Scrutiny* with the essential means to a sustained and coordinated critical effort: an analysis of the present conjuncture and an interventionist critical strategy designed to unlock [poetry's] cultural potential" (*Scrutiny* 150).[27] Poetry offered a particularly complex "test for life," which was one of the core concepts Leavis himself developed when he proclaimed the central role of the literary critic as the guardian of cultural continuity.

The editors of *Scrutiny* announced in its opening "Manifesto" (May 1932) that "a review is necessary that combines criticism of literature with criticism of extra-literary activities," and additionally that they "take it as axiomatic that concern for standards of living implies concern for standards in the arts" (2). The magazine would "desiderate a cultivated historical sense, a familiarity with the 'anthropological' approach to contemporary civilization . . . and a catholic apprehension of the humane values" (3). Sean Matthews, in his entry on *Scrutiny* for *The Oxford Critical and Cultural History of Modernist Magazines*, highlights the language in the prospectus that circulated prior to the magazine's publication. Of special interest is the language on the magazine's intended "pervasive interest": "[It] might be described as 'anthropological': there will be disinterested surveys of some departments of modern life, in an attempt to increase understanding of the way in which civilization is developing" (qtd. in Matthews 835 fn. 5). The editors' loose sense of the "anthropological" will be attended to further along, but here it should be stressed that in the manner they use it here they are advocating a comprehensive form of cultural observation and analysis, which in their estimation is best served by literary reviewing. The reason for such an approach lay in the literary tradition's ability to act as a form of communication and cultural organizing.

> The task of *Scrutiny* was to extend this small-scale intimacy of reader and writer, or of student and teacher, into a larger consensus embracing an entire literary minority, reorganizing it upon the basis of tested values. The consensus is already there, as Leavis insists so often in [his] essays; his dialogue of the deaf with the Marxists is really intended only for the ears of those for whom his arguments are already obvious. The aim is . . . not so much to convince anyone else as to recognize one another and to organize themselves into an effective force. (Baldick 174)

The critic, as an elite and specially trained minority, discovers what the significant meanings in certain texts are, and simply shows the reader these moments. The reader can share in the significance of these meanings, as they are a part of a commonly held experience. With this theorization of the role of literature in society, *Scrutiny* desired to salvage a culture that was perceived as lost or corrupted by industrialization and imperial aspirations.

## "A Very Barren Decade": *Scrutiny* and Poetry Reviewing

*Scrutiny*'s role in shaping poetic discourse in the 1930s has been underaddressed for two reasons: (1) the magazine's relevance to the histories of literary criticism and British cultural Marxism have been more obvious and more fully developed, which results in only token mention of its "poetry" function, and (2) Leavis's own rhetorical displacement of the "poet" for the "literary critic" as the one at the forefront of public perception by the mid-1930s means that the retrospective view of the magazine focuses on the latter and not the former. In the wake of this displacement, the magazine shifts from a tone of cautious hope (1932) to absolute cynicism (1940) and ossifies into the loud voice of the English "great tradition" for which the magazine is primarily remembered.

There is ample reason to think that *Scrutiny* should not be considered a poetry magazine: while the poetry of Ronald Bottrall, Isaac Rosenberg, Richard Eberhart, and several others was published in the pages of the magazine, after 1937 it publishes only two poems, both by Bottrall. Despite *Scrutiny*'s willingness to review contemporary poetry throughout its run, by 1937 a specific negativity had formed in the tone of the reviews. If we take a selective look at some of the contemporary poetry reviewing between 1932 and 1937, we see a trend toward rejection, but a trend with a purpose that will be analyzed in the following pages.

"This Poetical Renascence" was the first extended review of the field of contemporary poetry that *Scrutiny* published (June 1933). In the review, Leavis walks through 13 publications and in the process elucidates an argument for poetry that combines the rhetoric of both *New Bearings* and *Mass Civilization and Minority Culture*. The review mostly concerns itself with the poetry produced by the "Auden Group" (so named by Leavis in the review), but most importantly how their poetry reflects on a larger question for Leavis, namely, whether or not there is an intelligent public for literature. For Leavis, the answer to that question either proves or disproves his thesis established in *Mass Civilization and Minority Culture* that modern society has lost its structural cohesiveness, and that because of the "perpetual avalanche of print [the ordinary cultivated reader] has had to acquire reading habits that incapacitate him when the signals for unaccustomed and subtle responses present themselves" (*New Bearings* 171). Not surprisingly, then, Leavis's initial assertion in this review is not hopeful.

> *Poetry, New Verse, New Signatures, New Country,* the *Hogarth Living Poets*... journals specified because of their intelligence—all go to show that there is not in any serious sense a public for poetry. A real public for poetry would be a public in some degree educated about poetry, and capable of appreciating and checking critically the editorial standards; a public embodying a certain collective experience, intelligence and taste. The good editorial critic would be the representative of the highest level of such a public... And if one says that the contents of the publications referred to make it impossible to believe that such a public exists, that is not to disparage insultingly those editorially responsible. (66)

The assignation of blame is significant here: the "public," as read by Leavis, indicates the limits of poetry, and not the other way around. If, as Leavis worries in *New Bearings*, "the poetry and the intelligence of the age lose touch with each other, [then] poetry will cease to matter much, and the age will be lacking in fine awareness" (20). The relationship between the editor or critic and the public must be mutually determining: it is the role of the editor/critic to serve as the "middleman" of ideas, but it is simultaneously the educated public's responsibility to discern and select intelligently from these ideas.

> Favorable reviews and a reputation are no substitute for the conditions represented by the existence of an intelligent public—the give-and-take that is necessary for self-realization, the pressure that, resisted or yielded to, determines direction, the intercourse that is collaboration... The individual artist to-day is asked to do far too much for himself and far too much as an individual. ("Renascence" 72)

The lack of an editorial approach akin to *Scrutiny*'s, which can educate its readership on the signal importance of the poetry it publishes, appears from Leavis's point of view to be these publications' major failing. As we have noted, Leavis reads "modernity" as the dissipation of a perceived organic whole, and modernist poetry's tendency toward complex allusion and difficult meaning is merely an indicator of this dissipation. These publications are thus required to mediate this complexity, or they are otherwise complicit in the general failing of the age. Auden's poetry is "too personal—relying too much on private associations" (69); Spender's "technique is very immature and unstable" (70); Day Lewis's poetry exhibits "uncertainty of purpose and [a] level [of] confusion" (73); George Reavey, whose poetry is "so free to experiment in idiom and technique," which results in an "individually created language," thus "has no public, and is the product of conditions in which no public for poetry exists" (75); and Harry Crosby "uses a completely private language" (75–76). If poetry's role is to communicate the "most conscious" aspects of a universal experience to a homogeneous public, then these writers can only ever be judged by their failure to match this ideal.

By June 1934, Leavis's view of contemporary poetic production had hardened with what he took to be fresh evidence of modernity's disintegration. The review entitled "Auden, Bottrall and Others" assesses the titular poets under review in relation to both Eliot and Pound.

> If there is not a "definitely modern" technique, one might gather from the explicit preoccupations of Mr. Auden, Mr. Bottrall, Mr. Mavrogoradato, Mr. Muir and Mr. Turner that there is at any rate what could without too violent an abstraction be called a distinctively modern mode of contemplating life—that which dictated the use of anthropological themes in *The Waste Land* . . . A "mode of contemplating life," however, has, as something abstract and general, no great interest for the critic of poetry; he has his eye rather upon technique, for it is in the successful technique that concrete particularity of realization is manifested. (73)

For Leavis, as we noted above, "the resort to anthropology is justified in a realization of the Life theme—unity, continuity and renewal, in a communicated sense of the mystery" (83). The limit that contemporary poetry hits in its so-called "anthropological approach" can be exceeded by criticism, which can see what else is required of the poem. These poets apparently fail in their ability to provide a "successful technique," and it is in their attention to the abstractions of the "anthropological method" that their detachment from "life" can be found. This failure in technique has direct cultural consequences for Leavis. A poet like Ronald Bottrall, whom Leavis had been advocating on behalf of since *New Bearings*, and who in this review is praised for "his tough idiosyncrasy and the resoluteness of his technique," has that same technique criticized for a "tendency to intellectual forcing" and a "lack of rhythmic variety," which results in the conclusion that his poetry "involves something like a shift from the plane of poetry to the plane of political manifesto" (80–81). These poets are all assessed, and fall short of, criteria established by and for Eliot's poetry. "In *The Waste Land*, with the rhythmic shifts, we pass from datum to datum, each compellingly 'there' and not merely pointed to or schematically represented; and the significance of the poem resides in what stands finally given—the data with their implicit relations" (81).[28] In one year, Leavis has transitioned from critiquing poetry editors for not offering their audiences a critical apparatus to critiquing the poets themselves for the limits of their technical abilities.

However, in all of this, Leavis seems to miss how Eliot himself understood anthropology's use for poetry. As David Chinitz notes, Eliot took from anthropology the idea that "art originated not for purposes of pure aesthetic pleasure but as a component of ritual . . . [and furthermore that the] lessons of early anthropology thus dovetail with [his] concern that art could not survive if it persisted as an autonomous cultural practice" (238). In other words, Leavis "aimed to democratize, not anthropologize, the old high literary culture . . . [whereas] Eliot . . . turned in the end to national culture as a means to reverse, or at least mitigate, the social autonomization of art" (Esty 184). Jed Esty understands these contending attitudes as representative of divergent attitudes on the part of Leavis and Eliot toward the collapse of the Empire, arguing that Leavis (among others) links imperial decline with national decay, whereas Eliot pursues a cultural revivalist approach zeroed in on "Little England" (215–17). If Eliot was pursuing the "romance of retrenchment," then for Leavis, he fails to deal with the "living tradition" of the present-day cultural situation, which Leavis read as one of irreversible disintegration and not as a return to a new organic whole.

Following these divergent attitudes, by late 1934, the hope for poetry following Eliot and Pound had dwindled and was replaced by an increasingly agitated tone of rejection and refusal. By September 1934, from the perspective of *Scrutiny*, Pound had ceased to be useful as a critic and poet. H. A. Mason finds that Pound's *ABC of Reading* "should finally discredit [him] as a critic," owing to his inability to "listen to criticism and distinguish among his opponents those who appreciate his labors . . . from those who seize on the weakness of his recent work in order to discredit and repudiate the re-orientation of tradition for which he was so largely responsible" (192). Neither Eliot nor the poets he advocates fare any better. In the June 1935 issue, Marianne Moore's *Selected Poems* is seemingly reviewed only because of T. S. Eliot's introduction, as the bulk of Leavis's review deals with Eliot and not Moore's poems directly. He concludes the review with the following observation:

> I ought, perhaps, in differing with so distinguished a critic, to have examined passages of Miss Moore's verse in detail. But such examination would have taken more room than can be spared, and those readers most likely to have commented on the deficiency will, for the most part, in any case insist on reading so authoritatively sponsored a book for themselves. (90)

The conversation throughout is with Eliot. Leavis cannot countenance Moore's lack of "intensity of feeling" (88) and uses the occasion of his introduction to attack Eliot's inability to properly assess contemporary production. In short, Leavis cannot be bothered with the poems, only the critic who endorses them.

Even when a poet is favorably reviewed, he or she is carefully bracketed out from an English tradition, with the implication that the success of the work does not alter Leavis's thesis about modern disintegration. In the December 1935 issue, Leavis briefly but approvingly reviews Hugh MacDiarmid's *Second*

*Hymn to Lenin and Other Poems*: "MacDiarmid exhibits a truly fine disinterestedness . . . [The book] is an impressive product of the endeavor to recreate a tradition—to find some equivalent for the advantages that Burns enjoyed." If we follow Leavis's logic that the "poet is the most conscious point of his age," then MacDiarmid seemingly fits the bill. However, Leavis is dismissive of a specifically Scottish tradition: "Had there been such a tradition actually alive MacDiarmid might have done a great deal more with his talent" (305). MacDiarmid can only be read and understood from within a Scottish tradition, and thus it is implied not only that he offers nothing to the English tradition but also that the Scottish tradition limits MacDiarmid. This aligns precisely with Leavis's notion that the poet's vitality and relevance are wholly conditioned by the cultural situation they find themselves in, but it also illustrates the inconsistency of the borders of Leavis's canon: i.e., Eliot and Pound (and Dante) can be considered within the English tradition, but MacDiarmid is only for the Scottish.

On the other hand, the *Scrutiny* group could blur definitions of national belonging if it helped illustrate their point. In the case of the March 1937 review of the W. B. Yeats–edited *Oxford Book of Modern Verse*, the review is titled "Yeats and the English Tradition," and H. A. Mason treats the advent of the anthology as an opportunity to reflect on the contemporary reception of Yeats himself. Mason's most damning criticism of Yeats is configured in terms of distinguishing between the role of poet and that of critic.

> Nothing so much marks the distinction between the ability to criticize in the act of writing a poem and the power of criticizing the poems of others, as [Yeats's] remarks on Eliot and Hopkins. It is almost as though he did not understand the tradition of which he is a part. (450)

Mason interestingly co-opts Leavis's tradition of Yeats, Hopkins, and Eliot to attack Yeats's inability to recognize "where he belongs" (i.e., within a specifically prescribed English tradition).[29] As a result, Mason's condemnation of Yeats-as-critic is extended to Yeats-as-poet, as if Yeats does not recognize his "age" appropriately, such that he is of no use to the progenitors of this tradition. As with Pound before, Yeats is tossed on the heap of failed promise.

Mason's ability to reflect Leavisian principles was not limited to just Pound and Yeats. The review "Poetry in 1936" (June 1937), written by him, is final in its condemnation of contemporary poetic production. Mason claims that "the samples given here do nothing to mitigate the judgment which is enforced by the examination of their whole published works—that one and all of those who on their first appearance were 'promising' have failed to come up to that promise, or, more grimly, have fulfilled the tendencies which could be detected from the start" (77). In and of itself, this condemnation of the work under review could be treated as an isolated instance of disapproval of a particular batch of works. However, Mason makes sure this rejection of the books at hand speaks to an irreversible cultural trend.

> The way in which Hopkins and Eliot are here used to give significance and an air of universality to what is in any case petty . . . is fairly common. Common enough, indeed, to lead one to reflect that the way in which the refounders of poetic tradition are being used, so far from leading to a continuation of that tradition, is positively harmful. (80)

The trend in the attitudes for contemporary poetry from 1932 to 1937 is thus one that begins with a tone of cautious hope and then moves from mild approbation to increasingly strident disapproval and ultimately to wholesale rejection. *Scrutiny* would never again adopt anything resembling an encouraging attitude toward new work, if indeed they reviewed it at all. With some exceptions, such as Eliot, reviews of contemporary work disappeared almost completely after 1937.[30] As the trend in the tone of the reviewing develops, it is clear that the one path for poetry would have been to navigate the waters of Eliot and Pound, but in ways that were not simple mimicry, such that the poetry could in turn offer its readership a singular perspective of its "contemporary sensibility." As Leavis made clear, this role had become the responsibility of the literary critic, and one way of reading this shifting attitude toward poetry is as a strategic choice. In other words, the poetry under review from 1932 to 1937 was treated and engaged with to firm up Leavis's replacement of the poet with the literary critic as the guardian of the English tradition.

## Ways Forward: Poetry as a Form of Cultural Practice

The arc tracked in this chapter approaches the development of poetic thought from the highly restricted viewpoint of poetic production in the service of intellectualizing conceptions of English culture and tradition. One result was the eventual displacement of poetry from such conversations, as the claims for poetry were based on essentialist notions of poetry as a form of communication as well as an undisturbed link to cultural practices from the past. Both such understandings, as has been demonstrated, were effectively critiqued, but as a result culturalist readings of poetry were devalued for decades to come.

Another way to approach this phenomenon requires us to look at how poetry was treated in the pages of more overtly self-declared poetry magazines in the aftermath of *Scrutiny*'s disavowal of the value of contemporary poetic production; this will be the focus of the following chapters. In magazines such as *New Verse* and *Contemporary Prose and Poetry* (among others), poetry that dealt directly with the social and political concerns of the time was advocated. Additionally, the role of poetic form in relation to political action climaxed in a debate over the relevance of Surrealism for British poetry. One surprising consequence of this debate was the development of a cultural anthropology movement—Mass-Observation—that arose from an attempt to pursue a culturally minded Surrealist practice.

# CHAPTER 2

# THE ENGLISH IN ENGLISH SURREALISM

The 1930 spring–summer double issue of Eugene Jolas's *transition* 19–20 featured a section entitled "Cambridge Experiment: A Manifesto of Young England." Prefaced with an unsigned manifesto, this section collected many of the contributors to the Cambridge-based magazine *Experiment* (1928–31), and this event has served for several literary historians of English Surrealism as an early instance of the Paris-based movement's engagement by British writers.[1] Yet, it is clear from the selection in the pages of *transition* that its British adherents would treat Surrealism very differently. None of the work published could be described as "automatic writing" or in any sense engaged with avant-garde formal experimentation. "Experiment: A Manifesto" establishes the following ground:

> A sense that literature is in need of some new *formal* notation: an attempt to show how such a notation can be built out of *academic notations*, where academic means perhaps no more than non-moral and is after all best explained in our poetry: a belief in the compact, *local* unit: and in the *impersonal* unit: a belief finally, and a disbelief—for it is about this mainly that we are at odds—in *literature* as a singular and different experience, something more than an *ordering* of life. (106)

This passage bears the strong mark of I. A. Richards's influence, who, as we saw in the previous chapter, had laid out a rationalist-empiricist model of reading poetry. Specific echoes in the above passage can be found in statements in both *Practical Criticism* and *Principles of Literary Criticism*. In the former, Richards argued that the "whole use of intellectual belief is to bring *all* our ideas into as perfect an ordered system as possible" (258). In the latter, Richards asserted that the "artist" is capable of a higher level of ability in the organization of his thoughts than those around him.

> His work is the ordering of what in most minds is disordered. That his *failures* to bring order out of chaos are often more conspicuous than those of other men is due in part at least to his greater audacity; it is a penalty of ambition and a consequence of his greater plasticity. But when he succeeds, the value of what he has accomplished is found always in a more perfect organization which makes more of the possibilities of response and activity available. (55)

The contributors, many of whom either studied with Richards or attended his lectures (William Empson being the most notable of, indeed, all of Richards's pupils),[2] clearly borrow his valuing of "belief" as an "intellectual belief" over a moral or religious use of the term.[3]

The following piece in this issue of *transition* was by Jacob Bronowski; entitled simply "Experiment," it continues toeing the Richardsian line. Following Richards's strong Arnoldian emphasis on poetry's replacement of religion as the central organizing morality of culture, Bronowski argues that literature must import from criticism new values (107–8), as the "axioms of morality" have become "anomalies," and thus literature "has lost that tradition by which a work could be made significant by weighting it with a certain stable morality" (109). He goes on to conclude, echoing language found in the manifesto, that "we must find a *notation* to replace the old moral tradition," and he further identifies how the *Experiment* group understands formal innovation differently from anyone else.[4]

> In a sense that is a formal problem . . . [as well as] in the sense in which it means "to be solved in terms of the literary medium."

And the medium of literature is the sum total of all its relevant contents: outlook, narrative, "objects," and then the words symbolizing objects. These are of one unity; and the writer's problem is to convert his adjustment to the world into literature in terms of this unity. That is a problem of the ordered use of this medium, and it is for a discipline for this use that we are looking. (111)

The emphasis throughout is on order, organization, and the empirical framing of literature as a means to express lived experience. The previous chapter addressed the end logic of such an empiricist understanding of poetry and criticism as it manifested and was developed by F. R. Leavis and the *Scrutiny* circle. It is important to identify this tendency with the *Experiment* group not so much to reemphasize the well-known fact of "Cambridge English's" logico-empiricist approach to literature; rather, as many contributors to, and editors of, *Experiment* would go on to be involved in the Surrealist movement, early understandings and prejudices those writers carried with them need to be established, considering that they selectively took on broad aspects of Surrealism that were convenient to preset theories that were fully formed in their own minds by the late 1930s.[5] In other words, contrary to the popular consensus of Surrealism's "failure to take" in Britain, it is more useful to characterize the advent of English Surrealism as a stage in the development of British poetry that ultimately had little to do with the orthodox tenets put forward by its Parisian counterparts. Read in this way, we can more fruitfully understand Surrealism's belatedness in Britain as a part of a larger condition of British poetry in the late 1930s: namely, that Surrealism was only fully countenanced once it had developed a culturalist approach to literature that paralleled a similar shift in British poetry,[6] which itself became more broadly politicized as the decade wore on.

The final piece to be addressed from the "Cambridge Experiment" section of *transition* was written by Hugh Sykes Davies (who himself would become centrally involved in the English Surrealist movement—publishing a novel (*Petron*) and writing widely in support of the movement, albeit, as will become evident, from his own particular point of view). In an essay entitled "Localism," Davies, while describing the process of the artist's relation to the society in which he or she produces work (in an attempt to synthesize Eliot's and Richards's conflicting notions of value and belief), makes a prescient claim about the impact and influence of international trends in writing on a writer's local situatedness.

> National self-consciousness . . . arises in its most productive form after wars, when men look back from a previous present to a past that has been full of effort and glory . . . The effect of this self-consciousness is to solidify national tradition in all spheres. Ideology tends to become fixed for a time . . . And though new, foreign influences are admitted, by contact with the enemy and by commercial expansion, they are not strong enough to disturb or obscure the local tradition. They act only as a fertilizing agency. The advantages to the artist are obvious: he is presented with definite material—definite ideas, mythological, moral and religious. (114)

Davies has identified the structural form that would prevail in the following years in which continental modernist avant-garde practices would be imported and recoded according to localized concerns. Nick Hubble characterizes this piece as "captur[ing] a nodal point in cultural politics . . . [as] it celebrates localism as the possibility of representing the complex in the simple" (42).[7] But it also identifies a conscious nationalist attitude expressed by a member of a group desiring international recognition.[8] Davies's trumpeting of the local carries echoes of a disciplinary perspective developing since the early 1920s—anthropology. In effect, Davies is reflecting the interdiscursive development between literary criticism, psychology, politics, and of course anthropology that would find an uneasy, and temporary, expression in late-1930s British poetry.[9]

This chapter, then, will not take English Surrealism as a brief flirtation with continental modernism, which has been a view long upheld mainly on the evidence of the spectacle of the 1936 International Surrealist Exhibition in London (which will be addressed below) and the relative paucity of Surrealist publications following the Exhibition compared to continental Surrealist movements. Rather, it will be read as part of a broader structural development in British literary practice that can be characterized by the shift away from high modernist aesthetics to late modernist culturalism. I identify this shift as developing unevenly among multiple considerations and debates regarding the fate and direction of British letters. With that in mind, "periodical formations" best illustrate the contentiousness and uncertainty of these ideas in process. Raymond Williams uses the term "formations," whose "internal organization" can be characterized by "formal membership," by "conscious association or group identification," or, and most relevant here, by some "collective public manifestation": "such as an exhibition, a group press or periodical, or an explicit manifesto" (68). The nationalist impulse of Davies, for example, who conflates the "local" with the "national," exhibits a tendency in late modernist British writing to synthesize the complexity of emerging discourses into a unitary model of knowledge. This tendency, often characterized as "empiricist," inflects the development of Surrealism in Britain with a populist tone, and in turn, the overarching feature of this particular formation is its drive to treat its project as involved in an understanding of culture, where "culture" is read uniformly as a national one.

English Surrealism's moment will be reviewed, but with a specific eye on how long-simmering literary debates combined with emerging political concerns overrode considerations of the movement simply as an aesthetic practice. As the literary magazines involved in the conversation about Surrealism will illustrate, the movement was not taken on board "wholesale" but rather was used in service of the aforementioned literary and political developments. As a result, Surrealism never flourished as a writerly practice in Britain. Instead, it was treated as a weak form of Romanticism, or dismissed as a bourgeois practice that could not service the political Left, with whose cause it most identified itself. The rejection of Surrealism was not a provincial rejection of the continental avant-garde but rather the unique development of a parallel, yet ultimately disparate, more writerly practice.[10]

## Surrealism and Its Import(s)

David Gascoyne's *A Short Survey of Surrealism* (1935) popularly marks the beginning of a short period of intensive focus on Surrealism by British writers. Surrealism's belatedness in Britain meant that writers seriously engaged with the movement were faced with the difficulty of reviewing over a decade of contentious claims concerning what Surrealism was and how it was to be practiced. Furthermore, the advent of Surrealism in France came soon after World War I, and the revolutionary social and cultural claims by Breton and others had undergone transformation as the movement's French practitioners took on board the theories of Marx and Freud (to be discussed below in more detail). Finally, the late modernist transition that witnessed the "weaken[ing of] the relatively strong symbolic forms still evident in high modernist texts . . . also register[ed] the ways in which intense social, political, and economic pressures of the period increasingly threatened the efficacy of high modernist form" (Miller 20). As opposed to previous attempts to understand the development of Surrealism in Britain simply as a process of cross-cultural exchange, which in turn frames this development ahistorically, this chapter will also attempt to consider how the structural development from high to late modernism impacts on the particular character of English Surrealism.

One way to understand the particular shape of this development requires a revisiting of the initiating documents to see how people such as David Gascoyne and Herbert Read framed their writing in terms of "order" and "tradition" and thus appealed to what Perry Anderson has identified as core aspects of English national character: tradition and empiricism.[11] Following Jed Esty's articulation of the "anthropological turn" in the late 1930s and 1940s that describes a process by which artists and writers "begin to deemphasize the redemptive agency of *art*, which, because of its social autonomization, operates unmoored from any given national sphere, and to promote instead the redemptive agency of *culture*, which is restricted by national or ethnolinguistic borders" (2–3), this chapter will engage with English Surrealism as the domestication of selectively convenient claims from the movement's orthodoxy (represented here by Breton's two manifestos) by writers involved in a broader trend that sought political and cultural solutions in literary form. Before the chapter engages with Surrealism in Britain, it will be useful to review how Surrealists envisioned their practice. In Andre Breton's first and second manifestos of Surrealism (1924 and 1930, respectively), Surrealism is initially defined as "psychic automatism in its pure state, by which one proposes to express—verbally, by means of the written word, or in any other manner—the actual function of thought" (26). Surrealism primarily embraced "automatic writing" as a key into the mind's subconscious, thus revealing to writers aspects of their selves previously unnoticed. Peter Nicholls understands automatic writing as "provid[ing] an *unmediated* experience not of the body . . . but of the unified self, the self in its waking *and* dreaming life" (*Modernisms* 285). The problem that arises for the Surrealists in this process is that the "word gives us, then, the meaning of the thing, but in doing so replaces what it names, thus condemning the thing to a kind of non-being" (285). This "negation" presented the Surrealists with their "political aesthetic, for language's negation of the real, the absence which always echoes within it, is potentially a rejection of reality-as-it-is, that world which, codified by law and logic, exists by exiling what-it-is-not to the fantastic realms of art and the imaginary" (286). It is with this view of language that Surrealists felt that their approach blurred the distinctions between discourses of art, literature, politics, and science, as "our interaction with the world may bring us back to a full sense of ourselves by disclosing the ways in which reality is shaped by and responds to our desires" (288). Furthermore, this attitude brought Surrealists into engagement with other rigorously codified discourses without their ever fully embracing the ideology of these discourses.

By the time of the second manifesto, many Surrealists had joined the Communist Party, an action Breton defends thusly: "I really fail to see . . . why we should refrain from supporting the Revolution, provided we view the problems of love, dreams, madness, art, and religion from the same angle they do" (140). Breton had discovered a compatibility between the ideas of Marx and Freud and those of Surrealism and joined the party to express his solidarity.

> As Marx, entirely preoccupied with the need to modify the external conditions of social life from top to bottom . . . [as well] as Freud, with his ever-increasing emphasis on the primacy of the superego—considering all this, I doubt that anyone will be surprised to see Surrealism turn its attention, in passing, to something other than the solution of a psychological problem . . . It is in the name of the overwhelming awareness of this necessity that I believe it impossible for us to avoid most urgently posing the question of the social regime under which we live, I mean of the acceptance or the non-acceptance of this regime. (139)

Breton, as the major theorist of Surrealism, never rigorously engages with Marx's or Freud's writings and treats them rather superficially (as evidenced above). Yet, Surrealists deliberately did not embrace any political or psychoanalytical practice or ideology too intensively and merely employed those discourses' claims to scientific objectivity as a means to address self-knowledge. Ben Highmore characterizes this move as a way for Surrealism to "negotiate its way out of the enclave 'art.'" Furthermore, Highmore sees the Surrealists' use of "the rhetoric of 'science' . . . as effect[ing] a refusal of both art and science; or rather it rendered both terms inoperable within conventional use." Such a use of "science" in literary production, then, deliberately subverts the autonomy of art and the empiricism of science, and it provided the Surrealists with "a resource that countered the 'rationalism' of science with the possibility of a science of everyday life that would operate in the murky waters of myth and ritual" (47). As for their political involvement, Surrealists felt that "contemporary social organization (capitalism) hadn't eradicated the marvelous in the everyday . . . [as] the existence of the marvelous in the everyday was alienated from consciousness by forms of *mental organization* . . . [that required] a systematic attack on such mental bureaucracy" (49). It is precisely because Surrealists saw their project concerned with the everyday that discursive compartmentalization was viewed as a symptom of a society that needed radical rethinking. Finally, Breton's inability (or unwillingness) to take Marxist theory fully on board in a systematic fashion means that there is another aporia in Surrealism's methodology and reception: namely, its neglect of understanding how the "Surrealist image is historically conditioned" (Jameson 104). For Fredric Jameson, Surrealism manifested in a historical situation when the "traditional city [was] on its way to becoming extinct" and when "the human origins of the products of this period . . . in their production . . . still show traces of an artisanal organization of labor" (104).[12] This sheds light on the philosophical and literary tradition the Surrealists lay claim to as successors: "The Romanticism of the Surrealists becomes clearer, for their nature was precisely the city itself, to which they attached themselves with all the profound longing which the Romantics satisfied through the presence of landscape" (106). For the purposes of this writing, following Jameson, English Surrealism will be read as a cross-cultural exchange between its French and British practitioners, but additionally, one that was historically situated. For Britain, this entails addressing how the French romance of the city becomes recoded into the "romance of retrenchment." Put another way, Surrealism in France arose out of a metropolitan high modernist sensibility that, when it arrived in Britain in the mid-1930s, was faced with a late modernist trend that saw writers invested in a culturalist approach that prioritized national identity.

## Madge, Gascoyne, and *New Verse*: Surrealism Comes into Focus in England

The bulk of Surrealist writing, and writing on Surrealism, in Britain in the late 1930s primarily occurred in the pages of literary magazines. While there are examples of attention to Surrealism in magazines such as *Experiment* (Cambridge), *This Quarter*, and *Criterion* before 1935, it was not until *New Verse* brought sustained attention to the movement that it became a central part of literary conversation in Britain.[13] Subsequently, magazines such as *Contemporary Poetry and Prose*, *Arson: An Ardent Review*, and the *London Bulletin* regularly published Surrealist work, and magazines such as *Twentieth Century Verse* and *Left Review* adopted serious, if critical, attention to the movement's aims and efforts. Beginning with *New Verse*, I will analyze this early phase in Britain to illustrate how explanations of Surrealism configure it as a nationally differentiated aesthetic, and thus paves the way for subsequent writers to selectively choose those aspects of Surrealist theory that best suit the English writing of poetry.

*New Verse* is best remembered for W. H. Auden's presence and Geoffrey Grigson's editorship—and scant attention has been paid to other equally interesting and significant aspects of the magazine's makeup.[14] Contrary to the hegemonic narrative, *New Verse* was not the hermetically sealed core document of the Auden Generation, but rather a complex, often contradictory, and heterogeneous expression of poetic trends that occupied Grigson's attention.[15] *New Verse*'s own success facilitated wider attention to topics under review, even if they were not centrally trumpeted. Even though *New Verse* was neither a Surrealist magazine in the strict sense of it being the sole focus of its editorial agenda nor the first to pay attention to the movement, the confluence of Grigson's interest and, as we will see, Gascoyne's sustained advocacy generated the conditions in which Surrealism briefly became *the* topic of conversation in literary Britain.

Surrealism is first addressed in the sixth issue (December 1933). Charles Madge used the occasion of some art exhibitions in London (those of Joan Miro and Max Ernst) to address the growing interest in Surrealism in England.[16] His essay "Surrealism for the English" makes the argument that if Surrealism were to become relevant to English writers, then it would need to arise out of cultural and literary conditions in England. "Close study of the philosophical position of the French surrealists is needed to extract the essential purpose from the formal appearance of their work. But English writers will need something more: namely, a knowledge of their own language and literature" (14). For Madge, English writers need to turn to their own writing traditions and the development of English poetry to gauge the appropriateness of Surrealist practice in a specifically English context: "In France, the history of the poetic word has been very different from its history in England" (17). For this reason, Madge doubts the arrival of Surrealism as a workable practice in England, as a "contemporary period of poetic acceleration must needs be part of the same historical process as gave rise to the surrealist group in Paris" (18). It is notable that at this point Madge does not name any contemporary examples of Surrealist writing in English, but it is also equally notable that he frames his discussion around nationalist lines, as he conceives of literary tradition and development as occurring from within specific language groups (French, English, etc.). What is important to stress here is that Madge's nationalist framing is by no means novel, and indeed, as will be shown, future discussions of Surrealism in England follow his framing.[17]

In the meantime, another frequent contributor to *New Verse*—David Gascoyne—published the first sustained study of Surrealism in English. *A Short Survey of Surrealism* consists of an introduction to the movement by Gascoyne as well as his translations of a small selection of writings by Breton, Paul Eluard, and Tristan Tzara, among others. Gascoyne's introduction is divided into six sections, which account for the majority of the pages in the publication.[18] In this writing, Gascoyne not only outlines Surrealism as a "French" movement but also argues for its "internationalist" potential.

> For a writer, or anyone else, to object to an attempt to establish Surrealist activity in England, on the grounds that this would mean an "importation from Paris," is just as stupidly provincial as a doctor would be if he objected to the practice of psychoanalysis in England because it originated in Vienna. Surrealism itself, as it is today, is by no means wholly the product of previous French culture; there is a very strong element both of German and of Spanish thought in it, synthesizing as it does the philosophy of Hegel, Feuerbach, Engels and Marx, and the distinctly southern "lyricism" of painters such as Dali, Miro and Picasso. For Surrealism transcends all nationalism and springs from a plane on which all men are equal. (94)

Despite Gascoyne's explicit rejection of nationalist logic, he characterizes Surrealism's influences within nationalist categories. "English Surrealism" would potentially be a unique process within Britain and could furthermore develop out of a nationally conceived literary tradition. Gascoyne takes pains to cite English precursors—"Shakespeare, Marlowe, Swift, [Edward] Young, Coleridge, Blake, Beddoes, Lear, and Carroll" (94)— and thus frames Surrealism not so much as the revolutionary practice he desires but rather as a logical development of an English tradition.[19]

The book also includes work in translation by seven Surrealists totaling 21 pages. Given the vast output of Surrealist texts by 1935, one might expect some variety, but surprisingly, again and again, the texts published contain a recurring feature: references to nature and landscape. Andre Breton's three selections—"On the Saint Genevieve Mountain . . .," "The Spectral Attitudes," and (with Paul Eluard) "Force of Habit"— name various locations, but most are pastoral. In "On the Saint Genevieve Mountain . . .," the title itself sets the scene, with lines such as "[the] flora and fauna of this country" (99). "The Spectral Attitudes" moves through various settings. Initially urban—"The circus always enchants the same tramlines"—the poem quickly moves to the fields, mountains, and seas: "I have a boat detached from all climates"; "I cut and cleave the wood of this tree that will always be green"; "In the gorges which hide themselves between two mountains" (100–101). Finally, "Forces of Habit" is full of nature references: water, leaf, flower, weather, stream, river, plants (119–20). Rene Char's poems variously name swamps, a rose garden, a "quarry of unworkable ochre," leaf, foxglove, "and mountain weeds wither[ing]" (102–3). Paul Eluard's "At the End of a Long Voyage . . ." includes boats, storms, and voyages, while "What the Workman Says Is Never to the Point" contains lines such as "take the landscape by force" and "flower of flax," along with references to plantations and harvest, all set against imagery of the city (parks and buildings) (107–9). Georges Hugnet's poems mention chrysalis, fern, sea, beaches, ponds, tree, river, and a Barbary fig (110–11). Benjamin Peret's "Three Poems" references honey, protozoans, sea horses, a cowshed, a field, hedges, and harvest and contains lines such as "[the] rains and the winds will bless you" (112–13). Tristan Tzara's "The Approximate Man" portrays a violent and treacherous landscape: "the mountains' whooping-cough charring the escarpments of the gorges"; "whose typhoon stigmatizes your forehead"; "it means suffering when the earth remembers you and shakes you off" (114–18).[20]

This list is selective and does not pretend to present a complete analysis of each individual text; however, the consistency of nature or landscape references in each of the selections does reflect on Gascoyne's editorial choices. David Matless, in his *Landscape and Englishness*, argues that landscape works "as a vehicle of social and self identity, as a site for the claiming of a cultural authority" (12). The 1930s saw a marked increase in the publication of domestic travelogues as well as travel and nature guides in Britain. Esty interprets this development thusly: "As English culture moved from expanding imperial modernity to preservationist national past, the island itself became one large museum" (42). This preservationist mode was ruralist in nature, and while Gascoyne never claims Surrealism as a kind of neo-agrarian movement, his selection illustrates a canny understanding of the mode of English life in the 1930s. In short, Gascoyne's mission throughout his *Survey* had been to "sell" Surrealism to the British. It is my contention that he accomplishes this in a twofold manner: first, with an extended rationalist and historical justification of Surrealism, especially by emphasizing its validity within an English literary tradition; and second, by supplying examples of the movement's leading names, whose work contained traces of a ruralist theme that may have appealed to a culture "becoming self-consciously historical" (Esty 42).

One of the earliest reactions to the book was a review printed in *New Verse*. In *New Verse* 18 (December 1935), Charles Madge returns to the topic of Surrealism with a review of Gascoyne's book.[21] While Madge is not dismissive of Gascoyne's effort (he describes it as "really admirable" [20]), he finds a lot to fault in the book, arguing that Surrealism's revolutionary claims seem anachronistic in a period of history that Madge reads (ironically from our vantage point) as largely stable and peaceful. He concludes with the thought that "Surrealism is now in its academic period—the period of explanation and anthologies" (21). Madge's cynicism about the book is curious, as up to this point (outside of Gascoyne), he had been the most visible proponent of Surrealism in the pages of *New Verse*. Madge's objection may be rooted in his misreading of the contemporary political situation, and thus he finds the revolutionary rhetoric overblown. Yet, in two ways Madge would be largely prescient about the future of Surrealism in England: "the period of explanation" and "the wider public" would be two ways to characterize Surrealism's presence in England in the two following years. The well-attended and widely reviewed International Surrealist Exhibition in London in the summer of 1936 brought broad attention to Surrealism in Britain; it was followed by a series of talks, debates, and publications assessing Surrealism's role in English literature as well as engaging with its revolutionary political potential (or lack thereof).

## The International Surrealist Exhibition and the Debate over Surrealism

The International Surrealist Exhibition was organized by a committee that included Hugh Sykes Davies, David Gascoyne, Herbert Read, and Humphrey Jennings and had received official sanction from Andre Breton, who was in attendance for its opening.[22] The event opened on June 11, 1936, and during its run through July 3 it hosted over twenty thousand attendees (according to Paul Ray, "the largest number ever to attend an art show in London up to that time" [141]). The commercial success of the event, combined with the largely incredulous and dismissive reviews it received in the press, resulted in a general sense that the Exhibition was nothing more than spectacle.

In an effort to explain the Exhibition to its audience, a series of lectures and poetry readings were given throughout June.[23] A series of lectures occurred in conjunction with the Exhibition that were later collected in the Herbert Read–edited *Surrealism*.

The book was published in lavish fashion and featured an introduction by Read with essays by Andre Breton, Hugh Sykes Davies, Paul Eluard, and Georges Hugnet, with accompanying illustrations. Read's introduction attempted to demonstrate Surrealism's relevance to the English Romantic literary tradition, naming English precursors to the movement and stressing Surrealism's English qualities. Read even goes so far as to translate *surrealisme* as "superrealism." In Read's attempt to frame Surrealism's appropriateness to an English literary tradition, he devalues the movement's more radical claims for the form's revolutionary potential and reduces it to the reiteration of a historical literary form.

Davies's emphasis in "Surrealism at This Time and Place" is on the "tradition" of Surrealist writing within English literature. Davies's key phrase in this essay is "dialectical materialism," a concept that he sees the Surrealists valuing "for [the] critical examination of the history of all the arts; and as a matter of course they accept the principle of the continuity of history" (123). This way of understanding Surrealism devalues the change explicit in dialectical materialism in favor of an organic and naturalized understanding of the past. Davies defends this focus by arguing that Surrealism, rather than being the "fag-end of romanticism," has "enlarged, coordinated and enriched" Romanticism's "inchoate, disorderly, [and] intuitive" structure (168). Davies, similarly to Read, has defined Surrealism not as an internationally developing literary form but rather, in an effort to rationalize its function in Britain, as a logical outgrowth of an English literary tradition represented by Coleridge (and thus, again similarly to Read, he needs this tradition to be a Romantic one).

Read's and Davies's collective emphasis on Surrealism's logical presence within an English Romantic tradition accomplished two things: it muted Surrealism's revolutionary potential as an aesthetic form and political philosophy and rendered it obsolete as a "new" development in writing by emphasizing its relation to Romanticism. In Alan Young's estimation, "So much of the English literary past has been cited in support of Surrealism that the new movement was almost comically revealed as a very small and unoriginal aspect of Romanticism from which the English poet, fully aware of the literature of his past, could have very little to learn" (186–87). Peter Nicholls concurs with this assessment, asserting that "Davies and Read managed to develop this lineage so as to obscure the avant-garde character of Surrealism and to make it instead something thoroughly domesticated and familiar" ("Surrealism" 405).

The most rigorous critique of the rhetorical moves found in *Surrealism* came from a magazine that itself was concerned with both the aesthetic and the political—the *Left Review*. By the time of the Exhibition, the magazine's editorship had been primarily taken over by Edgell Rickword, who since closing *The Calendar of Modern Letters* had become a member of the Communist Party, and while he had shifted his own focus toward political concerns, it was not at the expense of his interest in literature. Rickword's personal adjustments found reflection in *Left Review*'s editorial policy. As David Margolies characterized it, *Left Review*'s attitude stressed that "more fundamental than their immediate role, writers in their activity *as writers* were considered to be political," and further that "literature was not merely a reflection but a part of life, an agent of revolutionary change and an activator of the great reserves of human potential" (2). As such, the magazine became affiliated with the British Popular Front and published writers with broadly left-leaning or anti-Fascist positions.[24]

The poetry and fiction published in *Left Review* was generally thematically concerned with the class struggle in England. Jack Lindsay, whom Margolies identifies as "a phenomenally productive writer and frequent contributor to *Left Review*," wrote a poem, entitled "Not English," that was published in the May 1936 issue, just before the Exhibition. It was so popular that the issue sold out within a month, and the front matter advertising in the following June issue announced a pamphlet publication of the poem, now entitled "Who Are the English?" The poem reads as a straightforward piece of propaganda, decrying the ruling class and exhorting the workers to rise to reshape England. "Who are the English, / according to the definition of the ruling class? / . . . keep then the recompense of a sounding name, for you have nothing else" (353). The poem proceeds to argue for an alternate English tradition and namechecks a series of historical radical movements or individuals: John Ball, Jack Cade, Wycliffe, Lollards, Oliver Cromwell, Anabaptists, Levellers, Muggletonians, Bedlamites, Luddites, and William Morris. The exhortation climaxes with "England, my England — / the words are clear / *Workers of the World, unite!* / The voice comes pealing through the trumpet of the night, / *You have nothing to lose but your chains!*" (original emphasis) and culminates with "the disinherited are restored, our mother, / England, our England, / England, our own" (357). Aside from the use of line breaks, it is difficult to discern any other formal features that would distinguish this as either a poem or prose. Margolies notes that Lindsay "tend[ed] toward reductive thinking," and in one review for the magazine he missed Bertolt Brecht's use of caricature in *A Threepenny Opera*, instead reading the play as a critique of capitalism. Margolies concludes that "it is not so much that Lindsay neglect[ed] particularity but that he neglect[ed] the literary experience . . . for a general political conclusion" (10). Further, an essay Lindsay published in the May 1938 issue, entitled "The May-Day Tradition," closes on a similar theme found in his poem.

> The unity of culture lies in the continuity of man's productive energy, his courageous attempts to merge dialectically with nature through work. Culture has a unity and a persisting significance in so far as it vitally reflects the productive tensions. Only by realizing the truth can we assume the role of the defenders of culture. (966)

Lindsay's poem and essay are typical of what Margot Heinemann identifies as the magazine's "stress on the 'cultural heritage' [that] laid great emphasis on recovering episodes of struggle in which the common people had played an active role." Poems such as "Not English" partook in a drumbeat of editorials, cartoons, and creative writing that reasserted a "great tradition . . . but it was not much like that of Eliot or Leavis . . . [in that it] provided an inspiration and a sense of historical process, rather than a model of how to write" (Heinemann 123–24). If we recognize his blindness to the very simple notion that form affects meaning in poetry, and further, if we accept Lindsay's poem as representative of the kinds of poetry and fiction produced in the magazine, then the ensuing exchange on Surrealism should unsurprisingly reveal that radical poetic form did not find sympathy in the pages of a magazine that read that formal experimentation as a kind of obscurantism, and thus as counterrevolutionary.[25]

The *Left Review*'s attention to Surrealism prior to the Exhibition was mainly skeptical, with a disparaging review of Gascoyne's *Short Survey* (January 1936), as well as an interview with Louis Aragon, who had by then broken with the movement and joined the Communist Party (May 1936). The 1936 exhibition served as an occasion for further comment, mostly reserved and cynical, with a few contributions by Anthony Blunt and Alick West (July 1936 [as a supplement]). Blunt is critical of Surrealism's "bourgeois" origins and counters that "propaganda" is the "new art . . . [and] the product of the proletariat, which is again performing its true function" (vi), and he stresses that "[Surrealism] pretends to free language and thought from all conventions, but takes no account of the fact that [it is] using bourgeois conventions in a negative form all the time" (viii). When Herbert Read, himself a regular contributor to *Left Review*, published *Surrealism*, the full force of the magazine's critique of the movement was brought to bear. A. L. Lloyd's review (January 1937), entitled "Surrealism and Revolutions," judges Surrealism broadly as counterrevolutionary given its individualist, as opposed to a favored collectivist, focus. For Lloyd, responsibility to the proletariat is of the utmost importance, as the "masses are only passive, inasmuch as they have illusory consciousness of activity within the frame of the bourgeoisie, *individual* activity" (148). Lloyd invests in an idea of political revolution that necessarily entails a cultural revolution collectively experienced and expressed. In his estimation, English Surrealism fails because, despite its radical formal pronouncements, it still announces a poetics of self-investment.[26]

Read and Davies were given an opportunity to reply to Lloyd's review (February 1937), and they chose to zero in on the latter's charge of Surrealism's nonrevolutionary "lyrical impulse." It is necessary to note that Lloyd never uses this precise phrase, instead using "lyrical capacity," "lyrical bases," and "discreet interior lyricism," all implying an internalized emotionality set in contrast to rational processes (145, 148). Additionally, the term does not appear in *Surrealism* itself, so the duo's use here is unique to this reply, which presents the reader with the challenge of deciphering their specific use. Read and Davies argue that the way they think about the lyrical impulse is in relation to "other impulses and other kinds of human activity," yet they only cite English writers who illustrate such a combination (Wordsworth, Tennyson, and Browning) (149–50). Their sense of the "lyric" is vague as well, but Read has elsewhere defined this term in two ways: (1) "in lyrical poetry what is conveyed is not mere emotion, but the imaginative prehension of emotional states"; and (2) "we might define the lyric as a poem which embodies a single or simple emotional attitude, a poem which expresses directly an uninterrupted mood or inspiration" (Preminger 715; Read *Form* 62). Despite their taking issue with Lloyd's characterization of Surrealism as a manifestation of a lyrical impulse, their thinking on this phrase appears to fall in line with his: the lyric is presented as a byword for the emotional and irrational aspects of individual expression.

In the last analysis, their reply reworks their original claims in the book: namely, they defend Surrealism within the tradition of English Romanticism and thus fail to counter the critique of their domestication of the movement within a limited understanding of English writing. They further argue that they "found it necessary to step outside the bounds of bourgeois criticism, and to study the 'lyrical impulse' not from a literary point of view of general psychology, taking evidence from mental disease, other abnormal conditions, from anthropology, and from actual experiment" (150). This claim is misleading as they primarily cite literary figures and literary production in the book, and in this reply as well. Ultimately, the thrust of the review and the reply tars Surrealism's literary potential with the brush of bourgeois complacency and favors the political as the test for any literary production. In this way of thinking about Surrealism, the movement's justification in terms of literary development has been handcuffed to the past (and thus critiqued as not a development at all), which results in a faultily conceived backup defense of its political revolutionary potential. The result is that Read and Davies alienate those who value Surrealism's innovatory aesthetic potential, and they fail to convince the more hard-line leftist radicals of Surrealism's role in a cultural revolution.

Roger Roughton, editor of *Contemporary Poetry and Prose*, on the other hand, avoided the pitfalls of wedding his Communist sympathies and his interest in Surrealism. While, on the surface, the magazine never explicitly argues for a nationally defined Surrealist movement, it conceives of itself as arising out of a need for a domestically grown Surrealist practice intertwined with a need for a revolutionary class uprising in Britain. *Contemporary Poetry and Prose* began its run around the time of the Exhibition and achieved the tag of the "only Surrealist" magazine of the 1930s in the United Kingdom.[27] The magazine is interesting not only for the high frequency of Surrealist contributions from British and French writers (in translation) but also for its unstinting support for the anti-Fascist cause in the Spanish Civil War.[28] With this complex combination of focuses, *Contemporary Poetry and Prose* was better able to handle the "political" side of Surrealist claims than Read or Davies, but it also more generously considered Surrealism's formal potential than the *Left Review*. The particular shape of the editorial focus was in part due to where the magazine was published: The Arts Café on Parton Street, a street that also housed the David Archer Bookshop (which was a "hot spot" for like-minded leftists in London), as well as the offices of Wishart and Co. (the publisher of *Left Review*).

Despite Roughton's eventual inability to establish a convincing wedding of Surrealism and Communism, he did manage to publish a wide variety of poetry across an international spectrum. That said, the magazine retained a nativist perspective in its editorial selections. Rod Mengham has noted Roughton's "attempt to locate Surrealism in terms of its relationship with other traditions of writing," and thus his publishing of non-English writing can be better understood as a comparativist move in an effort to legitimate an English brand of Surrealism. He points to "Roughton's own choice of English-language texts from earlier centuries," such as the traditional English ballad "Little Musgrave" and other versions of English ballads found in Labrador, Tennessee, Louisiana, and New South Wales, as evidence (691–92).[29] It might be said that publishing English ballads that traveled with the expansion of the British Empire actually displays the privileging of English cultural exports and thus simply reinscribes authentic Englishness mapped onto imperial belongings. Joseph Roach states that such acts of "orature"[30] illustrate an "alternative historical model of intercultural encounter, one based on performance . . . [and] such a model would emphasize the truly astonishing multiplicity of cultural encounters in circum-Atlantic America, the adaptive creativity produced by the interactions of many peoples [Native Americans, Europeans, those of African descent, and white American settlers]" (189). Roughton's inclusion of these versions of traditional English ballads is thus provocative but ultimately reactionary, as Roughton seems to want to reclaim these versions as part of an English canon. Alternatively, their inclusion can be viewed as implicit markers of the impact of colonization that also ignores the new identity formation these ballads "creatively adapt," as they are folded back into an English tradition (indeed, they are labeled as "traditional"). Even though Mengham argues that the inclusion of these ballads "effectively celebrat[ed] tradition as a focus for continuous transformation . . . [a] poetics of version" (692), the ballads displace their cultural production as ineffably adapted elsewhere in favor of claiming English as a reiterable concept. Granted the ballads rub against the "authentication" that Read and Davies used to legitimate Surrealism in English, but their inclusion does not overthrow the idea that the English past is the underwriter of such adapted identities. *Contemporary Poetry and Prose*, while offering a more culturally complex vision of writing, in actuality highlights the core tension predominant in discussions surrounding Surrealism in Britain: the condition and development of an English literary tradition.[31] The evidence of Surrealism's presence in British poetry in the 1930s can be mainly found within the pages of literary magazines: Gascoyne's *Survey* and a few small books of poetry, Davies's novel *Petron*, and Read's *Surrealism* represent the main extent of nonperiodical publications. There has thus been a lasting insistence that given the ephemerality of literary magazines, it follows that English Surrealism itself was an ephemeral matter as well. This writing hopefully dispels this notion to some extent. The periodical formation outlined here cannot be reduced simply to an English variant on a French theme. English Surrealism's production and theorization within magazines, which themselves did not hold an overtly orthodox Surrealist editorial mission, meant that the shape of that production was inflected by debates over the role of tradition in contemporary English writing, as well as the cultural politics of literature. As will be explored in the following chapter, these debates produced another interdisciplinary-minded movement—Mass-Observation—that, as well as involving some of the names that were associated with English Surrealism, has an equally misunderstood poetic history.

CHAPTER 3

POPULAR POETRY AND
MASS-OBSERVATION

Humphrey Jennings recognized the irreconcilability of Surrealism and leftist politics, and in his review of Herbert Read's *Surrealism* (*Contemporary Poetry and Prose* 8 [December 1936]), he takes issue with the claim to "universal truths" that Read and Davies proffer. "The elevation of definite 'universal truths' of classicism is not only a short-sighted horror, but immediately corroborates really grave doubts already existent about the *use* of Surrealism in this country" (167). In essence, Jennings finds Read and Davies's logic for Surrealism culpable for the same consensus-building ideology of political discourse and dismissively rejects their thesis. "Is it possible that in place of a classical-military-capitalist-ecclesiastical racket there has come into being a romantic-cultural-*soi-disant* cooperative-new uplift racket ready and delighted to use the 'universal truths of romanticism—co-eval with the evolving consciousness of mankind' as symbols and tools for its own ends?" (168). Jennings finds that they have missed the core use of Surrealism, which lies in the theory of "coincidences." "'Coincidences' have the infinite freedom of appearing anywhere, anytime, to anyone: in broad daylight to those whom we most despise in places we have most loathed: not even to *us* at all" (168). It is the accident of occurrence that gives the value to what he terms "coincidences." In reaching for "universal truths," Read and Davies have argued for a programmatic understanding of Surrealism that Jennings illustrates to be antithetical to the movement's theories and aims. Jennings's alternative—locating "coincidences" in daily life—would form the root of Mass-Observation, a movement he, and his friend Charles Madge, would create. They thought that these coincidences could be observed on a large scale and thus reveal a map of British society.

Characterizing M-O as "ethnographic surrealism" has, in effect, become the most popular way of dealing with the movement's early interdisciplinary approach, as it explains its borrowing of rhetoric from both art and science. However, this approach is limited by a too simplistic connection of shared personnel involved in both English Surrealism and M-O. In his discussion of a group of Surrealist writers interested in anthropology and ethnography, James Clifford coined the phrase "ethnographic surrealism" to describe "a theory and practice of juxtaposition" that "studies, and is part of, the invention and interruption of meaningful wholes in works of cultural import-export" (147). Clifford thinks of ethnography as the "general cultural predisposition that cuts through modern anthropology and that this science shares with twentieth-century art and writing" (121). In his definition, ethnographic surrealism is an interdisciplinary approach to cultural observation. Taking his cue from a provocative footnote in Clifford's text that suggests a link between M-O and the French authors he is examining, Ben Highmore reads M-O as "employing Surrealism for an ethnographic project," and in his doing so, "the 'will to order' of anthropology is seriously undermined, while at the same time Surrealism's tendency to revel in mythic individualism is effectively countered" (82). M-O has been traditionally linked to Surrealism through Jennings's involvement in both movements, as well as Madge's attention to Surrealism in *New Verse* (reviewed in the previous chapter), and the two movements' parallel interest in anthropology (as noted by Clifford). Yet, given Jennings's critique of Surrealism referred to at the opening of this chapter, and the general absence of any mention of Surrealism in the M-O documents, the link between the two movements is tenuous at best.[1]

The movement that became known as Mass-Observation was organized primarily by Charles Madge and Humphrey Jennings and initially included members such as David Gascoyne, William Empson, Kathleen Raine, and eventually and most influentially, Tom Harrisson. It was envisioned as a project that would collect everyday observations of the British people, in the hope of identifying a "collective image" from the mass of contributions. M-O has been characterized as "autoethnography" (James Buzard, Jed Esty), "ethnographic surrealism" (James Clifford), and a "science of everyday life" (Ben Highmore). More recently, Nick Hubble has cautioned against such approaches, as they "often struggle to maintain focus and can become subject to historicist pressures that reduce complexity to the product of a particular time and place," and has alternatively argued that the movement needs to be addressed in terms of "major cultural, political, and historical themes" (1, 3).[2] The very hybridity of M-O has led to much analytic confusion over the group's aims and practices, and, as will be shown, M-O did indeed sample from various discourses to explain its project. Too often lost in the mix of these competing descriptions of M-O are the movement's literary origins. Originally named "Popular Poetry" by Madge in one of his diaries, M-O, from the very beginning, mixed poetry and certain developing sciences (anthropology, psychology, and sociology). M-O could have continued theorizing a new radical poetics, instead of tending toward a more systematic, albeit for the time unique, form of anthropology. Rehabilitating M-O's literary origins not only corrects this aspect of its historical narrative but also more accurately explains M-O's project as an argument for reading British society textually, as one would a poem.

    This chapter will first pursue a revisionist approach to M-O's literary antecedents. To do so places stronger emphasis on M-O's aesthetic claims than is found in previous scholarship, as well as reasserts those claims as a vital, and not misbegotten, portion of M-O's self-theorization. This approach will involve addressing how extensive was the influence on M-O's project of I. A. Richards's writings and teachings on theories of poetic value, as well as emphasizing how Coleridge's definition of "imagination" is a more correct starting point in the way of understanding M-O's definition of the "image" and "coincidences"—both core terms in M-O's attempts to theorize how the public could be read expressively. With this shift in emphasis, M-O can be rightly understood as initially participating within the discourse of the English poetic tradition. This approach also corrects the misconception that "poetry" and the "poetic" were flimsy terms used to generically mean "creativity" or "expression."

Periodicals, in short, have been the unused marker of M-O's development, and as a result, previous approaches have provided an incomplete picture of M-O. M-O's eventual shift toward a more rigorously scientific approach has led to a general sentiment that the "poetic" in M-O's early stages was part of a misguided attempt at a politicized aestheticism, led by Jennings and abandoned when he himself left the group. This chapter will attempt to explain the failure of M-O's poetics not simply as an inevitable shift toward scientific legitimacy but also as a notion lost in the competing discourses that made up M-O's vision.

M-O's stages of development can be easily marked by the types of articles that appeared in periodicals throughout 1937 and the early part of 1938. The articles covered here have been noted and discussed in other studies of M-O, but the question of the forum of their appearance has never been addressed. In other words, what difference does it make whether an article appeared in *New English Weekly*, *The Daily Worker*, or *Left Review*? The answer to such a question may be obvious: in selecting periodicals with interdiscursive interests (mainly in the form of politically left, culturally progressive, aesthetically informed publications), M-O instinctively latched onto a specific, established periodical formation in which to promote a likeminded project.

This overview of M-O's development will be followed by an examination of perhaps M-O's least understood publication—*May the Twelfth*—which has been popularly treated as a work of "ethnographic surrealism." As a collage of a heterogeneous mix of cultural expressions and artifacts, *May the Twelfth* has been commonly pointed to as evidence of M-O's direct lineage from English Surrealism. However, the book can also be shown to adhere to Pound's ideogrammic method as well: namely, by compiling images of lived experience without obvious transitions, it allowed for an interpretative openness and engagement on the part of the reader. *May the Twelfth*'s complex form thus does not originate from any single influence, and this complexity indicates more likely a movement in the process of figuring out its methodology than a production of any coherent school of thought. That it was regarded as a failure by its editors says more about the direction in which M-O was moving in terms of its methodology than the viability of the book's intent.[3]

M-O's failure as a sustainable poetics was finalized in its 1938 publication *First Year's Work*. The book concluded with an essay by Bronisław Malinowski, who in his general praise for Mass-Observation rebuked its practitioners for their experimental approaches and challenged them to pursue their research in a more orthodox anthropological manner.[4] This essay served as the impetus for M-O's revision into a more mainline form of anthropology—a version of M-O that is much better remembered today. The moment of this publication also marks the beginning of M-O's absence from periodicals of any kind and can thus also be read as the end of a very brief periodical formation.

Finally, in its self-description from the very beginning as an "anthropology of ourselves," M-O uncritically adopted the phrase to mean an undifferentiated national grouping (much like Richards's "reader" and English Surrealism's "tradition").[5] M-O took "ourselves" to mean the British people, thus envisioning a unified nationalist expression. Ben Highmore has pointed out, following Perry Anderson's "Components of a National Culture," that M-O flourished as an anthropology movement, and not a sociology movement, precisely because its delimiting term—Britain—remained unanalyzed (Highmore 99), or, as Anderson put it, "British society was never challenged as a whole from within" (Anderson 92). One immediate effect of this aporia that will be briefly addressed in the conclusion of this chapter, and more extensively analyzed in the next, is how the construction of a national identity in late modernist Britain relied on assumptions of racial and ethnic homogeneity. As Tony Kushner has stressed, M-O's "humanistic approach, although allowing insights into minority life and relations, was heavily racialized and hierarchical" (100–101). In M-O's development into a disciplined social science, it ignored the ideological ramifications of proposing an anthropological survey of "home." By recuperating the "poetic" in M-O, we find that in approaching British society "textually," M-O was culpable for maintaining a "privileged position" in relation to its object of study, while ignoring the fact that "society is not a text that communicates itself to the skilled reader . . . [as] society is the cultural condition in which speakers act and are acted upon" (Asad 155).[6] The origins of this attitude can be found in the writings of I. A. Richards, who assumed a culturally homogeneous "reader" and in the process ignored the cultural situatedness of texts and readers.

## SCIENCE AND POETRY

Humphrey Jennings provided M-O with the idea of the "image" to describe the collection of people's observations of their everyday lives. Jennings never set down a precise definition of the word, which has produced much confusion. Kathleen Raine writes that Jennings "held that 'the image' . . . was valid just in so far as it was not invented, but discovered: never must the poet invent an image: because the kind of truth poetry communicates was for him collective, public, and historical" (*Defending* 49). Charles Madge, as late as 1982, declares that Jennings's use of the word was akin to "gestalt" without providing any evidence to support this similarity, instead relying on a Michael Faraday diary entry that Jennings had used in his manuscript version of his book *Pandemonium*. Nick Hubble succinctly paraphrases this passage to claim that the image "involves metamorphosis rather than literary substitution." The image, in Jennings's sense, is metonymic or contiguous—it presents a found object in a provisional context. Hubble elaborates on this distinction by declaring that "rather than freely signifying and so perhaps evading the imposition of external meaning, the image holds both one meaning and the sense of its self-transition to another meaning, equally its own" (74). The overlap in all this exegesis is the historical and cultural situatedness of the image. In this way of understanding the image, it shares much with Ezra Pound's own 1913 definition of the image as an "intellectual and emotional complex in time" ("A Retrospect" 4). This is not to argue for an Imagist genealogy for M-O, nor is it an attempt to replace Surrealism with Imagism as the literary forebear of M-O, but the compatibility of Jennings's and Pound's mutual understandings of the image underscores the fact that M-O was as well informed by what poetry could offer their self-definition as by any other discipline. Pound, later in that same essay, argues that the poet should "consider the way of the scientists rather than the way of an advertising agent for a new soap," as "the scientist does not expect to be acclaimed as a great scientist until he has *discovered* something" (6). In his essay "The Serious Artist," Pound declares that the serious artist is "scientific in that he presents the image of his desire, of his hate, of his indifference as precisely that, as precisely the image of his own desire, hate, or indifference. The more precise his record the more lasting and unassailable his work of art" (46). While it is outside the focus of this project, the prevalence of Pound's pre-1922 declarations on art and poetry, and their subsequent influence on I. A. Richards, appears to be rather substantial and provocative. The point here is that Madge and Jennings most likely received their ideas about Pound directly or indirectly through Richards.

I. A. Richards, in *The Principles of Literary Criticism*, proposes six definitions of "imagination." The sixth, which Richards states that he takes from Coleridge (and which concerns us most here in answering the question of how Humphrey Jennings defined the "image"), asserts the following:

> That synthetic and magical power, to which we have exclusively appropriated the name of imagination . . . reveals itself in the balance or reconciliation of opposite or discordant qualities . . . [and] the sense of novelty and freshness, with old and familiar

objects; a more than usual state of emotion, with more than usual order; judgement ever awake and steady self-possession with enthusiasm and feeling profound or vehement. (Coleridge qtd. in *Principles* 227)

In Richards's view, Coleridge's "imagination" operates as a synthesizing function—folding the unknown, or the otherworldly, into the known and the present. In essence, Coleridge posits interiority as a reproduction of the object world in the process of establishing subjectivity. This, by now, is a familiar concept and can be found differently approached by Hegel, Marx, and Freud, but Coleridge's version of subjectivity would be the best known and understood by Madge, Jennings, and Empson. What is more, Richards's filtering of Coleridge through his writings would have had the most direct impact on these men.

Richards's influence on the thinking of Madge and Jennings has only ever been superficially tracked, most recently by Nick Hubble, who, while providing provocative biographical connections, does not engage with Richards's writings extensively.[7] To track Richards through M-O would not merely provide historical detailing but in actuality would bolster the claim that M-O's project was initially Richardsian and concerned with the poetic in its methodology. More precisely, across Richards's three key books—*The Principles of Literary Criticism*, *Science and Poetry*, and *Practical Criticism*—he developed contrasting definitions of scientific and poetic language that M-O would directly adopt, albeit in an unacknowledged fashion.

In *The Principles of Literary Criticism* (1924), Richards differentiated "scientific belief" from "emotive belief": whereas the former involved the "readiness to act" as if the proposition were universally and infallibly true, the latter is relational, circumstantial, or "narrowly restricted." "Poetry . . . [is] chiefly conversant of universal truths . . . [and therefore] beliefs . . . are entertained only in special circumstances of the poetic experience," and thus "they are held as conditions for further effects, our attitudes and emotional responses, and not as we hold beliefs in laws of nature, which we expect to find verified on all occasions" (260–61).[8] Initially, these terms are distinguishable by universality and provisionality alone. By the time of *Science and Poetry* (1926) two years later, in a chapter entitled "Poetry and Beliefs," Richards had modified "propositions" and "conditions" to the terms "statements" and "pseudo-statements."

> [There is a] fundamental disparity and opposition between pseudo-statements as they occur in poetry and statements as they occur in science. A pseudo-statement is a form of words which is justified entirely by its effect in releasing or organizing our impulses and attitudes . . . [and] a statement, on the other hand, is justified by its truth, *i.e.* its correspondence, in a highly technical sense, with the fact to which it points.[9] (59)

Pseudo-statements, while restricted to poetry in Richards's system, are contrasted with statements in a manner that bears parallels to connotation and denotation. In other words, pseudo-statements include any ambiguous expression (hence Empson's *7 Types of Ambiguity*). It is the looseness of Richards's terminology that later allows M-O to apply his idea about the organizing power of pseudo-statements in the argument that they can be read in the "dominant image of the day."

Richards later fleshes out his ideas for how impulses are organized through poetry when he publishes *Practical Criticism* in 1929. He retains the term "emotional belief," but he has switched from "scientific" to "intellectual" belief as the apposite term, which allows him to treat more broadly the full stretch of rational thought: "*Neither belief nor disbelief arises*, in this intellectual sense, *unless the logical context of our ideas is in question*" (original emphasis) (258). On the other hand, "this acceptance, this use of the idea—by our interests, desires, feelings, attitudes, tendencies to action and what not—is emotional belief" (259). In essence, intellectual belief is simply the acknowledgment of objective and observable facts, whereas emotional belief is closer to Coleridge's definition of the imagination—as that which internalizes and reproduces those facts into something completely other (e.g., a poem and a response to a poem).[10]

It is important to stress here that Madge himself is often vague or ambiguous in his use of the words "science" and "poetry," as if he assumes that he and the reader will share the same understanding. The best explanation lies in the fact that he is writing to and for a coterie of writers who would have no doubt read, or been familiar with, Richards's writings, and thus Madge's default definitions of these terms come from his former mentor. Richards was not only well known in Cambridge, but through his books—and his essays published in magazines like Eliot's *Criterion*, or the attention he received in Leavis's *Scrutiny* or Grigson's *New Verse*—his ideas were widely felt. The precise relevance of laying stress on this point is that one of the effects of the "long shadow" of I. A. Richards is how deeply internalized and naturalized his influence was, to the extent that someone like Madge, 40 years later in an interview with Angus Calder, cannot clearly distinguish his own ideas from those of Richards.[11]

M-O articles never identify Richards as an influence or forebear, but the definitions reviewed above filter into M-O's discussions of art, science, and everyday life. How exactly M-O treated Richards's terminology, and evolved its own treatment of these same terms, can be found predominantly in the pages of periodicals. In its first 16 months of existence, M-O, as it only published two books and a pamphlet, mainly existed in the pages of periodicals, where at least 30 articles either advocating or reviewing M-O were published.

## A Periodical Formation: The Role of *New Verse*, *Left Review*, *New Statesman*, and *Life and Letters To-day*

When a chronology of M-O–related publications is made (from January 1937 to April 1938), it becomes clear that there were three clearly demarcated stages in the types of publication. From January to June 1937, articles promoting M-O predominate. In June 1937, a pamphlet, simply entitled *Mass-Observation*, was published, followed by the Coronation observations—*May the Twelfth*—on September 23, 1937. From June to December

1937, then, reviews of these two books consist of the bulk of publication. In November 1937, *New Verse* published a special "Auden Double Number" (November 1937, nos. 26–27), in which Charles Madge offers a terse critique of Auden's recent writings and invites Auden to partake in observations of his hometown of Birmingham; later, in the February issue of the Oxford-based *Light and Dark*, Tom Harrisson continued this attack on Auden (and his "circle") while claiming to use M-O techniques to read the Auden's poetry. This final stage can be characterized mainly by Tom Harrisson's very public disavowal of the literary in M-O, as well as the fallout from his aggressive stance toward his critics. As has been noted above, this final stage immediately precedes the publication of *First Year's Work*, a book that marks M-O's complete shift away from the literary as well as its total absence from periodicals.

In this first stage, where precisely M-O chose to publish—*New Verse*, *New Statesman and Nation*, *Left Review*, and *Life and Letters To-day*—reveals the community that they wanted to reach. While, as Ben Highmore has pointed out, M-O advertised in the *Daily Express*, the *Daily Herald*, and the *News Chronicle*, it was in these four periodicals that M-O's project can be found to be most clearly explicated (76). *New Statesmen and Nation* was founded in 1913 by the Fabians Sidney and Beatrice Webb, and by the 1930s it had become more editorially radicalized, having incorporated the *Nation and Athenaeum*. The *New Statesmen*'s main focus was mainly politics, but it also published articles focused on cultural concerns, and occasionally creative writing ("About *New Statesmen*"). For example, Tom Harrisson's only published poem—"Coconut Moon"— appeared alongside the first M-O announcement in the January 2, 1937, issue, thus famously drawing Harrisson's attention to Madge and Jennings's project. *Life and Letters To-day*, originally run by the *New Statesmen*, by the late 1930s was publishing mainly poetry and some fiction (authors included Auden, Dylan Thomas, Marianne Moore, and Stevie Smith). In the 1940s, it became more engaged with the New Apocalypse poets and ultimately found a focus in publishing regional writing (Tolley 2007 48–52). The editorials, such as one found in the issue before the one containing the M-O article that will be discussed below, would occasionally express political sentiment. The editorial in question, for example, challenged its readers to think about the impact of the fact that four thousand Basque children had already died in fighting in the Spanish Civil War (Summer 1937 1–2).

*New Verse* and *Life and Letters To-day* focused on literary publications, but all four periodicals (along with *Left Review* and *New Statesman*) published writers linked with the Popular Front. In other words, M-O deliberately aligned its project with the concerns of politically conscious artists and writers and, in turn, not only portrayed M-O's focus on "mass society" as a class-conscious effort to critique institutions of power but also implicitly sought like-minded people who understood the idea of using literary principles to analyze cultural conditions. This, too, can be gleaned from the rhetoric in the individual articles, but what is most telling is the relatively short time frame in which these articles appeared. After June 1937, no M-O articles were published in these magazines, and the reappearance of M-O in *New Statesmen* in February 1938 (to be reviewed below) came about only in response to one critic's attack on a Tom Harrisson article. In short, M-O identified a periodical formation compatible with its aims, and when those aims shifted (or did not "take" within the formation), its presence in these periodicals ceased. By addressing this set of publications in these four periodicals, a clearer motive and methodology can be ascribed to M-O's early instantiation than has previously been possible. Most significantly, the central role that poetry played in M-O's early formation can be more assuredly stressed than before.

The earliest Mass-Observation publications can be found in two short announcements (January 2, 1937 and January 30, 1937) by Charles Madge, Humphrey Jennings, and (for the second article) Tom Harrisson, who declared M-O to be devoted to an "anthropology at home," which would collect "coincidences" to profile the "mass wish" or "mass fantasy" of the British people and then plot "weather-maps of public feeling" (January 2, 1937 12; January 30, 1937 155). The announcements also served as a call for volunteers to collect data: "The artist and the scientist each compelled by historical necessity out of their artificial exclusiveness, are at last joining forces and turning back towards the mass from which they had detached themselves" (January 30, 1937 155). In these two articles, M-O had announced an interdisciplinary approach for studying British society. As Ben Highmore notes, M-O's use of the word "science" can be read multiply: as "science as objectivity," but also as "aimed at the emergence and circulation of an effective economy of representations, a social imaginary made up of mass images that can be treated as dream elements and wish fulfillments of a social unconsciousness" (83–84). These proclamations could also be read as an attempt to synthesize Richards's division of beliefs—i.e., collecting statements of the world as it is seen (emotional belief) and treating them collectively as an image of the world as it is (intellectual belief). The *New Statesman* announcements are provocatively vague in this respect, though, and only in subsequent publications are the ideas framing M-O's project made clearer.

Charles Madge published two essays in the *Left Review* related to M-O: "Magic and Materialism" (February 1937) and "The Press and Social Consciousness" (June 1937). In the former, Madge accuses "bourgeois science" of ignoring centuries of myth, religion, and ritual, and he praises anthropology, psychology, and sociology for treating these cultural traditions seriously. He goes on to claim that poetry, in particular, shares with these "nonbourgeois" sciences the ability to "light up, in fitful flashes, a scene on which the full day of science will presently dawn" (32). Echoing the claim in the second *New Statesmen* article, Madge argues for the compatibility of the goals of poetry and the sciences sympathetic to magic, myth, and ritual. The result of collecting data on the "needs and wishes of the masses" will be "a poem or thesis [that] becomes a report of this collective achievement" (33). Madge also describes this process as an "observation of images," following Jennings's sense of the word, that once again Madge claims will "form a mass-picture . . . [or] weather-map" (34). In effect, Madge argues for overturning the division of art and science in an effort to present "revelation" as "fact," images as patterns. Poetry, following Richards's claim of the organizing impulse of emotional belief, serves as the justification for treating nonprofessional observation of daily occurrences as significant data.

"The Press and Social Consciousness," while not specifically naming M-O, engages in similar rhetoric as is found in the article above. Madge critiques the "social homogeneity" produced by the popular press and cites Coleridge's description of the imagination when confronted with the poem—"the willing suspension of disbelief"—as a way to describe how the news is written not as "objective fact but as poetic fact" (281). Madge's concept of the "poetic" here is flexible. While he is not arguing for an expanded definition of what could be termed "poetry," he is emphasizing (via the poetic analogy) that the news employs similar structural features as poetry. Aside from the obvious claim that both the news and poetry are language acts and thus carry a denotative and connotative level, the analogy foregrounds the constructedness of news stories. He argues that the news should not be treated as objective but rather as "poetic memory, affecting our feelings but not our actions" (282). For Madge, "speech, language, the written and spoken word" are all forms of "social consciousness . . . [that] has varied in different cultures" (279). Compare this last claim to Malinowski's in his supplement to Richards and Ogden's *Meaning of Meaning* (1923):

> All words which describe the native social order, all expressions referring to native beliefs, to specific customs, ceremonies, magical rites—all such words are obviously absent from English as from any European language. Such words can only be translated into English, not by giving their imaginary equivalent—a real one obviously cannot be found—but by explaining the meaning of each of them through an exact Ethnographic account of the sociology, culture and tradition of that native community. (299–300)

Malinowski's "functional" approach (as he terms it) is a response to a perceived cultural isolationist focus in Richards and Ogden's book, and he reminds the reader not only that the specificity of linguistic expression is unique to each culture but also that this specificity is rooted in the practices of that culture.[12] Madge, following Malinowski, reads linguistic expression as cultural action, and by studying that culture through its language, one can come to a full understanding of how it behaves.[13] These two articles taken together propose that "poetry" and the "poetic" can refer broadly to the creativity people have in shaping their idea of the world they inhabit through language. Poetry and the poetic are treated in these articles as cultural effects. Yet, as with the following article in *Life and Letters To-day*, Madge appears to be adapting his terminology to suit his audience. In other words, it is more likely that a former student of Richards would have an informed understanding of these two terms, and thus he is savvily "tweaking" their formal definitions to appeal to a readership primarily concerned with cultural politics. Madge has also established here the early methodology of M-O: its practitioners will study British habits and expressions, but always through the medium of language.

This functional approach toward language is also expressed by Madge and Jennings in the autumn 1937 issue of *Life and Letters To-day*. In an article entitled "They Speak for Themselves: Mass Observation and Social Narrative," the authors emphasize the "natural" language they are capturing in the reports and even play up the anthropological angle by engaging in a colorful description of their project.

> This is hardly a "well of English undefiled" since into it continually flow more or less muddy streams from press, radio, advertising, film, and "literature." But in actual social usage, all the jungle of words grow up together in Darwinian conflict until they establish their own ecology and functions. Contrast this functional value with the use of words by sensitive, stylist writers . . . [and] there is a general wish among writers to be UNLIKE the intellectual, LIKE the masses. Much "proletarian fiction" is a product of this wish. But it is enough for such fiction to be ABOUT proletarians, if they in their turn become a romantic fiction, nor even for it to be BY proletarians, if it is used by them as a means of escaping out of the proletariat. (37)

Here Jennings and Madge directly employ William Empson's definition in *Some Versions of Pastoral* of "pastoral" as a form of proletarian literature: "The wider sense of the term [proletarian literature] includes such folk-literature as is by the people, for the people, and about the people. But most fairy stories and ballads, though 'by' and 'for,' are not 'about'; whereas pastoral though 'about' is not 'by' or 'for'" (6). The book follows Empson's idea that literature as a "social process" attempts "to reconcile some conflict between the parts of a society . . . and also [attempts] to reconcile the conflicts of an individual in whom those of society will be mirrored" (19).[14] Following Empson, Madge and Jennings present M-O as a means toward reconciling intellectual practice with everyday life. Nick Hubble finds Empson's contributions through this book to be central to the shaping of M-O. According to Hubble, Empson's claim that proletarian literature is "usually Covert Pastoral" provides M-O with an "imaginary solution"[15] for bridging the divide between bourgeois and proletarian consciousness. Hubble argues that in one of the main features of "pastoral" that Empson outlines—"comic primness" (or "getting the joke at both levels—both that which accepts and that which revolts against the convention that the speaker adopts primly" [211])—M-O found the seeds for their participatory observation. That the individuals being observed "were in on the joke" meant that M-O had negotiated around how the anthropologist "escapes context . . . his value and his meaning is to be found in the way he moves from context to context with a freedom that is the very antithesis of the social embeddedness of the social facts he studies" (North 52). With Mass-Observation, the observer, as a so-called member of the society in which he or she observed, could not escape that context in his or her observations. The importance of this connection to Empson's "imaginary solution" (as in Richards with "emotional belief") is the literary provenance for some of its core ideas.

The poetic in M-O, however, was most explicitly expressed in the pages of *New Verse*. The February–March 1937 issue opened with "Poetic Description and Mass-Observation," which was an essay introducing M-O to *New Verse*'s readers by Charles Madge and Humphrey Jennings (Madge is credited with writing the essay, and Jennings with collecting the examples). The piece began with three examples of writing: an excerpt from a contemporary novel, a historical account, and an observation by a Mass-Observer noted in their diary. Madge claims that the third is "(i) scientific, (ii) human, and therefore, by implication, (iii) poetic" (2). The third example by the Mass-Observer:

> Coming home on a Midland Red 'Bus from Birmingham (a distance of approx. 6 miles) I was sitting on the front seat, near the large sliding door. There was a cold easterly wind blowing through the door, and after having some cigarette ash blown in my eyes, I touched the Conductor on the sleeve to attract his attention, and said "May we have the door closed, Conductor?" He turned round and leant towards me in a confidential way, and then said in a most insolent manner "Yes, when I'm ready to shut it!" I was too surprised to make any reply. The door remained open until I left the 'bus. (2)

Madge claims that this passage is both subjective and objective, as the observer's own subjectivity is being observed, and thus illustrates what M-O achieves, that is, as a "technique for obtaining objective statements about human behavior . . . [that supplies] an interchange of observations being the foundation of social consciousness" (3). Madge, in other words, is proposing a wedding of two concepts Richards held apart, meaning that M-O offers both the pointing to and the organization of social reality. These observations operate "poetically" as they "produce a poetry which is not . . . restricted to a handful of esoteric performers" (3). In doing so, he democratizes poetic performance as a public performance that can be managed by anyone, at any time. M-O, in effect, treats poetry in the abstract, as a term that defines a kind of socially aware practice not limited to formal conventions, or specialized training, or even individual talent. While the idea of a "popular poetry" was not novel to Madge, M-O, as is outlined here, presents a nonpoetic poetry, or a poetry freed from traditional conventions of poetic form.[16]

Yet, M-O only ever attempted one poem. In the following issue of *New Verse* (May 1937), Madge presented the "Oxford Collective Poem"—an 18-line poem written in an irregular rhyming pattern, in three six-line stanzas.[17] The poem was preceded by over three pages of explanatory notes detailing the method of composition. Using a basic feature of M-O, that is, establishing the "dominant image of the day" from the collected reports, 12 Oxford observers collected "images" over a three-week period.

> We selected the six images which appeared most . . . Next we met and composed each a single pentameter line dealing with each in turn of the chosen images . . . We each put a mark against the line we preferred, provided it was not our own; and so took a vote to select one line for each of the six images . . . The task now was to integrate these lines and their ideas into a unified poem . . . [with] the stipulations made that the poem was to be in pentameters, not being less than twelve lines, not exceeding eighteen. One or two people chose to use a stanza form, some wrote in rhymed couplets, and there was one unrhymed poem . . . Each poem went round the circle and we were all expected to make any alteration we thought fit . . . [and ultimately] the poem which emerges is much more a collective account of Oxford than of any single person in the group. (17–18)

The following is the result:

> Believe the iron saints who stride the floods,
> Lying in red and laboring for the dawn:
> Steeples repeat their warnings; along the roads
> Memorials stand, of children force has slain;
> Expostulating with the winds they hear
> Stone kings irresolute on a marble stair.
>
> The tongues of torn boots flapping on the cobbles,
> Their epitaphs, clack to the crawling hour.
> The clock grows old inside the hollow tower;
> It ticks and stops, and waits for me to tick,
> And on the edges of the town redoubles
> Thunder, announcing war's climacteric.

The hill has its death like us; the ravens gather;
Trees with their corpses lean towards the sky.
Christ's corn is mildewed and the wine gives out.
Smoke rises from the pipes whose smokers die.
And on our heads the crimes of our buried fathers
Burst in a hurricane and the rebels shout.

The traditional formal features of this poem belie the social experimentation of its production. This fact, compounded by its uniqueness as the only poem produced by Mass-Observation (and not by individual members), has lent credence to the idea that M-O's attitude toward poetry was little more than a dalliance. Subsequent criticism of this piece has reinforced the ephemerality of not only the poem but also M-O's poetics. A. T. Tolley, who in addition to misidentifying Tom Harrisson as "Hopkinson" and erroneously claiming that M-O ended at the start of World War II, likens the experiment to the Surrealist "exquisite corpse" (*Thirties* 283). The experiment does bear similarities to the game of individuals in a room contributing their own words or phrases to what will be constructed as a single poem, but the "Oxford Collective Poem" could also be characterized by its use of cut-up, collage, found objects, and stream of consciousness, as well as iambic pentameter, a chartable rhyme scheme, and poetic diction. Valentine Cunningham, after reproducing the poem in full, condemns the poem as "extremely trite," "conventional," and "highly bourgeois" (339–40). The contributors are faulted for being Oxford undergraduates with a classical education that is reflected in the form and content of the poem. Samuel Hynes offers a more generous assessment when he argues that the poem is "interesting because it *is* collective . . . [as it is] an anthology of the image-content of undergraduate minds, and so a kind of document in the shape of a poem" (287). Yet, even Hynes is reticent about this poem, as he reads M-O like most others: as a social movement with possible anthropological applications, but at no point a literary movement.

Most recently, Nick Hubble's study on M-O is content to unproblematically quote Cunningham's and Hynes's comments on the experiment, without providing any further insight (64). This experiment is an early example of what would be more fully realized by the chance operations of John Cage and Jackson Mac Low. To use the example of the poet Mac Low, he attempted throughout his career to remove authorial intention as fully as possible from the writing process to produce poetry that would level the hierarchy of author over reader. Charles Bernstein reads his work this way:

> I think the work is grounded in this dichotomy: that "self" if it is to mean anything at all is to be found from the outside in, in the structures and materials that make up, in constantly changing ways, the world. World not an assumed prefix form to be revealed but a series of possibilities to be realized. ("Jackson at Home" 254)

What Bernstein recognizes in Mac Low's poetry is the effort to foreground the cultural materials used to construct a poem, any poem. In Mac Low's case, he would often use source texts (such as Ezra Pound's *The Cantos* and James Joyce's *Finnegans Wake*) and perform readings through these texts based on procedures that guarantee "chance" selections over authorial intent.

Steve McCaffery characterizes Mac Low's poetry in terms very similar to Madge's self-description of M-O in "Poetic Description": "There is a radical questioning of the position of the subject in a language considered to be sovereign and external. No longer present to the productive moment of meaning, the subject situates as a witness to—and experience of—a particular outcome or method" (191). What both Bernstein and McCaffery identify in Mac Low's work is an iteration of a similar methodology employed in the "Oxford Collective Poem," namely, a process by which poetry can not only reflect but also illustrate its cultural conditions. While Mac Low more successfully realized his own particular methodology, it bears a strong similarity to M-O's attempt to objectively convey, via a subjective medium, the society that it inhabits.

It is necessary, then, to view the "Oxford Collective Poem" as one piece of the movement's complex self-description, and not the failure of a new poetic movement. The various M-O publications examined thus far all demonstrate a willingness to recalibrate the movement's claims ever so subtly to adjust to the established readership of the magazine. So, as discussed above, *New Verse* readers encountered an emphatically strong claim about poetry's relevance to M-O and vice versa. Both the *Left Review* and *New Statesman*, as culturally and politically leftist publications, read presentations of M-O as more anthropologically or sociologically motivated, with the *Left Review*, as a self-proclaimed site for cultural and political commentary, reading pieces by Madge that deal with "poetry" as a sociocultural effect. As for *Life and Letters To-day*, a periodical that published mainly poetry and fiction but was not averse to making cultural comments in its editorials (as evidenced above in its references to the Spanish Civil War), there is a direct, if unacknowledged, reference to Empson's definition of "proletarian literature" in an effort to differentiate M-O's project from the constraints imposed on individual artists in representing the masses. Madge and Jennings's decision to publish in these magazines reflects their sense of M-O as a progressive movement. Taken together, these magazines were all involved in the Popular Front politics of the late 1930s, and in some ways this fact defines them collectively as a periodical formation. This periodical formation can also be characterized by a mutable sense of poetry and the poetic: M-O never provides a "correct" sense of these terms; rather, it applies several definitions to appeal to the broadest possible audience. The aim in doing so was to recruit interested participant observers from the readership of these magazines, who would be called upon to contribute to a singular, wide-scale observation effort that remains unique in the combination of its focus, methodology, and results.

## *May the Twelfth*: The Poetic Document of Coronation Day

*May the Twelfth*—edited by Humphrey Jennings, Charles Madge, T. O. Beachcroft, Julian Blackburn, William Empson, Stuart Legg, and Kathleen Raine—similar to the "Oxford

Collective Poem," compiled the observations of Britons on Coronation Day, May 12, 1937. The book contains two parts: the first is divided into four sections and covers Coronation Day itself, while the second presents a collection of "Normal Day Surveys," conducted on the 12th day of the three preceding months. The four sections in the first part are divided as follows: (1) "Preparations for May 12" contains a collection of press clippings under headings like "One Big Family," "Troubles," and "Rumors and Adaptations"; (2) "London on May 12" has a combination of three types of sources: observations by Observers who had participated in the previous "Normal Day Surveys," thousands of respondents to a circulated questionnaire about the day, and a "Mobile Squad" of 12 Observers who called in reports to the M-O office; (3) "National Activities" is a series of reports from Observers and questionnaire respondents outside of London (with some international respondents included as a "control"[18]); and (4) "Individual Reactions" initially presents reactions to radio broadcasts, continues with an examination of "popular feeling," and culminates with the presentation of people's reported dreams. Aside from occasional footnotes clarifying, or commenting on, the reports, press clippings, and observations, the editors do not present an argument for the overall significance of their collected data. This aspect of the book became the central focus of critique in its reception (which will be examined in the next section), but it also leads to an uncomfortable question about what exactly this book is—or, in other words, How do we classify *May the Twelfth*?

It is, in fact, a document that defies easy classification. It contains many features that one would expect in an ethnographic project, but it lacks any rigorous scientific analysis. Given Jennings's ever-increasing involvement in making documentary films, it could be argued that the book, which was the only M-O publication he had a central hand in compiling, is a print version of a documentary film.[19] While *May the Twelfth* does bear similarities in form to Jennings's films, the book can be more rightly claimed as a collaborative effort; thus, while Jennings in his role either as filmmaker or book editor ultimately controls the selection and combination of material, the book presents such a diffuse range of materials that it ultimately exceeds the range of meanings possible in a film. One way to characterize *May the Twelfth* that would manage to explain all of its formal complexity and ambiguity is by thinking of it as a poetic document. Madge and Jennings asserted in their *New Verse* article "Poetic Description and Mass-Observation" that observations as "objective statements about human behavior . . . [are] a poetry which is not . . . restricted to a handful of esoteric performers" (no. 24 3). M-O worked from Richards's idea of the poet's "vigilance" that is more than "usually organized," which results in "original connections . . . [as] so much more of his past comes to be freely revivable for him at need" (*Principles* 169). M-O has democratized Richards's restrictive claims so as to pronounce a "poetry of everyday life" that remains rooted in Richards's core requirement of the poet's "vigilance." As for *May the Twelfth*, the collected observations can be thought of as poetic texts, as they vigilantly document daily life and, according to Derek Attridge's classification of poetry, include "a sense of its real-time unfolding" (*Singularity* 71). Arranged without an overarching narrative, the various observations combine into a heterogeneous set of images that keep the reader in the presentness of the moment of reporting. Furthermore, there is an implicit invitation for readers to sample observations as they wish. Explicitly, some observations are footnoted with references to other compatible observations.[20] These footnotes anticipate hyperlinks, destabilizing the linearity of the text and encouraging the reader to treat the text nonsequentially. In other words, as Jennings argued for the suddenness and unplannedness of "coincidences," the text itself becomes a site where readers can engage at random and possibly find their own "coincidences" in the act of reading.

*May the Twelfth* resembles numerous postmodernist textual experimentations. The emphasis on the everyday has antecedents in Frank O'Hara's "I do this, I do that" poetics. The "hyperlinks" anticipate more radical experiments found in bpNichol's *The Martyrology* Book 5 or in Mark Z. Danielewski's novel *House of Leaves*. Furthermore, the notion that anyone can generate poetic texts echoes Fluxus's deconstructing the line between art and everyday actions, as well as various chance generation procedures performed by John Cage, Jackson Mac Low, or, more recently, the Flarf poets. Like M-O, these latter-day experimentalists challenge the notion of the formal boundaries of poetry, as well as who can be a poet. To return to Madge and Jennings in *New Verse* 24 once again, they see M-O as critiquing the notion that "the term 'poet' [applies], not to his performance, but to his profession, like 'footballer'" (3). In defining the poet based on a criterion of "performance," as opposed to profession, M-O encouraged the perception that anyone could produce poetry. Furthermore, a nation of vigilant poets would provide a network of connections previously unseen, and thus a more thorough "image" of the nation could be constructed than through the work of canonical, or publicly recognized, traditionally formal poets.

Benedict Anderson, with his example of the daily newspaper as one means by which an individual imagines himself or herself as part of a larger community, argues that "the newspaper reader, observing exact replicas of his own paper being consumed by his subway, barbershop, or residential neighbors, is continually reassured that the imagined world is visibly rooted in everyday life" (35–36). In *May the Twelfth*, Part 1, Chapter 1, the editors introduce a collection of press clippings by declaring that they "played the double role of both describing the preparations which were made and also of being . . . one of the main instruments for preparing the people [for the Coronation]" (4). While Madge, in particular, was suspicious of the press's tendency to produce "social homogeneity," M-O's compilation of press clippings provides the ground on which the day's activities and perceptions are measured.[21] In the variety of responses that are written, the heterogeneity of the public is laid bare, but as part of a shared ceremony, its unity is underlined. In other words, *May the Twelfth* is akin to Anderson's notion of the newspaper, as they both reveal to each participant that "the ceremony he performs is being replicated by thousands (or millions) of whose existence he is confident, yet of whose identity he has not the slightest notion" (Anderson 35). In producing

*May the Twelfth*, M-O provided the British public with a textual representation of its complex unity. The book "works" as poetry as each individual imagines a connection between himself or herself and the collective past of Britain as they all experience the events around the Coronation.[22] Again, if, as Richards states, the imagination brings "the sense of novelty and freshness, with old and familiar objects" (*Principles* 227), then the combination of the coronation-as-ritual and the specific Coronation in 1937 permits the observers to imagine themselves as part of a nation that is both its legacy and its present. Reading *May the Twelfth* as a poetic document gives more credence to the notion that the work is a collective creative expression and, as a result, reproduces the nation as an imagined whole.

This is not to say that M-O should be read strictly as an outgrowth of Surrealist practice in Britain. Highmore has used this historically assumed link to declare that the book "could be characterized as a practice of understanding society as a *totality of fragments*: the montage of incidents seen as symptomatic of repressed forces" (82). In treating the book as an example of montage, Highmore argues that "a critical totality of fragments is possible that attempts to see the world as a network of uneven, conflicting, unassimilable but relating elements," and as a result the book "suggests a different relationship between reader and text: rather than being the recipient of knowledge, the reader is left to make their own connections within a work that appears to have no ordering principle apart from disorder" (95). Highmore's liberatory claims for M-O imply a solution to the main challenge to Surrealism: namely, its tendency to become a quasi neo-Romanticism that celebrates the isolation of the artist's vision from the rest of society's. The problem with this analysis is not so much its inaccuracy but rather its simplistic attitude toward aesthetic forms. To restate Talal Asad's dictum, "society is not a text," and however innovatory *May the Twelfth* is in its structure, it does not radicalize the society it represents.

As a way of demonstrating this comparatively, montage bears similarities to Ezra Pound's proclamations on the "ideogram" and what he called the "ideogrammic method" in poetry.[23]

Perhaps the most concise definition of the ideogrammic method that Pound offers can be found in *Guide to Kulchur*: "[It] consists of presenting one facet and then another until at some point one gets off the dead and desensitized surface of the reader's mind, onto a part that will register." In Pound's acerbic rhetoric, the value of this method lies in the active participation and revelation it potentially provides to the reader. Akin to Jennings's "coincidences," ideograms offer the "newness of the angle" to the reader (51). The variety of revelation theorized in Pound's ideogram parallels Jennings's sense of the "image" as well, as they both rely on the idea of the historical and social contiguity of the text or object in question. According to Sanford Schwartz, in *The Matrix of Modernism*, the ideogram "directs attention away from the poet's own voice and toward the historical documents themselves, . . . [and furthermore, it] would also establish an essential bond between imagination and truth, presenting the imaginative apprehension of new relations without sacrificing historical veracity" (91–92). While this accounting of the ideogram echoes Jennings's sense of the image and suggests a close affinity between Pound's and M-O's work, there is a key distinction in approach. Pound's use of montage was deliberate and consistent, whereas M-O's use of coincidental juxtaposition was not programmatic. In short, the comparison to Pound illustrates that M-O cannot be described simply as an outgrowth of Surrealist practice but is itself a unique approach to poetic experimentation, which was prevalent at the time.

Additionally, more recent scholarship has underlined the stark differences between montage and collage and has even illustrated the unsettled nature of any attempt at definition. Charles Bernstein's distinction, for instance, between montage and collage reads the former, through Sergei Eisenstein, as using "contrasting images in the service of one unifying theme," whereas the latter "juxtaposes different elements without recourse to an overall unifying idea" ("Pound" 160).[24] For Bernstein, *The Cantos* exhibits the use of montage, as Pound's "appropriation of prior texts . . . [was] intended as an evaluative, 'objectively' discriminating—and hence hierarchical and phallocentric—'ordering' of these materials" (161). The very scope of *The Cantos* is precisely what makes it problematic, then, as "it took the arrogance of Pound's supremacist and culturally essentialist ideology to give him the ambition to imagine a work on [this] scale, . . . [that is,] a poem that theoretically encompasses nothing less than the story—history of the determinately *seminal* strains of human culture" (161). *May the Twelfth*, it could be argued, is distinct from *The Cantos* on this last point, as the editors of the former text intend to display all the arcane, ephemeral, and mundane practices of the British people on one day and thus do not engage in Pound's elitism toward cultural artifacts. However, *May the Twelfth* does share with *The Cantos* this "culturally essentialist ideology" insofar as it claims to portray Britain, in all its varied behavior, as a nation unified in a single activity—Coronation Day—and it thus structures all this variety as an expression of a singular people.

Both projects rely on the selection and combination of material in an attempt at a unifying theme. If, as Ben Highmore stresses, M-O, taken in its historical context, was engaged in a "critically dialogic response to the image of a society where diversity was being brutally and systematically eradicated (Nazi Germany)" (92), then, in its aesthetic context, *May the Twelfth* can be read as a political and poetic response to the "objectively discriminating" *The Cantos*. In other words, montage should not be treated with any political equivalence automatically, just as it should not be treated with any aesthetic equivalence. *May the Twelfth* engaged in a kind of formal experiment that gave permission to the reader to openly draw his or her own conclusions, but it was not free from ideological designs.

*May the Twelfth*'s reception was mixed, contradictory, and marked by a persisting confusion over what the book intended to be and how it should be read.[25] Nick Hubble reviews the early print reception of M-O, but he focuses almost exclusively on the criticism and development of its scientific methodology (142–50). He usefully points out that while the perception of hostile criticism to *May the Twelfth* is rooted in three reviews, there were also generally positive reviews.[26] Yet Hubble, who throughout his own book downplays the poetic in M-O, here too fails to address these reviewers' oversight regarding the poetic potential of *May the Twelfth*. Maurice Richardson, one early reviewer, frames his impressions similarly to most *Left Review* writing, i.e., situating the common man as in some way oppressed by official institutions, by praising the quality of the observers' writing as opposed to "the false and specious over-simplifications" of the press (November 1937 625). He closes by asserting that "from an anthropological point of view some of the aspects of crowd-behavior noted are fascinating" (626). The book's value, this review suggests, lies strictly in what it offers the class struggle. E. C. Large, in the December 30, 1937, issue of *New English Weekly*, does point out that "actors, novelists, and dramatists" also engage in observation, but he implies a contrast in these professions in relation to what occurs in *May the Twelfth*, warning that "if the observations [of *May the Twelfth*] are supposed to be scientific observations, [then] it is a form of cheating" (231). He concludes by declaring that certain facts seem to have been suppressed and that there can be "no science" when that is the case (232).[27] The reviewing does not countenance *May the Twelfth* as a poetic, or even more generally a literary, document, and the subsequent proclamations by Tom Harrisson would expunge the poetic from M-O for good.

In two articles—"Mass Observation and the W.E.A." (*The Highway* [December 1937]) and "Mass-Opposition and Tom Harrisson" (*Light and Dark* [February 1938])—Tom Harrisson effectively rejects the notion that M-O will continue as a literary endeavor. In the former, he claims that Madge felt that "the problems of the press and poetry" were connected to the fact that "neither showed any signs either of accuracy or effect" (47). Harrisson thus characterizes Madge's concern as rooted in social dynamics, not poetic form. Even though, Harrisson allows, the collected observations "result in one sense anthropology, in another literature," he insists that the overall methodology of M-O is not literary in nature, claiming that "a far more accurate picture of life [is produced] than any novelist can hope to give" (47).[28] In his 1938 publication, Harrisson then definitively stakes out M-O's ground as a science in solidarity with the working class against a perceived bourgeois poetry. In "Mass-Opposition and Tom Harrisson," Harrisson takes the occasion of the *New Verse* "Auden Double Number" (nos. 26–27) to rigorously attack Auden and his peers for writing poetry out of touch with the language of everyday society. He addresses several recent publications in which Auden appears, and he performs a selective reading of poems by W.H. Auden, Charles Madge, Kathleen Raine, Stephen Spender, C. Day Lewis, Kenneth Allott, and several others, noting the prevalence of "fish" or "water" references in their poetry.[29] The crux of Harrisson's defensive complaint is that "artists are resenting a 'science of ourselves' because they have, for some time past, got away with claiming that title for their own work" (11). Furthermore, the "poet's laboratory is entirely inside him or her," and thus poetry only "provides us with a promiscuous self-documentation" (13). Throughout Harrisson's ill-tempered attack on Auden and his contemporaries, he treats poetry as inherently the property of an insulated few, and not as representative of a nation.[30]

Harrisson disavows poetry wholesale as a suitable means to examine British society as it exists, and to return to Empson's discussion of the pastoral, "though 'about' is not 'by' or 'for'" the people (6). As Harrisson works his way through the contributions to *The Year's Poetry (1937)*, he notes a reference to the ocean in Madge's "Delusions" series, which leads him to charge that Madge used "M-O to write Mass Poetry, a horrible perversion and one which is now a part of the unforgettable past."[31] He continues by claiming a new solidarity between his own and Madge's approach to M-O, and he insists that they "are no longer concerned with literature—[Madge] got rid of that in the Coronation book" (10).[32] Or, indeed, Harrisson has taken Empson a step further by arguing that poetry is not about, by, or for the people, and thus it is not "proletarian," nor does it "attempt to reconcile the conflicts of an individual in whom those of society will be mirrored" (Empson 19). Harrisson has instead argued that in eliminating poetry and the poetic from M-O, it has democratized its process.

The immediate response to Harrisson's *Light and Dark* article was made primarily by G. W. Stonier (whom Harrisson had attacked in his article) and two Oxford students—George Dudman and Patrick Terry—in a pamphlet entitled *Challenge to Tom Harrison*. In their pamphlet, the authors work through Harrisson's article point by point, and while the details of their critique will not be reviewed here, it was, in sum, damning and final in its judgment. They conclude with the point, which they say Harrisson misses, that "the fact that the poet uses Mass-Observation's materials does not mean, by any straining of the English language, that [he or she] consider the only purpose of Mass-Observation to be the provision of material for their poetry" (22). In essence, their "challenge" to Harrisson accepts his assumption that M-O and poetic form are mutually exclusive pursuits through which to "speak to" British society. Consequently, they make no effort to argue for M-O's poetic potential and instead unwittingly reify Harrisson's division of M-O and poetry as mutually exclusive endeavors. Even though they emphasize the cross borrowing of the two, they keep M-O and the poetic discrete and, in turn, reify Harrisson's claim that M-O does not produce poetic objects.

G. W. Stonier's response to Harrisson was published in the February 26, 1938, issue of *New Statesman and Nation*. Entitled "Mass Observation and Literature," Stonier's piece argues that Surrealism and M-O can be "bracket[ed] together," but only as they both "claim to be scientific . . . [and] spring from the same fundamental distrust of the arts" (326). Alluding to the *Challenge* pamphlet, Stonier ultimately takes umbrage at what he characterizes as Harrisson's attempt to show how M-O proves poetry "decadent and [how M-O] will finally adjust the situation" (326). Harrisson's reply in the March 12, 1938, issue of the same journal simply reiterates the claim he made in *Light and Dark*, that "modern poet[s] had the habit of generalizing for humanity from their very limited personal experiences" (409). This exchange effectively and definitively established M-O as non-, or even anti-, poetic, along with firmly placing Harrisson as the face of M-O.[33]

At the heart of this exchange was how British society could be treated as a "knowable" object, and the discourse, regardless of the authors' respective attitudes toward M-O, situated the poet firmly apart from the broader public. M-O's culturalist push—treating people's behavior in a systematic fashion rather than seeing it as material for creative production—embodied a broader structural shift that has been identified before as late modernist England's "anthropological turn." Jed Esty characterizes M-O's "home anthropology" as a way "in which the national essence and the fractured present could be brought together . . . by the increasing cultural power of relativist, particularist, and realist beliefs about English boundedness and knowability" (45). Yet, M-O, in attempting an "anthropology of ourselves," never satisfyingly resolved who belonged to "ourselves" and who did not. While Observer reports were included in *May the Twelfth* from all over the Isles, there was a strong nationalizing tendency in framing their results. As Tony Kushner declares in *We Europeans?: Mass-Observation, "Race" and British Identity in the Twentieth Century*, "They [nonwhite Britons] were chosen because of their foreignness" (101). M-O, in Kushner's estimation, "failed to confront the possibility that an individual could be both black and British" (100). M-O's nationalist categories reinforced the perception that the "ourselves" of Britain were English, and they underpinned this perception by limiting their subsequent social surveys to cities inside England (primarily Blackpool and Bolton).

The structural shift that has been identified in the previous chapters—from high modernist aesthetic universalism to late modernist culturalism—resulted in an ever-increasing valuation of England as a nation populated by the English.[34] One effect of this drive toward retrenched Englishness was that by the 1940s there was a peak in regional periodical publications that proudly declared their locality as the defining marker of their respective literary publications. While Irish and Scottish nationalist-inspired publications had been prominent in the previous decades (such as *The Modern Scot* [1928–55], *The Irish Statesman* [1923–30], and *Ireland To-day* [1936–38]), it was not until the late 1930s that Welsh poets and writers joined this trend and pursued their own widespread cultural revival. Additionally, while 1945 has often been used to mark the beginning of postimperial Britain, from a literary perspective, there were several notable postimperial figures active in the British publishing community before that year. In one figure—Tambimuttu, a Ceylonese-born British émigré—we have an individual who brought together multiple forms of regional and colonial identities in his magazine *Poetry (London)* as well as in his book series. In addressing Tambimuttu's brief, but provocative, career in 1940s London, the categories of race and identity (categories often passed over as non-English) can be addressed to illustrate how Welsh, Scottish, Irish, and nonisland colonial identities came to be constructed through poetry and critical reviews in the little magazines, in opposition to a hegemonic English identity.

# CHAPTER 4

## THE POLITICS OF RECEPTION

By 1939, all of the magazines addressed thus far had ceased publication, or, as in the case of *Scrutiny*, were locked into an editorial vision that increasingly ignored contemporary poetic production. The Second World War, of course, had much to do with this, especially with the institution of paper rationing, which began in early 1940 and continued to 1948. The result was a significant decrease in any print production and more direct government control over what could be published (Gardiner 417–18).[1] Notable exceptions included John Lehmann's *New Writing and Daylight* (1942–46), printed under the Leonard and Virginia Woolf's Hogarth Press imprint that Lehmann ran by the 1940s, and Cyril Connolly's *Horizon* (1940–49), which enjoyed the patronage of a wealthy art collector (Latham "Cyril Connolly's" 857). Then there was *Poetry (London)* (1939–51). Run by Meary James Tambimuttu, whose "Letters" that opened most of the issues posed a challenge to the culturalist and political poetry of the 1930s and argued for a more expansive, and indeed "Romantic," vision for poetry. The "Letters" singled out Geoffrey Grigson's *New Verse* and W. H. Auden as the main representatives of the former tendency—a tendency Tambimuttu came to call "objective reporter" poetry.[2] Dylan Thomas represented the alternative to such poetry. Indeed, Tambimuttu came to find affiliations between Ceylonese and Welsh poetry, and he published work by Keidrych Rhys, Lynette Roberts, and R. S. Thomas, among several others. These Welsh poets writing in English would serve for Tambimuttu as an alternative to the so-called "objective reporter" poetry, as he came to construct this contrast along ethnic lines.[3] In other words, "objective reporter" served as a kind of code for the culturalist turn of late modern English poetry, a turn Tambimuttu read as exclusionary.

This chapter will demonstrate how Tambimuttu uses Eliot in establishing a translocal poetics. His heavy representation of Welsh writing in English in the periodical then will be read as a proactive editorial decision in light of his Letters and the claims for poetry in Britain we have encountered thus far. Finally, a very direct connection will be drawn between this editorial choice and the racial discourse in which the revived vision of exclusive Englishness is renovated as mature, ordered, disciplined, and, ultimately, canonized.

## THE EGREGIOUS TAMBIMUTTU

In 1948, Tambimuttu published *Natarajah: A Poem for Mr. T. S. Eliot's Sixtieth Birthday*. Originally intended to be called *Mr. Eliot's Circus*, the poem and its two titles (both published and rejected) embody many of the issues presented in a consideration of Tambimuttu. It can be read cynically as a means to gain cultural capital by using an internationally famous author as its *raison d'être*, more generously treated as an auspicious example of South Asian writing in Britain on the cusp of the massive immigration in the middle of the twentieth century, or regarded dismissively as weakly wrought pastiche. As Peter Riley noted about Tambimuttu, "people become their names," and Tambimuttu's evokes a disparate range of responses (169). Tambimuttu was seriously successful as an editor, aggravating as a business partner and friend, and annoying to those who viewed the role of poetry and literature as vital to bulwarking a threatened culture. Tambimuttu's reception and legacy is too often framed in terms of a narrowly considered poetic development or, owing to his Ceylonese birth, a representative example of the postcolonial subject. What these analyses elide is precisely how Tambimuttu manufactured a "Tambimuttu" who, in turn, attempted to voice an unwieldy critique of hegemonic literary and cultural forces at work. In other words, Tambimuttu's marginalization by the late 1940s was largely self-made, and while the financial factors are well documented, they do not account for why he was so completely and permanently silenced after eight years of running one of the most successful literary magazines in Britain. Tambimuttu, by addressing his use of an "American" Eliot, his own notions of culture and tradition, and his late attempt to reposition himself as "eastern," situated the entire narrative construction about himself firmly in opposition to the rapidly institutionalized Leavisite discourse in the late 1940s and 1950s that preached seriousness, maturity, and the "special case" of English culture. In short, rather than read Tambimuttu as an ostracized victim of a managed cultural insularity, it is more appropriate to consider the conditions under which he showed himself out the door.

Reading his poetics through a transnational lens corrects two reductive positions that have prevailed in regard to Tambimuttu: either he was the great charlatan and interloper who foisted mediocre talent on the British literary world, or he was the wise "oriental" whose ways could never be fully appreciated or assimilated by the closed-minded English. And these attitudes have persisted: for example, the *Festschrift* published in Tambimuttu's honor in 1989 is full of the latter position and even carries an orientalist theme in its title—*Bridge between Two Worlds*. But the title suggests more than it ever intended: a potential allusion to the line in Eliot's "Little Gidding" that reads "Between two worlds become much like each other" (141). The worlds in the poem are metaphysical and corporeal, past and present, but the title would be fitting for Tambimuttu's acknowledged, yet underanalyzed, appreciation for Eliot. He made an appealing model for Tambimuttu not only because of his acclaim, his editing of *Criterion*, and his position at Faber, but also as an American-born émigré who was the "only great English poet living" (100). For example, Tambimuttu made several broadcasts for the Indian section of the BBC's Eastern Service from 1941–42, with one on Eliot. He opens with a description of what it was like to enter Eliot's offices at Faber, and in an effort to emphasize Eliot's foreign origins, Tambimuttu refers to his subject as the "American wanderer" (103). Indeed, the narrative arc of the broadcast highlights what Tambimuttu calls Eliot's "search for foundations": Eliot became tired of the "spiritual bankruptcy of his American cultural background, . . . [so he] came back to the country of his origin, England, only to witness the death-struggles of a culture without values or stability." This construction provides Tambimuttu with an opening to disparage Georgian and Imagist poetry: "The idea of the Georgians as retrenchment . . . [as they] attempted to save tradition by limitation of subject-matter, and achieved wateriness, [and] the Imagists attempted the same thing by limitation of technique, and achieved hardness and precision even though these qualities were often accompanied by triviality" (101). Eliot transcends all these limitations, and "instead of trying to escape tradition . . . he returned to an older scheme of values which he expressed in his work" (103). The broadcast then concludes with a short analysis of *The Waste Land*, declaring that the poem "attempts to speak the voice of ages, using all tongues, using all myths, with the voice of universal man" (104).

What Tambimuttu is attempting to describe is best defined as "modernist bricolage," or, as Jahan Ramazani defines it, "the synthetic use in early twentieth-century poetry of diverse cultural materials ready to hand" (99). Ramazani has argued, in *A Transnational Poetics*, that "intercultural poetic forms of modernism, in particular, have been especially attractive to so-called Third World poets in their quest to break through monologic lyricism, to express their cross-cultural experience, despite vast differences in ethnicity and geography, politics and history, from the Western modernists" (99). High modernist texts such as *The Waste Land* do not fit the mold of a monologic imperialism, as their incorporation of intercultural material calls into question the dominance of Western perception and at least allows their materials to enter into view (114). Tambimuttu values "modernist bricolage" as a means to express complex, transcultural experiences, despite the fact that many modernist texts were written from within a European poetic tradition and were guilty of perpetuating imperial attitudes (99–100). His honoring of Eliot is not simply literary appreciation, then, but a transcultural position taking within the poetic discourse of the 1940s in Britain. The Eliot we meet in this broadcast is migratory but situated, and by opening the broadcast with a visit to Eliot's office at Faber, Tambimuttu doubles Eliot's "search for foundations." Tambimuttu is telling an immigrant's story with the twist that Eliot is emigrating back to fictive origins, and if America could be replaced with Ceylon, Tambimuttu may have been referring to his own reasons for moving to Britain.[4] As Tambimuttu was someone who was attempting to carve out a space for himself in the metropolis, the legitimacy bequeathed to the bricolage structure of *The Waste Land* would have made it an ideal poem to model after. In other words, if "hybridity" is the result of multiple cultures reined together by empire, then the "knotting together of countless already knotted together indigenous and imposed languages, images, genres—is not an aspect but the basic fabric of the postcolonial poem" (Ramazani 100). Indeed, Tambimuttu uses a concept similar to "knotting together" to describe the process by which he constructed his dedicatory poem to Eliot for the latter's 60th birthday: he states in the prefatory letter to Eliot that the construction of the poem was similar to his grandfather's custom of weaving "what he assimilated from poets of his acquaintance into birthday mats for them" (1). In *Natarajah*, Tambimuttu literalizes the "rebegetting" Ramazani reads in other poets like Kamau Brathwaite and Derek Walcott, appropriating lines and themes from Eliot's poetry. The poem contains certain obvious nods to some of Eliot's poems: it has five sections like *The Waste Land* and each part of *Four Quartets*; there is a frequent refrain (or "mantram") of "Between the . . ." throughout, echoing lines from "The Hollow Men"; the second section is entitled "And We Journeyed," a possible allusion to "Journey of the Magi"; Sweeney, a recurring figure in Eliot's poetry, is referenced; and "time" is mentioned at several points, including as the title of the fourth section, possibly an allusion to *Four Quartets*. Additionally, the text contains references to London, Hinduism, colonial spaces, and natural life (Thames, Natarajah, Shiva, shantih, Mohenjo Daro, Matto Grosso, Kandy, panther, mosquitoes, ravines, mountains, yew trees). However, even with its highly allusive structure, it requires very little of the footnoting needed in *The Waste Land* for the references to be transparent. Furthermore, given its rather haphazard structure, the poem's overall thrust seems to be no more than an homage—a point made even more obviously deliberate by Tambimuttu's confessed original title: "Mr. Eliot's Circus."

Both Ruvani Ranasinha and C. L. Innes have argued that Tambimuttu is "orientalizing" Eliot in this poem, but such an argument reproduces the frame they are surely critiquing (Innes 226; Ranasinha 112). In other words, it suggests that the only move available to Tambimuttu is to mimic Eliot's imperial perspective. *Natarajah* is better read as an instance of "translocalism," that is, rather than derealizing "the local . . . by silhouetting it against an Eastern alterity," Tambimuttu moves back and forth between locations, foregrounding "a more fully interstitial migrancy than that of the modernists, because of its layering upon a prior postcolonial dislocation" (Ramazani 102). The poem is Eliotic in the borrowing of lines and form, but it is also a self-declared repurposing of materials that are inflected by the maker's situatedness (e.g., from colonial Ceylon but in metropolitan London).

But there is the risk of homogenizing Tambimuttu as another colonial in the metropole, thus ignoring how the great weight of class privilege, educational background, and the specifics of his ethnic background informed how he received, and was received in, London. A retrospective account of his time in London in the 1940s gives a sense of how Tambimuttu negotiated "his" London. In 1975, he published "Fitzrovia" in *Harpers and Queen*, which is an account of his time in London in the 1940s. In the article, Fitzrovia is an area without borders and features a series of apparitional figures who flit in and out of the narrative, often reduced to a single characteristic: Charles Madge drives a sports car and picks up women, Stephen Spender is handsome, William Empson has a garden. It is also a tale of acculturation—the first day he was in London he was lost, wandered around, and confused a woman with Greta Garbo, but as time passes he finds that he "was shedding part of what England had given me in Ceylon" (223–24, 227). And ultimately it is a mastered space: a fish and chip shop is used to transition to his youth in Ceylon, where he remembers eating freshly caught fish and repeats the lie that he is a descendant of the kings of Jaffna.[5] All of this leads to his imagining that he has proprietary claims over the later waves of immigration to Britain: "The eternal migration and intermingling of cultures—and I feel I was the pioneer of all this hustle and bustle, this little Indian colony" (227–28).

In part, the story is structured as a *Bildungsroman*: he establishes that he and his cousin used to "play" the roles of Byron and Chesterton in Colombo, implying that later he no longer had to pretend. However, coming to London is a growing up that is not quite a growing into. Moments such as when a white colleague's face is darkened with makeup, but his not, before going on TV, and when his friend, the Ceylonese writer Subramaniam, was called back to Jaffna from London by his family following his own troubles in London, are used to mark his difference and distance from the native population (231, 234–35). It is a highly selective account: mention is made neither of his removal from the magazine and press he started due to his financial mismanagement nor of the people he alienated as a result of unkept promises to publish, but as he provocatively states in closing, Fitzrovia, an area he is widely credited with naming, was an "attitude of mind" (235).

The most impactful expression of his "attitude of mind" was not his poetry but his publishing *Poetry (London)*, establishing Editions Poetry London, and very publicly and directly laying out his vision for poetry in his "Letters." Tambimuttu opened most of the issues of *Poetry (London)* that he edited with a "Letter." The complex form of the "First Letter" (February 1939) lies somewhere between a manifesto and a conventional argumentative essay. The complexity of form is compounded by the abstraction of his terminology and the grandness of his claims. He has an organic vision of poetry: "Every man has poetry within him"; "Each poet is a leaf, a significant leaf of Poetry, the multifoliate tree"; "Poetry is a descent to the roots of life."⁶ Further, according to Tambimuttu, criticism should also be organic: "Criticism is only valuable when it originates from life . . . . If criticism has its origin in life, very little adverse criticism on modern poets needs be written." In Tambimuttu's usage, "life" expresses a humanist universalism that was, for example, valued in Eliot's *The Waste Land*. Indeed, he seems to be channeling some of Eliot's statements on criticism and tradition in this Letter. Tambimuttu's argument that the "function of a critic should be to point out to what extent a poet's work is a half truth" echoes Eliot's claim in "The Function of Criticism" that the critic is concerned with the "common pursuit of true judgment" and "the correction of taste" (69). Later in the "First Letter," Tambimuttu argues that "every poet is a culmination of influences," clearly expressing Eliot's analogy of the "catalyst" in his discussion of the effect of tradition on the individual writer: "The poet's mind is in fact a receptacle for seizing and storing up numberless feelings, phrases, images, which remain there until all the particles which can unite to form a new compound are present together" (41). Rather than read Tambimuttu as simply ventriloquizing Eliot, it is more apt to treat his allusions as part of an effort to rework Eliot's claims for an ostensibly European tradition into a transcultural one and thus expand the tent, as it were, to include Tambimuttu himself.⁷ If, as Ramazani has it, "postcolonial hybridity 'confirms yet alters,' reworks yet revalues modernist bricolage . . . [and] thus re-begets a poetic mode that helped beget it," then Tambimuttu's editorial claims and publishing agenda should transcend the orientalist binary that, in its reductive logic, would firmly place him outside of an English tradition (115). While Ramazani only theorizes within the genre of poetry, Tambimuttu demonstrates in these Letters that bricolage is not limited to poetic form.

That said, his Letters do engage in an orientalist discourse that seems at odds with how he used Eliot as a rhetorical fixture. The Letters quite often posed a dichotomous construction of poetry: Western vs. Eastern, intellect vs. emotion, rational vs. spiritual: "Parallel to his positioning of emotion and intellect as antithetical, were his repeated references to irreconcilable cultural differences between the East and the West, reproducing notions of the essential simplicity of the former versus the complexity of the latter" (Ranasinha 114). For example, Tambimuttu coined the phrase "objective reporter," mainly to describe a form of poetry he felt was popularized by Auden and Grigson, but it generally became a term of abuse for any poetry he did not approve of. In other words, it should be read as a term of convenience and not an accurate marker for any literary affiliation. The phrase is first used in the "Third Letter" to criticize Louis MacNeice's poetry, even though Tambimuttu was happy enough to publish a section of *Autumn Journal* in the first issue, and more poems by MacNeice in subsequent issues (65). But in this Letter, the problem with such poetry is that it "appeal[s] only to a limited public . . . [as it is] *too* mental, too cultural, over-burdened with too many formal values that emerged from various poetry movements of recent times" (66). Ultimately, Tambimuttu judges that "modern verse . . . [has] the onus of discovering and preserving the more spontaneous and traditional qualities in poetry" (66). He offers an alternative to the rationalist "objective reporter" poetry when he expands upon how he thinks about "vitality" in poetry.

> In the Orient culture has never dissociated itself from life, and attained a self-consistency of its own and power independent of life, but here in the Occident we have built up an objective world of culture and thrown life under its yoke. As we understand the term, culture in the West is undoubtedly more culture than in the Orient, but Oriental life is more perfect because its culture is founded on tradition which in turn proceeds from spontaneity . . . Culture has become separated from the vitality which created it. (66)

He situates the debate as intercultural; however, his condescending attitude vastly oversimplifies (to use another umbrella term like "objective reporter") MacSpaunday's rich, active, and varied production in the 1930s and early 1940s, in direct contrast to the (unnamed) poets of the East. In other words, despite his clear desire to integrate multiple cultures into a new vision of poetry, based on his publishing record this only involves poets from Britain and Ireland.

The problem with his formulation, then, in the practical sense of a workable poetic form, is that he leaves unresolved how the "vitality" of the East can be imported into Britain. For instance, despite his critique of "objective reporter" poetry, he published MacNeice in five separate issues; Stephen Spender reviewed *Autumn Journal* in the third issue and was himself in the second and fifth issues; and even Geoffrey Grigson had poems published in the eighth issue. Poets associated with the New Apocalyptic and New Romanticism movements, such as J. F. Hendry, Henry Treece, G. S. Fraser, Anne Ridler, D. S. Savage, Philip O'Connor, John Hall, and Nicholas Moore, all appeared in *Poetry (London)*, along with Dylan Thomas, Keith Douglas, and George Orwell. Even the notorious *Poetry (London) X*, with its eclectic mix that is very much in keeping with Tambimuttu's claim of *Poetry (London)*'s "catholicity" in the "Second Letter," does not stray from the British Isles. Even so, it led to the characterization of the magazine as "a vast junk shop, or oriental bazaar, in which you may pick up—among the curios—odd bargains, simple pots, and genuine Birmingham brass" (Porteus qtd. in Symons 65). Hugh Gordon Porteus's disparagement of *Poetry (London)*'s eclectic composition is framed in orientalized terms, so that even while the poets published were homegrown, as it were, it is viewed as a product from a colonial space. This very much illustrates Ranasinha's claim that Tambimuttu's "talents [were] always equated with, and perceived as inherently deriving from, the exoticism of his formative environment" (116). Tambimuttu, despite his rhetorical use of Eliot as a model for the kinds of transcultural poetry he envisions being written, reproduces in his geographically British and Irish publishing choices the very divide that would effectively be used to marginalize him.

## Welsh Writing in English: *Poetry (London)* and the Challenge to an Insular Englishness

If we take into account the fact that Tambimuttu published no fewer than 12 Welsh poets over the course of the 14 issues he edited, some of whom had poems appear in multiple issues, then we can read Tambimuttu's oppositionality as one reconstructed "closer to home." In other words, it was in the fledging "Anglo-Welsh" poetry tradition that Tambimuttu found an expression of the challenge to an insular Englishness. We get some insight into Tambimuttu's more expansive notion of an English-language tradition indirectly in the editorial to the first issue of *Poetry Scotland*. In his "Editorial Letter," itself a nod to Tambimuttu's Letters, Maurice Lindsay proclaims the following:

> While *Poetry Scotland* was still only an idea in my mind, I wrote to my friend Tambimuttu, the editor of *Poetry (London)* and told him of my plans. He was most encouraging in his reply. He envisaged cousin-periodicals all over Europe, each local in the sense that it featured home poets most strongly; each international in the sense that it featured the finest new poetry of all lands in a smaller measure. (3–4)

We can perhaps apply Tambimuttu's vision for other periodicals to *Poetry (London)* itself. While it did publish many English poets, it also represented Irish, Welsh, and Scottish poets to a great degree as, in Lindsay's parlance, "home poets." The stress, then, on the Welsh in this writing is not to claim the magazine as an organ of the "first flowering of the Anglo-Welsh" but rather to examine it as one approach to challenging the perceived English orthodoxy.

Tambimuttu's interest in publishing Welsh poetry most obviously stems from his great admiration for Dylan Thomas. Thomas was the first poet he named in his "First Letter," clearly endorsing the kinds of poetry Tambimuttu was invested in: "Dylan Thomas is a great poet and he glorifies a thoroughly personal form of analysis and exposition." While Thomas's Welshness is not explicitly noted in the Letter, Tambimuttu clearly places him within a Welsh tradition. Following his statement in the Letter that he has arranged the poetry in the issue into groups "to facilitate their communication to the general reader," he pairs Thomas with a poem by Keidrych Rhys. Rhys, one of the most vocal proponents of Welsh writing in English, specifically within the pages of his *Wales* magazine (1937–40), was published as often as his wife Lynette Roberts and Thomas himself.[8] Additionally, Alun Lewis, Glyn Jones, Vernon Watkins, Augustus John, Roland Mathias, R. S. Thomas, Idris Davies, Brenda Chamberlain, and Clifford Dyment were all published, and as a result, along with *Life and Letters To-day*, *Wales*, and *Welsh Review*, *Poetry (London)* was one of the most consistent voices for Welsh writing in English in the 1940s. In Tambimuttu's dichotomy of "objective reporter" vs. "vital" poetry, these poets clearly were placed in the second category, and their specific challenge to the English tradition of poetry suited Tambimuttu's critique of cultural insularity.

Welsh writing in English, while it has historically been dated back to 1450, only widely developed in the late 1930s, and it solidified as a coherent movement with the prominence of Thomas, as well as Rhys's *Wales* and eventually Gwyn Jones's *Welsh Review*. The so-called "first flowering of Anglo-Welsh" poetry mainly involved poets from the industrialized and anglicized southern part of Wales.[9] According to Tony Conran, Anglo-Welsh poetry is unique among English-language poetries for three reasons:

> First, it has, in its background, a different civilization—it is like English poetry written by Irishmen or Indians. Second, it shares its territory with another linguistic community which regards its tongue as the right and natural language of the country . . . Third, it derives from a special sort of society, which I shall call the *buchedd* from a Welsh word meaning a "way of life" or ethos. (1)

Conran goes on to stress that this third difference was the most definitive, not only because of Anglo-Welsh poetry's derivation from *buchedd* society but also because it was a product of "its defeat and breakup" (2). In the face of the disintegration of "*buchedd* loyalty," poets "offered themselves as international or colonial recruits to the London intelligentsia . . . [and] tended to attack the *buchedd* from a position of would-be rootlessness" (111). Chris Hopkins reads the London migration more pragmatically in terms of market forces. In his essay on *Wales* and *Welsh Review*, he quotes Sally Roberts Jones's claim that "it is difficult to see how that generation could have established their careers solely . . . in Wales" (715). Regardless of each writer's motivations, the general effect on the kinds of poetry they wrote and published involved a "dynamic between a modern metropolitan English style and Welsh pastoral modes of understanding Wales' own recent history [that was] a defining feature of these magazines' relation to the kind of modern writing they chose to publish" (Hopkins 715). Despite Glyn Jones's admonition that "attempts to impose homogeneity on these writers on a basis of race or style or identity of vision or philosophy are bound to fail," it is clear that Tambimuttu viewed the Anglo-Welsh poets collectively as an alternative to a strain of English poetry that had increasingly forsaken aesthetic experimentation in favor of a culturalist particularism (38).

The pairing of Keidrych Rhys and Dylan Thomas in the first issue was presumably driven by, among other things, an implicit logic based on their mutual friendship and Welsh background. Rhys's "Homage to a Split Man" is structured as a riddle, never naming the "split man" and challenging the reader in the final line to "guess."

> Blank birth in one of the four hotels; loathing both Eton, and, still more,
> Oxford: loving Cologne and music like a child upon sea shore
> That just simply would rather throw up modern ships of war than animals for
>     the Zoo [. . .]
> And the high dance; and the songs, published; and the paper he ran
> Are all part of ghost searching half-starved through an artist's ploughshare
> And now his drunkard rows in Chelsea over don enemies do reveal quite a
>     split man,
> Double remove from toughs with knuckle-dusters in a four-ale bar.

Rhys establishes the "split man's" life as a vacillation between the dominant markers of class privilege (Eton, Oxford, Chelsea) and the rejection of such in preference for a range of "unrefined" activities ("like a child upon sea shore"; "drunkard rows"; a hint at a past in "four-ale" or cheap bars). The tension in the poem involves the split man's sacrifice of his artistic abilities for a life of excess. As Rhys frames this poem as a "homage," there is also the possibility that his identification with his subject may have something to do with his own struggle to survive as an outsider within the London literary establishment. The split man's artistic tool is described as a "ploughshare," establishing a contrast of rural production against metropolitan excess. The split man is ultimately consumed by these excesses, and the poem as a whole could be read not only as Rhys's meditation on the situation of a Welshman in London but also as his characterization of the hybrid nature of Welsh writers in English. In other words, what Glyn Jones dubbed the "'beer and skittles culture' of the mid-twentieth-century British working class" became increasingly more prominent in Wales, and thus the poem can be read as a form of remorse for the disintegration of *buchedd* culture (Jones qtd. in Conran 10).

Dylan Thomas's poem, "Poem in the Ninth Month," was one of the first solicited for *Poetry (London)*.[10] The title and the opening line—"A saint about to fall"—envision a child's birth as a fall from grace.[11] The poem's locatedness—"his father's house in the sands, / The vanishing of the musical ship-work and the chucked bells" (a reference to Thomas's dwelling in Laugharne)—is what appealed to Tambimuttu.[12] This is even more evident when the woodcut image of boats in a harbor that follows the poem is considered. In short, Rhys and Thomas use the Welsh landscape in these poems to ground their respective rhetoric, and thus provide a counterpoint to the industrialized, and in Tambimuttu's parlance "rational," space of their English peers.

The Welsh landscape is more overtly referenced in Lynette Roberts's "Poem from Llanybri" in the sixth issue. The poem addresses Alun Lewis, a fellow Welsh poet and friend of Roberts and Rhys. In its invitation to Lewis to visit her in Llanybri,

Roberts names local vegetation and offers the promise of "cowl," "savori fach," and "Cwmcelyn spread"—all Welsh phrases. The poem is invested in denoting Llanybri by its local growth and geography: "A fist full of rock cress fresh from the bank / The valley tips of garlic red with dew / Cooler than shallots"; "The East and West Marches also have bogs"; "Pluck and draw pigeon with crop of green foil / This your good supper from the limetree fells." It ends on a note of welcome and an invitation to respond in a way in keeping with a Welsh tradition: "send an ode or elegy / In the old way and raise our Heritage" (180). Patrick McGuinness, editor of Roberts's *Collected Poems*, pointing to her birth in Argentina, her family's multigenerational residence in Australia, yet her Welsh heritage, argues that she was "Welsh by a combination of choice and imaginative will" and further that the poem "is a cosmopolitan's claim to a rooted culture that is also a culture of rootedness" ("Introduction" xii). John Wilkinson concurs, additionally claiming that "Poem from Llanybri" is a "short manifesto of her localism," but he argues that her usage of British colloquial "swank" and her "suppression of conventional punctuation" places her "poetics more with modernism than with the warmed-over Georgianism promoted even today in Britain and Ireland" (190). In his Letter that opened the sixth issue, Tambimuttu states that the "commonsense" attitude "popularly held in England by the young avant-garde poets . . . was the intellectual one that poetry should be ordinary reportage, in the language of everyday speech, of the external world of objects and events" (164). Roberts's poem counteracts this type of poetry in two ways: first, the poem's Welsh location defies the "commonsense" second-order universalism of English poets (i.e., claiming the particularality of England as a universal condition), and second, her poem does not simply report the local vegetation and geography but uses them to metonymically represent an image of Llanybri.[13]

But perhaps Keidrych Rhys's presence in *Poetry (London)* was most important for Tambimuttu. As the editor of *Wales*, Rhys was among the first to articulate, in a coherent and consistent manner, the notion of a movement of Welsh writers in English. Tambimuttu advertised the magazine in *Poetry (London)*, and as there is significant overlap in the names published between the magazines, there is no doubt that Rhys was centrally responsible for Tambimuttu's attention to Welsh poetry in English. Yet, this link between the magazines has historically been obscured, and a brief consideration of *Wales*'s editorial agenda would put the previous claims here of Tambimuttu's use of Welsh poetry into sharper focus.

*Wales* first came out in 1937 and continued sporadically until 1960. Commonly regarded as the unofficial marker of the beginning of the "first flowering of Anglo-Welsh" writing, the magazine published many of the figures associated with this literary movement—notably, Dylan Thomas, Vernon Watkins, and Glyn Jones. As Roland Mathias characterized Rhys's attitude toward the purpose of the magazine, it "must measure up to metropolitan standards, compete in the English arena, shed its parochialism . . . Keidrych felt that the Welsh heritage, while in general conservable, was splendidly strange material with which to assault metropolitan readers and mark a Welsh place on the map" (299–300). Unlike certain strains of Irish nationalism's emphasis on Celtic language and culture, the Anglo-Welsh were largely unable to speak or read in Welsh and instead were invested in providing the "anglicization of Wales with respectability" (Harri Webb qtd. in Macdonald Smith 68). Glyn Jones best encapsulates the complicated nature of characterizing the Anglo-Welsh as figures caught in the conflicting strains of being from Wales but knowing only English.

> The Anglo-Welsh are the often unwitting, as the Welsh-language writers are the conscious, inheritors of a specific culture. What happened to split the writers of modern Wales into two groups? The answer is, the same forces have split our whole culture, our whole nation into two, namely anglicization. (37, 40)

For Jones, Welsh poets writing in English carry with them the implicit mark and crisis of their cultural tradition. To write in English is to testify to the impact of colonization, even if one is not thematically dealing with the issue. With this notion in mind, Jones continues to argue that *Wales*, then, was not "the complete and dynamic expression in English of a new Welsh awareness of national identity; the influences behind the writing of much of it were English and American rather than Welsh" (44–45). Much like the English, who "do not feel their language to be under relentless pressure from a powerful and attractive next-door neighbor," the Anglo-Welsh writer "would not feel his first responsibility to be to the English language as such, or to the community, or to his nation, or to a tradition" (127). The crisis that is thus addressed does not register the concerns of a linguistic minority but rather being a twice-marginalized group: being monolingual English speakers in a historically Welsh-speaking nation as well as being culturally Welsh in a state that was increasingly rooting its identity in an exclusionary sense of Englishness.

Rhys's statement in the first issue of *Wales* reflects this crisis. Written in the curt and aggressive rhetoric of a manifesto, it declares the magazine's contribution to English culture in terms very similar to Tambimuttu's.

> British culture is a fact, but the English contribution to it is very small. MacDiarmid told the Scots that they could gain nothing by joining forces with the English and aping their mannerisms. There is actually no such thing as "English" culture; a few individuals may be highly cultured, but the people as a whole are crass. Welsh literature is carried on, not by a clique of moneyed dilettantes, but by the small shopkeepers, the blacksmiths, the non-conformist ministers, by the miners, quarrymen, and the railwaymen. The Kelt's heritage is clear as sunlight, yet the burden of English literature has also fallen upon him. The greatest of present day poets are Kelts. We publish this journal in English so that it may spread far beyond the frontiers of Wales, and because we realize the beauty of the English language far better than the English themselves, who have so shamefully misused it. We are beyond the bigotry of unintelligent fascist nationalism. In case the English should claim our contribution for their own, we produce this pamphlet, calling it "Wales" in defiance of parasitical adoption. Though we write in English, we are rooted in Wales.[14]

As with Tambimuttu's concern with the rational overload of "objective reporter" poetry, Rhys visualizes *Wales*'s cultural contribution as the most recent in a long line of "Keltic" ones to so-called "British culture." Chris Hopkins reads this passage as Rhys arguing for an additive contribution to British culture, stating that "the notice mounts a strong critique of the very idea that there is any genuine 'English' culture, asserting instead that the national culture of the United Kingdom is better termed 'British culture' because it largely stems from Celtic inspiration" (721). While he notes the class dynamic of Rhys's definition of culture—"moneyed dilettantes" set against various tradesmen—he fails to note the allusion Rhys could have been making to the eisteddfod tradition in Wales, where, as part of the annual national festival, a poetry competition is held and the winner is not necessarily a poet by trade.[15] In other words, Rhys is here encapsulating one of the core schisms between English and Welsh culture that is bound up in the very notion of the word "culture": the English invest in culture as acquisitional and the Welsh embrace a more egalitarian notion. The rhetoric in this opening proclamation clearly resonates with Tambimuttu's inclusionary notion of poetry as the "multifoliate tree." In Rhys's narrow definition, it is the Welsh as "Kelt" who contribute to a British (and not English) tradition. In Tambimuttu's sense, he reflected a received English tradition that, in Viswanathan's terms, "sought to return [the colonial subject] to an essential unity with himself and reinsert him into the course of development of civilized man" (141). What Tambimuttu saw in Thomas, Rhys, Roberts, and other Welsh writers working in English was a similar ideology that itself was a product of their respective anglicizations. Rhys's and Tambimuttu's respective rhetorical strategies, while critical of insular Englishness, do not position themselves as anti-English. Rather, they reflect back onto the English a notion of a pure state of being, or an idealized notion of the individual, that was inculcated in the English education mission. Thus, it is ironic when Rhys in the second issue complains of "Newbolt-Fascism," referencing the 1921 Newbolt Report that enshrined English literary studies as the cornerstone of education reform, precisely as his rhetoric confirms the success of an anglicized education in the colonial sphere (36).

## WELSHNESS, MATURITY, AND INSULAR ENGLISHNESS

In light of a cultural nationalist discourse that is unambiguously voiced by Rhys and condoned by Tambimuttu, it is unsurprising that the backlash directed toward Tambimuttu, while fueled by poor interpersonal skills, takes on the character of stake holding in an English cultural tradition. In other words, while there were practical financial reasons why Tambimuttu was ousted from his own magazine and press, his monetary ineptitude does not explain why his ability to make claims for poetry were written off altogether. There were always detractors, but a public epistolary exchange he had with Geoffrey Grigson in 1947 begins a very public disavowal of Tambimuttu's abilities as a critic. In his 11th Letter (September–October 1947), Tambimuttu wrote a response to an article written by Geoffrey Grigson on Dylan Thomas that was published in *Polemic* 7 (March 1947). In his Letter, Tambimuttu spends four pages not only disparaging Grigson's ability to read Thomas's poetry correctly but also using it as more evidence of the faults of the "destructive criticism" he blames Grigson for employing. And suggestively, the advertisement that faces the opening of the Letter is for three Editions Poetry London publications, one of which is the Gwyn Williams–edited collection of poems translated from the Welsh entitled *The Rent That's Due to Love*. The connection between the ad and the Letter is obscured primarily by the fact that while Tambimuttu cites the editor in reference to Dylan Thomas, the anthology would not be published until 1950. In the Letter, Tambimuttu claims that Thomas employs a "free use of *cynghanedd*, . . . [which is] typical of his verse." Tambimuttu, after characterizing *cynghanedd* as "the foundation of Welsh prosody," goes on to state that it "is a fairly strict system of alliteration in which instead of one consonant being repeated, as in English verse, a series of different consonants is repeated in varying order" (6).[16] Tambimuttu's point in drawing out this formal aspect of Thomas's poetry is to illustrate his own aptitude in recognizing literary forms but also to implicitly fault Grigson's ignorance, and perhaps even indifference, regarding Welsh poetic forms; in doing this, Tambimuttu provides another piece of evidence for the faults of cultural insularity. He closes the Letter by arguing that if *Poetry (London)* "is to support any tradition, let it be the tradition of co-axial literature—different types of writing which are all facets of poetic experience." He continues by referencing Eliot: "I think it was Mr. Eliot who remarked that, today, we should expect to find different types of literature existing in the same language in the same country" (8).[17] This argument repeats the transcultural claims of his "First Letter"; however, as Grigson's response highlights, Tambimuttu was engaged in a literary milieu that was increasingly reading "tradition" in the singular, underpinned by a notion of a shared language and definitional standards.

Grigson's response mainly took issue with Tambimuttu's definition of *cynghanedd*. The passage is worth quoting in full, as it illuminates an attitude that would come to prevail about the magazine and Tambimuttu's editorials.

> It is hardly worth, for example, telling you that what you think is *cynghanedd* in a line of Dylan Thomas' is not *cynghanedd* at all, that *cynghanedd* is a strict "classical," formal usage, that a "free" use of it would be something as impossible as a free heroic couplet or rhymed blank verse. Still, one can feel the *drift* of your remarks. The axis which runs through *Poetry (London)* is that all poems are poems and equally worth printing. The only axis is to have no axis, beyond that faith in muddle and contradiction which has made *Poetry (London)* the most foolish (if representative) periodical of its time. (46)

For the purposes of the discussion, it is not so important to evaluate their competing views of Thomas and *cynghanedd*, as they are ultimately straw men for the deeper points of contention. Grigson adopts a conservative approach to poetic form, and this conservatism feeds into Tambimuttu's charge of objective reporter rationalist attachment to form over expression. Tambimuttu's catholicity is critiqued as an absence of critical discernment. Tambimuttu's response is exclusively invested in asserting Grigson's failures: "[His] habit . . . of disguising a failure to appreciate the real qualities of a poem with abusive language, ill manners and a patronizing and petulant tone, seems to be fairly clear in its silliness" (46). The debate appears to end at an impasse, with the discourse reduced to mutual dismissal and petty point scoring, and if anything proves Grigson's charge of a lack of maturity and seriousness in Tambimuttu and *Poetry (London)*.

While there were the aforementioned financial reasons that explain why the next issue—the 14th—would be Tambimuttu's last as editor, his leaving did supply this exchange with an air of finality regarding Tambimuttu's influence as a critic and publisher.[18] This finality was further solidified by the subsequent editor of *Poetry (London)*—Richard March—who, in an editorial opening the 16th issue, declared a radically different vision for the magazine. Entitled "Questions in the Silly Season," the editorial makes no mention of Tambimuttu, yet it notes the magazine's ten years in production.[19] The tone of the editorial is entirely directed toward staking out new ground for the magazine, and the editorial ends by posing a series of questions to would-be contributors to *Poetry (London)*: "Why do we still want to write poetry today?"; "Do you want him [or her] to merely read your poem?"; "Towards what?"; "To what end?"; "Are you doing this to 'express' yourself, or just to make poetry about yourself?" (2). With occasional possible answers interjected, the end of this editorial reads like a somber catechism, urging readers to self-reflect and seriously consider their own poetic production. The editorial closes with the hope that these questions "may help the poet to introduce a greater sense of immediacy, of necessity into his poetry-making than we have been able to discover of late" (2). The editorial never explicitly rejects Tambimuttu's editorial practice, but the serious tone of its reflective questions and the insistence on immediacy-through-self-examination implicitly runs counter to his proclamations of "vitality" and catholicity.

Indeed, Tambimuttu's lack of seriousness (read as immaturity) became one of the major themes in the critical leveling of his claims and his magazine. In Balachandra Rajan's article "Bloomsbury and the Academies" in *The Hudson Review* (autumn 1949), his main target is the lack of attention paid to contemporary writers by university English studies programs. Using as evidence the cessation of *Criterion* and the perceived solitariness of *Scrutiny*, he argues that Bloomsbury's lack of critical standards has contributed to this situation. Tambimuttu fits into this discussion when Rajan argues that the "typical names . . . [such as] Tambimuttu, Wrey Gardiner and Reginald Moore . . . differ from their elders chiefly in details of taste and in a greater readiness to print unestablished authors," and further laments that at present these names are unable to provide any substantial counterpoint to Bloomsbury's impact (454). Rajan goes on to theorize that "criticism is most difficult in an age of insecurity . . . [when] the clique becomes preferable to solitary honesty and evasion less threatening than the moral demands of defeat," and he subsequently charges that "Tambimuttu's contempt for criticism is well known and vehement" (454–55).

It is precisely this insistence on "seriousness" that frames a kind of rhetoric that developed in the late 1940s around poetry, a rhetoric that reflected broader social attitudes in the postwar condition of austerity measures and general deprivation. Eliot, in an essay published in the December 1944 issue of *Welsh Review* entitled "What is Minor Poetry?," argues that novice poets must first seek out smaller poetry magazines, as "a poet must make a place for himself among other poets, and within his own generation, before he appeals to either a larger or an older public." He characterizes a career in poetry as a maturation process, and smaller magazines are the place for fostering talent but are implicitly immature, as "their condition is precarious, their appearance at irregular intervals, and their existence brief" (257). Eliot's vision of literary development reflects a broader emphasis in English studies that was beginning to develop in the 1930s and 1940s that Brian Doyle argues was part of an effort to "accredit the Leavisian critical approach . . . [in which] the 'mature man' was thus placed at a distance equally from the 'blind' drive of the capitalist marketplace and a democratic process defined in quantitative or mechanical terms" (104). For

Eliot, the amateurishness of "minor" poets permits them to engage in the messy world of little magazines, but with an eye to transcending such market-minded publications, especially given their ephemerality and unreliability. While Eliot did not name *Poetry (London)* as such, his description of literary magazines' uncertain lives could easily characterize its state by the mid-1940s.

Furthermore, Doyle's reminder that the Leavisite program was very much behind the discourse of societal maturation through literary studies has relevance to the way in which Tambimuttu and his magazine were dismissed late in its run. By the end of the decade, the magazine came under review by D. J. Enright in *The Critic*. Enright's "The Significance of *Poetry London*" could be read as a kind of mission statement by a new generation of literary critics. Raymond Williams, one of the coeditors of the magazine, noted that "we were against supportive reviewing, which we thought characteristic of the London magazines" (69). While he names Cyril Connolly's *Horizon* as the "principal enemy," his characterization of the 1930s and 1940s literary scene could easily encompass *Poetry (London)*: "The peculiar tone of much thirties culture— descended from the Bloomsbury ethos—found its final expression in this magazine of the forties [i.e., *Horizon*]: above all, an extreme subjectivism, projecting personal difficulties of being a writer as central social problems" (72). In other words, while retrospectively Williams remembers Connolly and *Horizon* as the object of attack, it was Tambimuttu and *Poetry (London)* the editors of *The Critic* zeroed in on first.

Enright's article, which was released contemporaneously with the seventh issue of *Polemic*, in which Grigson's article on Thomas appeared in spring 1947, from the outset identifies *Poetry (London)* as the representative problem of post-1939 poetry.

Since 1939 (in February of which year the magazine *Poetry London* was inaugurated) something, it would seem, has happened to poetry. To suggest another aspect of the problem we might vary the proposition and say that since 1939 very little of any permanent value has happened *in* poetry. Never before have poets sprung up so thickly, never before has publication (given the right contacts) been so easy—but hardly ever before has accepted and recognized work shown such a striking uniformity of weakness. The question before us now is: Has that latter fact any connection with the former facts? Can it, even, be a case of effect and causes?

The obvious approach to an answer is by way of surveying the history and achievement of the periodical which has consistently and powerfully supported and encouraged the younger and youngest poets: I mean, of course, *Poetry London*. (3)

In short, *Poetry (London)* symbolizes a structural problem. After declaring that Tambimuttu had a "definite editorial policy . . . propounding a series of semi-philosophical, semi-aesthetic apothegms on the nature of poetry," Enright concludes that he "exhorts his audience to conduct their lives, as well as their poems, on a basis of catholicity as opposed to policy" (3–4). Later, Enright ungenerously likens Tambimuttu's catholicity to "a whale with a permanently open mouth," with the result that by "absorb[ing] young writers in their most impressionable years . . . [he] has turned them into dull facsimiles." Thus, for Enright, Tambimuttu, who "spoke of this as the formation of an 'anonymous tradition,' [forgot] that the men who mould a tradition, like those who make proper use of it, are rarely to be described as 'anonymous'" (6).[20] He emphasizes midway through his article that "I have written this article; not merely because I consider *PL* a rather uninspired collection of verse, but because I believe it has had a positively harmful influence on contemporary writing." That harm is once again conceptualized in terms of maturity (or the lack thereof): "The Editor's 'Letters' are so explicit in their self-revelation that it hardly seems fair to quote from them; clearly, honestly even, they display the weaknesses, the 'amateurishness,' and the false premises, that lie behind most of the poetry they accompany" (6). And later, "This premature approval of their adolescent exercises (and publication in *PL* is, for many people, the very seal of approval) will tend to substitute smug complacence, mutual admiration and group solidarity for that constant self-criticism without which they will never develop significantly" (9). The ultimate crisis of this situation, in Enright's estimation, is that *Poetry (London)*, as the representative case of poetry magazines in general, is "conducting a wholesale perversion of both the taste of the poetry-reader and the talent of the poetry-writer . . . [and in turn] has consigned 'the critic' to an unpleasant death and openly disclaimed any principle other than catholicity" (9–10).[21] Throughout the course of the review, Enright's purpose is to systematically dismantle every aspect of *Poetry (London)* and, with some rhetorical maneuvering, use the particular to critique the universal. In sum, *Poetry (London)*, and by extension the democratic inclusiveness and openness of the poetry it published, exhibits a cultural failing. While it is deeply embedded in this article, the critique of catholicity is rooted in the defense of a cultural particularism.

The central importance of Enright's review for the editors of *The Critic* is made obvious with the publication of its second issue in autumn 1947. The issue opened with an editorial entitled "The Reading Public and the Critical Reader" that dealt with the difficulty the editors faced in defining the role of criticism in contemporary society: "For while no one denies that intelligent people still exist, no one suggests that they exist as an *intelligent reading public* with the organic unity which that phrase suggests" (5). The editors use a *Time and Tide* review of their first issue that itself chose to critique Enright's article on *Poetry (London)* to lament that the "absence of taste in the general reading public is something which we can assume as proven, . . . [and] against this domination minority standards and minority magazines assert themselves only with great difficulty" (5). While the editors make clear that the first issue "did not contain a manifesto" and thus Enright's review was not technically a manifesto or an editorial statement, they claim in the second issue that the magazine "so far as methods are concerned [is] partisan rather than polemical, direct rather than oblique, in taste, puritan rather than catholic" (6). This final contrast, taken with the importance of the editors' return to its claims in their editorial, definitively situated *Poetry (London)* as the negation of everything that *The Critic* was striving for. The implications of this article, and its effects, can only be understood if we look at *The Critic*'s (and subsequently, *Politics and Letters*'s) intended audience. Williams stated that the "readership we hoped would extend from people still in the Communist Party to those who were in the orbit of Leavis, . . . [and] increasingly what for me became the decisive world was adult education, . . . [for if] there was a group to which *Politics and Letters* referred, it was adult education tutors and their students" (68–69). The debate over correct forms of criticism and tradition were part of a cultural turn in literary production in the 1930s and 1940s. As Brian Doyle has emphasized in his discussion of the 1921 Newbolt Report's chapter on adult education, "A sense of Englishness [was] linked to a mythology of medieval organic ruralism . . . [and] this mythology . . . offer[ed] a means of spiritualizing a policy of intervention into the disturbing cultures of modern industrial and commercial society" (61). Williams's aforementioned suspicion of metropolitan aestheticism fits neatly into an educational outreach program that attempted to link the correctness of ruralist nostalgia to literacy reform, with the effect of developing an insular cultural politics. *Poetry (London)* carried in its very title the antithesis of the ruralist nostalgia ingrained in the received Leavisite discourse.[22] As Alan Sinfield notes, Leavis's critique of modernism's "cosmopolitanism and internationalism; self-conscious experimentation with language and forms; the idea of the artwork as autonomous; and the concept of the artist as alienated by the special intensity of his (usually his) vision of the 'modern condition'" was carried on in journals such as *The Use of English* (1949–) and *Critical Quarterly* (1959–), but perhaps more lastingly in the burgeoning area of Cultural Studies (182–83).

Reading Tambimuttu's poetics as transnational helps put into focus his motivations for returning to Eliot time and again as a legitimating source, but the liberating thrust of such an analysis also needs to face the geopolitical reality of a retrenched and hegemonic Englishness within Britain, and within British poetry. That is, while the now too familiar narrative of the rise of the Movement and its victims remains the dominant framing device to discuss shifts in poetic production following the Second World War, in Tambimuttu's case, by attempting to base his platform on terms such as culture and tradition, he did indeed place himself at the very heart of a powerful and lasting discursive shift that marginalized him aesthetically and ethnically.

CONCLUSION

PERIODICAL FORMATIONS,
ANTHOLOGIES, AND CANONS

There are parallel developments in the late 1940s and early 1950s that are rooted in Leavisian criticism and Eliotic culturalism and come to dominate studies in English for decades to follow: namely, Cultural Studies and the Movement. The last chapter demonstrated how Tambimuttu became a convenient straw man both in terms of stated poetic production and implied cultural difference, yet Tambimuttu himself is not a known quantity in the histories of either of these movements. The relevance of the disciplinary rise of Cultural Studies to Tambimuttu's marginalization is indirect but illustrative. The particularist emphasis on a whole culture is clearly antagonistic toward the transcultural claims embedded in Tambimuttu's writings, especially his vision of a coaxial tradition. Cultural Studies nativism "relativizes England as one particular culture among many in a global system and relativizes the high aesthetic as one specialized element among many in a national culture, . . . [and if] this postimperial and relativist turn destabilized some of the epistemic privileges of aestheticism and cosmopolitanism, it also promised to restore some hope for a reconnection between high art and a socially deeper, but politically narrower, culture" (Esty 197–98). It is not that intellectuals like Raymond Williams articulated cultural wholeness as an explicitly exclusionary construct, but rather "the strategic silences in his work contribute directly to [new racism's] strength and resilience" (Gilroy 50). In short, with regard to Tambimuttu, the effective silencing of his work and his voice in the history of British poetry was largely accomplished through a discourse that countenanced cultural products that unproblematically fit a nationally constructed narrative and tradition.[1]

These conflicting notions of identity and culture are contested within the frame of a literary tradition, and by entering this discourse, Tambimuttu guaranteed his own marginalization. Donald Davie, more effectively than most, formalized this discursive shift within poetry in his first two books—*Purity of Diction in English Verse* and *Articulate Energy*. Davie's claims in these two books are well known, but it is precisely because of their canonical status that it is worth briefly rehearsing some of his claims in the context of Tambimuttu's reception. The main thrust of *Purity of Diction in English Verse* argues for a "chaste and pure diction" in poetry that "is achieved by judgment and taste, and [that] preserves the tone of the center, a sort of urbanity" (59). Davie borrows Matthew Arnold's sense of "urbanity" outlined in "The Literary Influence of Academies," arguing that it is "the tone or spirit of the center, embodying the best of a civilization" (Davie 164). Davie's nationalist frame is explicit throughout: e.g., "A pure poetic diction can purify the national language by enlivening metaphors gone dead" (54). Returning to Esty's point about the dual relativization of national culture and high art, Davie uses this discursive frame when discussing non-English poets, such as Synge and Goldsmith: "Not only does any given diction vary according to genre . . . and according to tone, but one scheme or structure of diction will vary from another because of the different cultures from which they spring" (9). Yet, Davie's borders are permeable. Using the unlikely example of the cucumber in a Cowper poem, Davie argues that the "gradual introduction makes a case which will bear scrutiny for seeing the cucumber in generalized terms" (50). In Davie's reading, there are two valences of meaning in the cucumber—the introduction of a nonpoetic word and the agricultural introduction of the physical object into Britain: "Cowper's humor plays round the ideas of modesty and ambition. His modesty is serious when he compares his poetic activity with that of gardeners who work, through generations, to acclimatize a fruit" (50).[2] The relevance of this passage to Tambimuttu lies along the lines of how tradition and national culture operate. The acclimatized cucumber becomes an English fruit at a time that is always already in the past. Tambimuttu's acculturation is a force of modernity—the geopolitical result of being an economically mobile imperial subject. Davie's "urbanity" is monocultural and should not be confused with Tambimuttu's pluralist metropolitan perception: "Plainly urbanity will come most easily to a poet who is sure of his audience, sure that he and his reader share a broad basis of conviction and assumption" (Davie 118). In short, Davie outlines a poetics that, while not rooting its claims in an antimodernist stance, clearly rejects the type of transcultural discourse on display in Tambimuttu's Letters.

I use Davie's claims for poetry and urbanity here because they are coded in an increasingly dominant discourse in postwar/becoming-postimperial Britain. Simon Gikandi, speaking about the "crisis of Englishness" in the "persistence and enforcement of colonial categories," argues "the foremost insignias of colonial culture overdetermine the making of what were supposed to be decolonized identities; in the metropolis itself, we see the same categories returning, in their phenomenality and ghostliness, to call into question the axioms of Englishness" (9). Tambimuttu, for example, who arrived in London with an English-language education, training in running a printing press, three self-published books of poetry, and an immediate knowledge of the London literary scene, perfectly represented this "crisis." Gikandi, for his part, uses the example of Indian and Caribbean cricket players' "entry into the field of cricket as the mark of both their mastery of the culture of Englishness and their transcendence of its exclusive politics" (9). The interlocked developments of Commonwealth immigration and retrenched Englishness became characterized by the rhetoric of warfare. Paul Gilroy, in *There Ain't No Black in the Union Jack*, has analyzed how the discourse of war was co-opted into the discourse of racism in postwar Britain, where the existential threat of the Axis powers was exchanged for the internal "threat" posed by immigrants (45). There is an analogous and contemporaneous discursive shift within poetry, and it is best embodied by the Movement poets of the 1950s, most especially in Robert Conquest's introduction to his 1956 *New Lines* anthology. The introduction does not specify individuals, but he opens by lashing out at poets of the 1940s (calling them the poets of the "id") and proclaiming that "in the late 1940's and early 1950's . . . a number of poets began to emerge who have been progressing from different viewpoints to a certain unity of approach, a new and healthy standpoint" (xiv).[3] This new poetry, contrary to its immediate predecessors, "submits to no great systems of theoretical constructs nor agglomerations of unconscious commands . . . [and] is empirical in its attitude to all that comes" (xv). While Conquest acknowledges the influence of Empson, Yeats, Muir, and Auden on the poets in his anthology, he reads them as poets unambiguously isolated from the period in which they wrote, as he concludes his introduction by declaring: "The stage needed sweeping" (xviii).[4]

There are two key reasons to focus on this particular anthology: (1) as the core publication of perhaps the single most influential literary movement in postwar Britain, it signals a clear end to the period under review in this project, and (2) it constructs its more specifically refined form of English identity in negation of the previous decade's writing.[5] Andrew Crozier argues that Conquest "sets the poetry of the fifties in reaction to that of the forties through a series of binary contrasts: empiricism versus theory, intellect versus feeling," and he underlines that the validity of these contrasts is less of a concern than the fact that "he codified a successfully assertive group position based on exclusion and prejudice" (212). It would be tempting at this juncture to slip into a discussion of how the Movement used Dylan Thomas and the New Apocalyptics as the representatives of all that was wrong with 1940s poetry, but that debate is almost as well known as Larkin's and Thomas's poetry. Rather, the ethnic exclusivity of this debate needs to be stressed: granted Thomas's lifestyle and complex metaphorical usage were abhorred, but these were just coded markers for

Thomas's "Celtic" background. By extension, Tambimuttu's ostracization from *Poetry (London)* may have been self-made, but his choice to leave London could be read as symptomatic of something else: what Crozier argues is "that [Conquest's] 'English tradition' is concerned less with any maintenance of traditional poetic decorum than with an ideological preference among self-images" (217). The rhetoric in Conquest's introduction reflects a new defensive expression of Englishness that would become more strident in Britain in the 1960s. For example, Antony Easthope quotes Conquest's dismissal of the influence of American poetry in his 1963 *New Lines* sequel—*New Lines-II*—stating that "British culture is receptive to immigration, if not to invasion, . . . [as it] is part of our experience, and for that no one else's experience . . . can be a substitute" (30–31). Easthope reads this as Conquest's defense of Englishness and concludes that the latter "appeals to individuals who simply experience Englishness as a direct access to the real, and this is the method of empiricism" (31).[6] Returning to the first *New Lines* anthology, as Robert Sheppard points out, "half of the poems in the *New Lines* anthology use the first person plural," and then he asks, "What model of community, if any, is being invoked, and who is included in the embrace of 'we'?" (22). He later argues that the Movement's "emphasis upon the demotic, upon 'tone' and upon the speaking voice, posited the existence of a stable ego, an author-subject, as the unifying principle of the poem; its rhetoric operated at a social level" (27). In short, the Movement's utter rejection of modernism, and its anxiety over social diversification on all levels, indicates a new periodical formation, sometimes referred to as "little englandism," that takes us outside the frame of this project.

Yet, what is most curious about writing on the Movement since the 1950s is that commentators tend to consider this grouping of writers as having existed almost entirely within anthologies. Jeremy Braddock, in *Collecting as Modernist Practice*, focuses primarily on modernist art collections and modernist anthologies and makes a salient point for us here about the authority that such collections enable.

If the collection is understood as a powerful determinant within a Bourdieuian "system of positions," or within the structure of the cultural field, we can begin not only to appreciate the collection as a powerful model for the originality of modernist art but also to see the way it could be fashioned as a provisional institution. As provisional institution, the modernist collection was a means of intervening in and reforming cultural practice, doing so on the basis of its form: the collection's aesthetic arrangement, as well as its inclusions and exclusions, was a representation of ideological position. (6)

He goes on to argue that art collections and anthologies are homologous in the sense that they "select a series of works to be included or excluded, create meaning out of their material association, and justify their collective meaning in prefatory apparatuses and critical writing" (14). One could add that by the 1950s, anthologies-as-collections had lost their "provisional" and gained their "full" institutionalizing function. Harding's point about consolidation in university textbooks seems especially significant in light of the fact that the first Movement anthology was compiled by D. J. Enright for his students in Japan and contains almost all the same poets Conquest would use a year later for his first *New Lines* (Bergonzi 161). Andrew Crozier's essay—"Thrills and Frills: Poetry as Figures of Empirical Lyricism"—is one of the most commonly cited articles on the Movement since its publication, and in it he constructs this anthology-centric vision: he outlines the so-called anthology "wars" that commence with Conquest's first *New Lines*; proceed with Howard Sergeant and Dannie Abse's *Mavericks* (1957); continue with A. Alvarez's *The New Poetry* (1962); and culminate in *New Lines-II* (1963). Robert Sheppard opens the first chapter of his study on postwar British poetry—*Poetry of Saying: British Poetry and Its Discontents, 1950–2000*—by arguing that the "official literary history of the period 1950–2000 has also been the history of its most strident poetry anthologies" (20).[7] He goes on to review several of the same anthologies as Crozier to establish an "orthodoxy" that the poets of the British Poetry Revival in the 1960s were reacting to and against. For different ends, Keith Tuma, after declaring the death of British poetry in America in the opening line of his book—*Fishing by Obstinate Isles: Modern and Postmodern British Poetry and American Readers*—works through the state of affairs of British and American poetry's reception in the United States since the rise of the Movement primarily through the optic of anthology publications.[8]

As David Miller and Richard Price's *British Poetry Magazines, 1914–2000* illustrates, while there is a common perception that literary magazine production decreased dramatically in the 1950s, the numbers indicate something more modest: 125 new titles in the 1950s compared to 152 in the 1940s (86). The editors refer to this downturn as "striking" but allow that it does not tell the whole story. Instead, they argue, since "many of the magazines that didn't last for thirty years still lasted for ten, fifteen, or twenty years, . . . it might be more accurate to see [the 1950s] as [a period]of cultural reconstruction with foundations that were usually pretty solid, even to the point of becoming Establishment or simply over-familiar titles of later years" (87). Furthermore, the rate of publication in university towns reversed the overall trend and increased the total number of new titles from the 1940s:

> These include Belfast, Keele, Hull, Newcastle upon Tyne, Manchester, Liverpool, and Oxford, all with slight increases and several, such as Keele and Hull, with their first appearance in the survey to date. Cambridge had ten new titles compared to six the previous decade; Edinburgh had seven new titles compared to only two before. (88)

If the Movement had helped move poetry into the university, it clearly did not signal the end of literary magazines, but rather contributed to an expansion of their production centers: i.e., no longer would one be obligated to be in London, such as many Welsh writers felt in the 1930s and 1940s, to be published. In fact, as Miller and Price point out, "only 24% of the titles in our survey were published from London [in the 1950s], compared to 41% previously" (89). The magazine did not go away, nor did it necessarily lose its visibility, but rather it became more localized in its circulation and specialized in its audience.

It is my contention, then, that thinking about the 1950s strictly in terms of anthologies is conditioned by the period itself—i.e., even though anthologies predate the 1950s, they come to be pedagogical tools precisely when the Movement contributes to the entry of a particular kind of English literary tradition into the university. As a result, much of what is considered here, including the early Leavis, has been marginalized. This marginalization is reproduced in subsequent poetry and criticism. Sheppard and to a lesser extent Tuma exemplify how narratives of the middle section of the twentieth century in Britain still generate misperceptions: broadly speaking, the narrative goes, the Movement served as the orthodox "bogeyman" for the so-called British Poetry Revival poets, and it was only with the resurrection of Basil Bunting's career, and the "rediscovery" of Hugh MacDiarmid, David Jones, Nancy Cunard, Joseph Gordon Macleod, and Mina Loy, that a "British modernism" could be newly claimed. The recuperative aspect of this narrative is to be lauded, as these abovementioned poets' work was shamefully neglected for too long and is quite worthy of renewed attention.[9] In other words, these are efforts to recuperate and rehistoricize traditionally obscured poets worthy of renewed attention, with the implicit assumption that the forces of the canon were instrumental in their obscurity (i.e., that this recovery is a political gesture in addition to being a literary critical one). The issue with such an approach is that it reproduces the high modernist, or even Romanticist, notion of "isolated genius" or "special talent"—a perspective this project aimed to unsettle by underlining the historical conditioning of such notions.

This project was initially inspired by the so-called Poetry Wars in the 1970s. Eric Mottram, a brilliant if controversial literary critic and editor, was appointed head of *Poetry Review* in 1971 and immediately proceeded to publish more formally experimental poets in a magazine that, since 1912, had been an organ of the establishment. The bitter and petty fights that ensued eventually led to Mottram's dismissal and the magazine's return to its original status quo.[10] The rancor produced by this debate persists, and as recently as 2005 I witnessed a paper being given on the topic by Robert Sheppard at the *Poetry and the Public Sphere* conference in Plymouth, UK, with several of the actors in the drama in attendance. Sheppard's claims were rather benign, but just discussing the topic led to angry muttering throughout, followed by a contentious Q&A. The point is, despite the ill feeling that persists, the conversation during the Q&A powerfully demonstrated to me the lasting impact a periodical can have on a poetry community. As an additional, and emotionally positive, anecdote, any time I visit Britain I have at least one person ask if I have had the chance to read the *English Intelligencer*—a now very difficult to find magazine produced out of Cambridge in the late 1960s by Andrew Crozier, Peter Riley, John James, and J. H. Prynne.[11] The hushed, reverential tone that accompanies this question, from poets with widely different interests and formal approaches, provides the magazine with an aura that I have not encountered elsewhere. This is the power of the periodical to form a reading community in action, and it is what this project attempted to highlight in a specific instance.

It is important to analyze periodical formations precisely because they illustrate broad structural developments as they occur. By analyzing how certain ideas are received or rejected, we can paint a more detailed picture of the period under review. More than that, in the period analyzed in this project, poetry was a central term in defining the singularity of Englishness. The four poetic periodical formations analyzed here all conform to a particularist vision of English culture. Edgell Rickword in *The Calendar*, and later F. R. Leavis in *Scrutiny*, developed and solidified a vision and an insistent belief that what was needed in Britain were "standards of criticism" to safeguard a disintegrating society. Simultaneous with Leavis's loss of faith in contemporary poetry's ability to offer an organicist version of English culture, a formation developed that considered Surrealism as viable poetic practice in Britain but only took on board what was relevant to a broader trend in the late 1930s—i.e., the culturalist turn of much of British poetry. Several of the key figures in the Surrealist formation then attempted to form an anthropology movement (i.e., Mass-Observation), but one that initially foregrounded poetry as a viable discourse through which they could analyze English culture. Finally, in the 1940s, a formation arose around Tambimuttu and his *Poetry (London)* that briefly challenged these previous formations, but as its vision of a more broadly inclusive English tradition ran counter to the restricted notions of Englishness popularly accepted, it never established a permanent influence. In other words, throughout these various periodical formations there was a shared vision of English culture and society as an imagined whole, and they all reflect a broader discursive trend that developed in Britain in the first half of the twentieth century: an increased culturalist emphasis that favored the expression of Englishness over the aesthetic experimentation of earlier modernist movements.

# NOTES

## INTRODUCTION

1. For more on the Romanticism and Classicism debate in the magazines, see David Goldie's *Critical Difference: T. S. Eliot and John Middleton Murry in English Literary Criticism, 1918–1929* (69–127). Harding's discussion in his book on Eliot's *Criterion* of the same debate is also worth reviewing, especially his chapter on Murry's *The Adelphi*; see 25–43.
2. Esty suggests that the "relativization of England as one culture among many in the face of imperial contraction seems to have entailed a relativization of literature as one aspect of culture . . . [as] the late modernist generation absorbed the potential energy of a contracting British state and converted it into the language not of aesthetic decline but of cultural revival" (8). In a similar fashion, despite Jason Harding's claim that Eliot's periodical had a "self-appointed role as a guardian of European civilization," his extensive study of the magazine, *The "Criterion": Cultural Politics and Periodical Networks in Inter-War Britain*, as the title indicates, takes *Criterion*'s "networks" to exist exclusively within Britain (6).
3. See Suzanne W. Churchill, *The Little Magazine Others and the Renovation of Modern American Poetry*; Eric White, *Transatlantic Avant-Gardes: Little Magazines and Localist Modernism*; Adam McKible, *The Space and Place of Modernism: The Russian Revolution, Little Magazines, and New York*; Mark Morrisson, *The Public Face of Modernism: Little Magazines, Audience, and Reception, 1905–1920*; Faith Binckes, *Modernism, Magazines, and the Avant-Garde: Reading "Rhythm," 1910–1914*.
4. Thompson writes, "*Making*, because it is a study in an active process, which owes as much to agency as to conditioning. The working class did not rise like the sun at an appointed time. It was present at its own making" (9).

5. Price and Miller record 236 titles in print at some point between 1914 and 1939 and 152 during the 1940s.
6. Scholes and Wulfman find sympathy with Ezra Pound's appellation "fugitive periodicals of 'small circulation'"; however, they do not take it on board as a solution, but merely an indicator of the complexity of the terms ("Small Magazines" 701).
7. "Internal organization": (1) those based on *formal membership*, with varying modes of internal authority or decision, and of constitution and election; (2) those not based on formal membership, but organized around some *collective public manifestation*, such as an exhibition, a group press or periodical, or an explicit manifesto; (3) those not based on formal membership or any sustained collective public manifestation, but in which there is *conscious association or group identification*, either informally or occasionally manifested, or at times limited to immediate working or more general relations. "External relations": (1) *specializing*, as in the cases of sustaining or promoting work in a particular medium or branch of an art, and in some circumstances a particular style; (2) *alternative*, as in the cases of the provision of alternative facilities for the production, exhibition, or publication of certain kinds of work, where it is believed that existing institutions exclude or tend to exclude these; (3) *oppositional*, in which the cases represented by (2) are raised to active opposition to the established institutions, or more generally to the conditions within which these exist. Examples of (3) include the Futurists, the Dadaists, and the Surrealists (*Culture* 68 70).
8. "Meter adds to all the variously fated experiences which make up rhythm a definite temporal pattern and its effect is not due to our perceiving a pattern in something outside us, but to our becoming patterned ourselves" (*Principles of Literary Criticism* 127).
9. "We may best make our analysis of the experience that arises through reading these lines from the surface inwards, to speak metaphorically. The surface is the impression of the printed words on the retina. This sets up an agitation which must follow as it goes deeper and deeper" (*Science and Poetry* 11).
10. *Science and Poetry* quotes the opening of Arnold's "The Study of Poetry" as its epigraph. Arnold quotes himself from the introduction to *The Hundred Greatest Men* as "uttering the thought which should . . . go with us and govern us in all our study of poetry" (Arnold 340).

11. In "Notes on the Practice of Interpretation," a response to a *Criterion*-published Montgomery Belgion review: "My critic finds for example . . . that in *Science and Poetry* I 'endorsed Matthew Arnold's familiar dictum that what is valuable in religion as in science, is art.' Readers of that little book will remember, however, that I endorsed no such dictum. My endeavor there was to set what is valuable in religion (and poetry) and what is valuable in science as far apart as such unlike kinds of activity with their unlike kinds of value should be set. The whole essay was, in fact, an argument against confusing them" (190). Retrospectively, he went as far as to dismiss the debate over the terminology in toto, calling it "a pillow fight in a fog of escaped feathers" (189).
12. Mass-Observation was often abbreviated to "M-O" by its participants and commentators, as well as by subsequent scholars. For this reason, and for the sake of brevity, the form "M-O" will be used for the remainder of the chapter.

## CHAPTER 1

1. This is, in part, how Leavis saw what he characterizes 30 years later as "an assertion of a kind of continuity of life with *The Calendar*" (qtd. in Lucas 391). While Leavis commonly acknowledged titling his magazine after this series of essays, it appears that the title was initially proposed in an organizational meeting with coeditors L. C. Knights and Donald Culver, when they were deciding how to go forward with the project: "We spent some time discussing a name for the new periodical before Leavis came up with *Scrutiny*, borrowed from the series of 'Scrutinies' in Edgell Rickword's *Calendar*: it suggested the severely discriminating eye and had a sufficiently rasping sound" (Knights 561). Rickword later reflected that the purpose of the "Scrutinies" was to establish "a clean break, or whatever you like to call it, and we wanted to say why these figures needed shifting" ("Conversation"). There were seven published throughout the run of the magazine: Sir James Barrie (March 1925), Walter de la Mare (April 1925), John Masefield (May 1925), Arnold Bennett (June 1925), Bernard Shaw (September 1925), "Ancients and Moderns" (February 1926), and H. G. Wells (July 1927). Barrie, for example, is dismissed by Rickword wholesale: "To go see a Barrie play is like going to see a sheep in a cage in the Zoo" (41).

2. Only after it becomes a quarterly in April 1926 does it simplify its name to *The Calendar*; however, for the sake of convenience, I will from here forward refer to the magazine, regardless of the issue referenced, as *The Calendar*.
3. The idea for initiating *The Calendar* arose out of conversations between Rickword, Douglas Garman, and others, following Garman's inheritance of a small amount of money, combined with assistance from Garman's brother-in-law, the publisher Ernest Wishart. Rickword would later serve as an editor for the Wishart and Co. book publisher. (Hobday 85–87)
4. This charge is made in the "Comments and Reviews" section of the opening issue, vol. 1, no. 1 (March 1925).
5. For a clarification of this attitude, see the following discussion on the statement of the magazine's interests.
6. However, at no point does Rickword champion advocacy or topical poetry, and indeed, even in this review when he criticizes Richards's assessment of the "normality" of the poetic mind, he uses the negative example of "occasional poets" to illustrate his critique (163). In sum, we see in this review that Rickword appreciates Richards's attention to poetry as a social mode, but he is wary of particular entailments of Richards's judgments when considering contemporary poetic production.
7. He further blurs the line between poetic form and other forms of communication by asserting that his notion of rhythm can be applied to the "plastic arts and architecture": "Temporal sequence is not strictly necessary for rhythm . . . The attention usually passes successfully from one complex to another, the expectations, the readiness to perceive this rather than that, aroused by the one being either satisfied or surprised by the other" (126). For Richards, rhythm is not strictly about sound, or, as noted above, in "temporal sequence"—rather, the experience of the individual in relation to the object produces rhythm.
8. According to Althusser, "interpellation" can be likened to "hailing": "*all ideology hails or interpellates concrete individuals as concrete subjects*, by the functioning of the category of the subject" [original emphasis] (173). The pertinence here is that interpellation describes the process by which we as individuals become subjects. How we identify, and are identified, is a result of a social interaction, and is not something innate in objects. We do not carry our identities in isolation from the world, but rather we are conditioned by our interactions in the world.

9. To list just a few of the more prominent instances: Edwin Muir's essay "James Joyce: The Meaning of 'Ulysses'" (July 1925); Edgell Rickword's essay "The Returning Hero" (August 1925); a review of poetry by Laurence Binyon and Alfred Noyes (September 1925) (a review that F. R. Leavis later flatteringly cites in his introduction to *Towards Standards of Criticism*); Edwin Muir's essay "The Zeit Geist" (*sic*) (October 1925); a review of poetry by A. E. and James Stephens by Bertram Higgins (October 1925); Edwin Muir's essay "The Present State of Poetry" (January 1926); a review of *The New Criterion* (February 1926); a note entitled "Euthanasia: Or the Future of Criticism" (July 1926); a review of I. A. Richards's *Science and Poetry* by Douglas Garman (July 1926); Edgell Rickword's essay "Some Aspects of Yahoo Religion" (signed as Jasper Bildje) (October 1926); and *The Calendar*'s sign-off by Edgell Rickword, "A Valediction Forbidding Mourning" (July 1927).
10. Muir, perhaps most famously known as a translator of Franz Kafka and fluent in German, consistently misspells "zeitgeist" as two words any time he uses it in any of his contributions to *The Calendar*. His reasons for doing so remain unexplained.
11. Under the masthead on the title page of the first issue, the text begins with the claim that the magazine "will be of value to all those readers who wish to keep in touch with the literature which reflects the spirit of the present day" (March 1925 ii).
12. "We lay down no programme as to *The Calendar*'s performance nor prophecy as to its character, since these things cannot interest our readers till they have a tangible existence, and then we shall be ready to join our own criticism with theirs" (70).
13. Following Arnold's claim of the lasting contribution of poetry to society over religion, *The Calendar*'s editors stage the debate as secular generosity opposed to religious insistence, in addition to painting old forms of criticism as ministers blathering in front of communities oblivious to them and meanwhile discussing amongst themselves regardless. This characterization encourages a preference for the secular, as it is based around community sharing and not so called ideological truths. Undoubtedly this passage was supplied by Douglas Garman, who had studied Classics with Richards at Cambridge before cofounding *The Calendar*; given Richards's use of Arnold in the epigraph to *Science and Poetry* the following year, and Garman's subsequent review of *Science and Poetry* (July 1926), it is clear that Garman would have picked up this idea from his former professor.

14. John Lucas describes this moment in the piece as "entirely democratic" and the tone as "take-it-or-leave-it" (396). I would argue that these two characterizations by Lucas of this passage are mutually exclusive, as "democratic" implies a more inclusive spirit than the aloofness of "take-it-or-leave-it." Judging by the tone of this piece as a whole, I am more inclined to agree with Lucas's latter characterization.
15. As they note further along, "agreement and disagreement are terms which mean little in such circumstances. The aim of writing is not to convince someone else . . . but to satisfy oneself" (71).
16. Rickword himself lost an eye in World War I, and many war veterans returned blinded by gas or explosions. While we must, of course, consider the fact that Rickword did not initially manage the finances (and by extension, one would assume, the solicitation of advertising), it cannot be accidental that the most frequently occurring advertisement in the full run of the magazine happens to be concerning books for the blind. Given the rhetoric in this piece, which disparages the "Victorian" mind-set, the war is a powerful absent presence in the pages of the magazine.
17. Leavis himself would regularly attend, despite no longer being a student at Cambridge at the time.
18. "This series was as much about the analysis of responses to poetry as about analysis of poetry itself. Richards handed out printed sheets of poems (four poems at a time), inviting his audiences 'to comment freely in writing upon them.' He then took back the statements, which he called 'protocols,' analysed them and lectured on the results. He wanted to know how people read poetry, but he had a larger project in mind. Poetry, he argued, belonged to the 'vast *corpus* of problems' that are addressed by subjective opinion, rather than scientific method or conventional rule of thumb: 'The whole world, in brief, of abstract opinion and disputation about *matters of feeling*.' Poetry invited subjectivity, so it was 'an eminently suitable *bait* for anyone who wishes to trap current opinions and responses.' His survey of the protocols was therefore 'a piece of fieldwork in comparative ideology.'" The book took a similar format, and even though the students who contributed are anonymously quoted, it is known that several of Leavis's own responses make their way in (MacKillop 74–75).
19. MacKillop underlines the signal importance of rhythm in poetry for Richards: "Richards showed that difficult rhythms slowed down or paced attention, enabling the reader to catch hold of

ambiguity, while blander modes of verse hurried on" (77–78). MacKillop claims that Richards's essay "Gerard Hopkins" (published in *The Dial*) was "basic" for Leavis and influenced Leavis's approach to rhythm in *New Bearings in English Poetry*.

20. Again, an attitude seemingly informed by Richards: "Only those unfortunate persons who are incapable of reading poetry can resist Mr. Eliot's rhythms. The poem as a whole may elude us while every fragment, as a fragment, comes victoriously home. It is difficult to believe that this is Mr. Eliot's fault rather than his reader's, because a parallel case of a poet who so constantly achieves the hardest part of his task and yet fails in the easier is not to be found. It is much more likely that we have been trying to put the fragments together on a wrong principle" (277–78). The onus here is clearly on the reader, not the poet, to handle the difficulty of the form of the poem.

21. Leavis seems comfortable casually brandishing the "anthropology" tag in regard to Eliot without ever demonstrating that he has anything more than a loose sense of the discipline (i.e., he never performs a critique of Eliot's work from within an anthropological discourse). However, we should treat this word as loaded in Leavis's corpus, as the discipline is ultimately a "science." Science's increasingly centralized role as a method of understanding the world was one indicator of modernity's disintegration.

> The part that science in general has played in the process of disintegration is a matter of commonplace: anthropology is, in the present context, a peculiarly significant expression of the scientific spirit. To the anthropological eye beliefs, religion and moralities are human habits—in their odd variety too human. Where the anthropological outlook prevails, sanctions wither. In a contemporary consciousness there is inevitably a great deal of the anthropological, and the background of *The Waste Land* is thus seen to have a further significance. (*New Bearings* 80)

Jed Esty argues that Leavis is outside such a discourse, as he "take[s] imperial decline to imply national decline," whereas writers such as Eliot "tend to use an anthropological language of culturalism . . . [that] rearticulate[s] value in terms of an integral national culture" (215). Esty's disambiguation of Eliot's and Leavis's attitude toward imperial decline is useful in distinguishing historical effects of their writing, but Esty's thesis points toward

the rise of Cultural Studies as a direct inheritor of the Eliot-style "little englandism," all but disavowing Leavis's central role in shaping Raymond Williams's early writings on culture.
22. For Leavis, again commenting on *The Waste Land*, contemporary life has reached a level of plurality that can only have limiting and confusing effects. "The traditions and cultures have mingled, and the historical imagination makes the past contemporary; no one tradition can digest so great a variety of materials, and the result is a break-down of forms and the irrecoverable loss of that sense of absoluteness which seems necessary to a robust culture" (*New Bearings* 78). *The Waste Land* can only point to the perceived disintegration of modern life and cannot retrieve a cultural wholeness, and thus Eliot's role as a literary critic and editor of *Criterion* served Leavis's understanding of critics as the special elite who could educate a broad readership.
23. As David Gervais additionally points out, for Leavis "'England' and 'Englishness' . . . are not things that are given, but changing, malleable concepts which the critic must strive to create afresh . . . [and he] had little time for the notion of a literary canon in the inert sense of a received orthodoxy . . . nor for any kind of 'Englishness' that presumed to pin down and immortalize the past" (143). Leavis had no time for criticism-as-memorialization and instead viewed criticism as an active agent in the world: a "test for life."
24. "Ille Ego," "Readers and Writers." *New English Weekly* (January 5, 1933), 282–83.
25. Leavis also namechecks *The Dial*, *New Adelphi*, the *Times Literary Supplement*, the *Nation and Athenaeum*, and *New Statesman*, but he is not exactly enthusiastic about their abilities to offer "intelligent reviewing" (32).
26. It is worth noting in the context of this discussion that the "impersonal living memory" argues for an objective and totalizing view of this poetic canon. This, in turn, obfuscates the fact that Leavis has constructed an ideologically specific canon that leaves out names we may consider important: John Donne "has had enough attention of late . . . [and is] more or less [an] understood quantity," and John Dryden is characterized as "so simple and familiar a quantity that he does not . . . need much particular treatment" (4). Furthermore, the canon he constructs is strictly English and does not discuss other culturally complex or hybrid figures: names such as Robert Burns (who does not appear at

all) or Edmund Spenser (Spenser is not dismissed but rather is claimed for English poetry as of "first importance . . . [but this] is too simple a fact to need examining afresh" [5]). In short, the idea that Leavis's account of the tradition of poetry is an "impersonal living memory" fails to hold up in the very manner of his selection of names to include and his reasons for excluding the figures he does.

27. However, Mulhern further allows that a look at the "critical record of the journal over the [first] eight years showed a growing inclination towards discouragement and exasperation" (*Scrutiny* 151). It is the intention of the following pages to track this trend in more specific detail than Mulhern manages, especially as Mulhern's focus on all aspects of *Scrutiny*'s reviewing mutes the very significance of the initial valuing of poetry as *the* genre of literature most suitable for the magazine's declarations on contemporary culture.

28. Leavis later quotes Eliot as asserting, in reference to his own work, that "the labor of an author in composing his work is critical labor; the labor of sifting, combining, constructing, expunging, correcting, testing" (79), and he turns it around to perform a critique of Auden's method.

29. He furthermore misses the irony of claiming an American and an Irishman for an English tradition.

30. Indeed, by 1937, there seemed to be a consensus among the *Scrutiny* reviewers that contemporary poetic production was not worth reviewing. In H. L. Bradbrook's September 1937 review of works by Ezra Pound, Louis MacNeice, Charles Madge, and Rex Warner—entitled "Tuesday's Hash"—he concludes that "poetry must be kept up—verse will still be turned out—despite the tedium and the effort . . . [as] we confront a depressing situation in which the elder poets seem to have spent themselves and the younger ones can achieve nothing" (226).

## Chapter 2

1. See especially Paul C. Ray's *The Surrealist Movement in England* (76–82); Alan Young's *Dada and After: Extremist Modernism and English Literature* (152–58); and Michael Remy's *Surrealism in Britain* (30–31).
2. The contributors include J. Bronowski, William Empson, Hugh Sykes, J. M. Reeves, Basil Wright, Julian Trevelyan, R. S. Alcock,

J. D. Cullen, Richard Eberhart, G. F. Noxon, George Reavey, John Davenport, William Archer, and Malcolm Griggs. Humphrey Jennings, while actively involved in the magazine, had by 1930 reduced his role and is not represented in *transition*. Of this grouping, Empson, Sykes (Davies), and Jennings were all centrally involved in the future developments of English Surrealism and/or Mass-Observation.
3. The intellectual debate between Richards and T. S. Eliot, while it colored many of the discussions regarding belief, value, and the roles of the poet and critic, is ultimately outside the scope of this writing. Jason Harding admirably covers this debate in his *Criterion: Cultural Politics and Periodical Networks in Inter-War Britain* (see especially 113–15).
4. Although Bronowski does not say as much, and despite the group's interest in the writing coming out of Paris, they do not explicitly embrace the Surrealist method. The tenets of Bretonian Surrealism will be addressed further along.
5. Humphrey Jennings and Hugh Sykes Davies (Surrealism) and Mass-Observation (Jennings again, as well as William Empson) are the figures in mind. Another such figure, Charles Madge, who was one of the founders of Mass-Observation and a reviewer of much Surrealist writing (see especially, below, his reviews in *New Verse*), did not arrive in Cambridge until just after *Experiment* folded (the last issue was released in spring 1931, and Madge began his studies in the fall). However, Nick Hubble notes that Madge had read Empson's review of Auden's play *Paid on Both Sides* in the final issue, which had prompted him to read Auden (whose writings Madge's own work has often been compared to) (43–44). Empson's piece may also mark Madge's introduction to Surrealism as a kind of "poetry of everyday life," as in that review Empson writes about the play that "it puts psychoanalysis and surrealism and all that, all the irrationalist tendencies which are so essential a part of the machinery of present-day thought, into their proper place; they are made part of the normal and rational tragic form, and indeed what constitutes the tragic situation" (61).
6. That is, taking on board the theories of Marx and Freud, and dabbling in the ethnographic method.
7. I am indebted to Nick Hubble's attention to this piece, as well as his reading of the manifesto dealt with above. See especially *Mass-Observation and Everyday Life* (41–43).

8. "[In late 1929] Bronowski took up the reins of *Experiment* and directed its course ever more vigorously towards a rapprochement with the exotic Parisian avant-garde. Indeed, many of *Experiment*'s editors and leading contributors visited Paris on travelling scholarships or working holidays; two French artists studying at Magdalene College, Louis le Breton and Henri Cartier-Bresson (together with Humphrey Jennings, who was part French), introduced the pages of *Cahiers d'Art* to Cambridge circles. The pervasive mood of Francophilia was recalled by the painter Julian Trevelyan: 'Our thoughts at this time were more and more directed towards Paris of which Cambridge seemed a sordid and distant suburb' . . . [George] Reavey and Trevelyan acted as *Experiment*'s envoys in Paris . . . By February 1930, *Experiment* was on sale in Sylvia Beach's bookshop in the rue de l'Odeon . . . And yet the nervous shifting demonstrated that a native strain of Cambridge rationalism could never quite be happily transplanted to the heady soil of Parisian bohemia—it is natural to wonder if the 'Cambridge Experiment' manifesto was received in avant-garde salons" (Harding "*Experiment*" 292–94).
9. Andreas Huyssen, in his discussion of "modernism at large," or the "cross-national cultural forms that emerge from the negotiation of the modern with the indigenous, the colonial, and the postcolonial in the 'non-Western' world" (9), identifies the issue contemporary critics face when dealing with received understandings of the "local vs. global." While the full extent of Huyssen does not immediately concern us here, one observation is relevant: namely, that in a classical anthropological context "'real' or 'authentic' culture . . . is seen as that which is subjectively shared by a given community and therefore local" (8).
10. The implicit focus in this chapter is on Surrealist texts. Surrealist painting in Britain enjoyed a more fruitful and diverse life than its poetic counterpart. See especially Michael Remy's *Surrealism in Britain* (2001) for an exhaustive treatment of English Surrealism across multiple aesthetic forms.
11. In his analysis of the "stagnation" of British society, and the lack of efficacy of the British Left in offering a challenge to the status quo, Perry Anderson argues in his seminal essay "Origins of the Present Crisis" that the "hegemony of the dominant bloc in England" is rooted in a sense of "traditionalism" and "empiricism": "Traditionalism and empiricism henceforward fuse as a single legitimating system: traditionalism sanctions the present by

deriving it from the past, empiricism binds the future by fastening it to the present. A comprehensive conservatism is the result, covering society with a pall of simultaneous philistinism (toward ideas) and mystagogy [or initiation] (toward institutions), for which England has justly won an international reputation" ("Origins" 31).
12. By way of contrast, he states that our contemporary condition of "postindustrial capitalism" means that "products with which we are furnished are utterly without depth: their plastic content is totally incapable of serving as a conductor of psychic energy" (105).
13. The full history of Surrealism's reception has been well documented by various authors: Paul C. Ray's *The Surrealist Movement in England*; Alan Young's *Dada and After: Extremist Modernism and English Literature*; and most recently, with an emphasis as well on the visual production, Michael Remy's *Surrealism in Britain*. While these books provide a deep historical perspective, their conclusions seldom reflect on the nationalist frame the original practitioners implicitly worked within.
14. Adrian Caesar argues that Auden's publicity, and not his poetry (as it was found in the pages of the magazine), contributed to this myth. He points to the statistic that "Gascoyne, [George] Barker and [Dylan] Thomas, three poets associated . . . with Surrealism in the 1930's, and whose work is often placed in the shadow cast by the Audenesque, between them published more poems in *New Verse* than Auden, Day Lewis, and Spender put together" (117, 119). Caesar does not go so far as to say that *New Verse* was a Surrealist magazine, but Surrealism's undeniably frequent presence in the magazine speaks to the diversity of form Grigson was willing to engage with (120).
15. Stan Smith has noted parallels to Grigson's and Leavis's respective editorial tones.

> Grigson acknowledged [in *New Verse* 4 (July 1933)] that the *Scrutiny* camp was "sincere," only to add "but sincerity by itself is not a very useful thing. Talking about taste does not create it." Leavis was too much the critic and academic . . . "If *Scrutiny* is not to be the perfect body-builder for prigs it must change its formula" . . . The evangelical tone shared with Leavis was, however, probably the most recurrent aspect of Grigson's activities. (657–58)

One could cynically conclude that part of *Scrutiny*'s success was in its confrontational and uncompromising rhetoric, and thus Grigson adopted this tone in the hope of gaining similar success.

16. In *Dada and After: Extremist Modernism and English Literature*, Young divides English reception of Surrealism into several phases ("English critics and French Surrealism" [1922–27], "English critics and post-Dada" [1927–36], and "Surrealism and English literature" [1935–50]), which suggests that awareness of the movement was present from the start but also that rather than perceiving a gap between French instantiation (1922) and English practice (1935), it is more useful to think of Surrealism in Britain as a development from critical (and distanced) reception to creative embrace. See especially pages 127–87.

17. However, Madge was by no means finished with Surrealism after his 1933 essay. In the tenth issue of *New Verse* (August 1934), he wrote a review of *Petite Anthologie Poetique du Surrealisme*. In the review, Madge describes Surrealism as a "science": "Moreover, surrealism is primarily so simple that it is as hard to be reconciled to it as to Copernicus. It is difficult, on the other hand, because it is the dialectical product of conflict with the mass of superstition and social prejudice commonly attached to the name of literature" (13). This particular emphasis on Surrealism's extraliterary function leads Madge to assert that "the value of surrealism is in providing the dialectical apparatus for salving certain treasures buried under the wreckage of literature" (14). For Madge, Surrealism can serve as a necessary corrective to literature by virtue of its "scientific" methodological claims. In doing so, Madge implies that Surrealism offers a kind of universal objectivity not possible within traditionally understood literary practice, given its socially produced, and thus subjective, character. However, Madge once again is frustratingly silent on the particular shape this could take within English writing.

During the same period, *New Verse* published some of the first English Surrealist poetry. In the fifth issue (October 1933), David Gascoyne's "And the Seventh Dream Is the Dream of Isis" was published. *New Verse* would continue to publish Gascoyne's poems and translations in subsequent issues: 6 (December 1933), 7 (February 1934), 12 (December 1934), 15 (June 1935), 16 (August–September 1935), 18 (December 1935), and 21 (June–July 1936). Yet it was the advertisement and review of Gascoyne's *A Short Survey of Surrealism* in the 18th issue (December 1935),

combined with the magazine's own success to that date, that provided Gascoyne's efforts with a wide audience.
18. "Ancestors of Surrealism," "The Dadaist Attitude," "The Period of Sleeping-Fits," "The First Manifesto 1924," "The Second Manifesto 1929," and "Surrealism Today and Tomorrow." The introduction takes up most of the space (in the 2000 reprint, it occupies 71 pages), and the original work in translation only 21 pages (again in the reprint edition).This proportion suggests that as a "survey" the examples found at the end are put into service to illustrate Gascoyne's framing of the movement, and not the other way around.
19. "The Surrealist cause is the revolutionary cause—in spite of the Surrealists' bourgeois origin, in spite of the attitude of certain dogmatic Marxists towards such phenomena as Freudian psychoanalysis and the more complicated developments of modern literature and art, and in spite of such apparent compromises on the part of the Communists as the Franco-Soviet pact and the recent rehabilitation in Russia of the bourgeois conception of the family" (Gascoyne 24–25). These are a lot of "in spite ofs" to overcome. As we will see later in this chapter, the debate over Surrealism's place within leftist thinking and practice in England would come to the foreground in the aftermath of the International Surrealist Exhibition and, simultaneously, the increasing attention paid by British leftists to the civil war in Spain.

If we understand Gascoyne's survey in this way, then we can see that despite his insistence on Surrealism's internationalist potential, he thinks along national lines, especially when he argues for Surrealism's revolutionary potential in England specifically. In other words, Gascoyne is not only presenting Surrealism to an English audience, but he also intends for this publication to act as an inspiration for Surrealism's development in England. By pointing to quasi-Surrealist forebears in England, he attempted to frame Surrealism in a way that could "make sense" in England. This is why he emphasizes the "dialectical" component of Surrealism so consistently: in arguing for Surrealism's historical materialist character, he is in actuality expressing the movement's natural outgrowth from a set of historical and cultural conditions already present (see especially pages 24–25, 48, 94–95). The concern here is not so much whether his position is defensible but rather to analyze the influence of its expression.

Paul C. Ray points out that Gascoyne's book was well received upon publication. In addition to the *New Verse* review, he points to reviews in *Criterion* 15, no. 60 (April 1936), *Times Literary Supplement* (January 4, 1936), *London Mercury* (January 1936), and *Left Review* (January 1936), which were largely favorable (the ensuing debate over Surrealism in *Left Review* will be detailed below). However, he inaccurately attributes two reviews, in *New English Weekly* 9, no. 14 (July 16, 1936) and *Poetry (Chicago)* 49, no. 2 (November 1936), of Gascoyne's late-1936 publication of his own poetry—*Man's Life Is This Meat*—to Gascoyne's *Short Survey* (96–97). In fact, Herbert Read reviewed *A Short Survey* in vol. 8, no. 10 (December 19, 1935). The review is largely favorable but objects to Gascoyne's "Englishing" of *surrealisme* and instead offers up for the first time the word "superrealism," which "on the analogy of super-natural would have been better and easier to pronounce" (192). The importance in mentioning all these reviews is that taken as a whole they represent a large reading audience in Britain, suggesting that Gascoyne's book would have been widely known if not read.

20. Salvador Dali's "Love and Memory" is the lone exception to this otherwise consistent set of nature or landscape references.
21. Grigson would often publish publication announcements for books or journals in *New Verse* and then include a damning review of the same title. The reader would less frequently find the two on the same page. However, what is curious about the review of Gascoyne's book is that the advertisement for the book is featured immediately following Madge's less than favorable review. The promotional language in the ad also, interestingly, directly contradicts the rhetoric found in the review: "This book is an explanation of one of the most important intellectual movements since the War. Mr. Gascoyne's work is not merely a history of the birth and growth of Surrealism but a thorough analysis of the main ideas which are embodied in the movement" (21). Contrast this with Madge's patronizing attitude toward Gascoyne's writing: "That difficulties of style are real" and that "the best way for him to begin will be to ask himself just what difficulties of style, grammar, vocabulary, even spelling, he feels arising within himself when he starts to write on the subject" (21).
22. In his book *The Surrealist Movement in England*, Paul C. Ray devotes a chapter to describing the planning, execution, and

fallout of the International Surrealist Exhibition. See "The Exhibition" (134–66). The Exhibition receives brief mention from most other writers who address Surrealism in England in the 1930s, but Ray's is the most exhaustive to date. See also Alan Young (171–72), Peter Nicholls's "Surrealism in England" (403–4), A. J. Tolley's *The Poetry of the Thirties* (227), and Samuel Hynes's *The Auden Generation* (219–20), and even a token mention in the most recent Dylan Thomas biography by Andrew Lycett (130–32).
23. June 16: Andre Breton, "Limits Not Frontiers of Surrealism"; June 19: Herbert Read, "Art and the Unconscious"; June 24: Paul Eluard, "L'Evidence Poetique"; June 26: Hugh Sykes Davies, "Biology and Surrealism" (later that day a reading was given by several French and British writers).
24. The Popular Front was an internationalist strategy to combine various leftist groups under one anti-Fascist umbrella. Andrew Thorpe emphasizes the "popular front" strategy as an official line originating from Moscow:

> The rise of the British Union of Fascists during the first half of 1934, and the Communists' prominent role in combating it, helped the party's fortunes, but it was due to the CI's [Communist International] adoption of the "popular front" strategy in August 1935 that the CPGB began seriously to expand. The new line was introduced because Moscow realized that with the consolidation of the Nazi regime, and its continuing hostility towards the USSR, the latter needed Western allies. In Britain, this strategy of seeking the unity of anti-Fascist forces was directed towards all opponents of the National Government, even Liberals. (44)

25. Rickword's biographer stresses that the former "considered the movement important enough to allow it to speak for itself, and to subject it to reasoned criticism" (Hobday 175).
26. Interestingly, despite Lloyd's skepticism about Read's book, he seems to not have been wholly dismissive of Surrealism. In the second issue of *Contemporary Poetry and Prose* (a magazine that will be addressed below), he translated poems by Paul Eluard, Salvador Dali, and Charles Cross.
27. Rod Mengham, following Adrian Caesar and Peter Nicholls, questions the characterization, as will be stressed below, that

Roughton's "working definition of Surrealism must have been extremely flexible, given the wide range of work that he published" (689).

28. The list of Surrealist poets published in translation is quite long. For example, in the second issue alone, dubbed the "Double Surrealist Number," 12 poets are published: Paul Eluard, Benjamin Peret, Andre Breton, E. L. T. Mesens, Salvador Dali, Georges Hugnet, Gui Rosey, Rene Char, Maurice Henry, Alfred Jarry, Charles Cross, and Edith Södergran.

29. Mengham seems to have missed an editorial note published toward the end of the following issue of *Contemporary Poetry and Prose*. Entitled "Misunderstood," it addresses the provenance of the version of "Little Musgrave" published in the previous issue.

> In the May issue of *Contemporary Poetry and Prose* the poem "Little Musgrave" was NOT, as some readers kindly thought, written by the editor; it is a traditional English folk ballad, probably of fourteenth century origin, which, like many others, was remembered by American colonials, who gradually substituted some anachronistic phrases and names. This particular Appalachian version was taken down a few years ago at Rabun Gap, Georgia. There is an English version in the Oxford Book of Ballads. (46)

Roughton explicitly establishes an "original" and "version" of the ballad, with the "version" containing anachronisms. In short, the ballad's inclusion is legitimated through its historical English version.

30. Roach explains that Ngugi wa Thiong'o's sense of orature "goes beyond the schematized opposition of literacy and orality as transcendent categories; rather, it acknowledges that these modes of communication have produced one another interactively over time and that their historic operations may be usefully examined under the rubric of performance" (11–12). In the context of Roughton's printing of versions of traditional English ballads found in North America and Australia, he is putting on display this coproduction of orality and print (from song exported and transformed, and then reimported and codified in print from a resituated origin). Roach further reads these acts as a process of "surrogation," in which "social or cultural differences exacerbate generational ones . . . [and] improvised narratives of authenticity

and priority may congeal into full-blown myths of legitimacy and origin" (3). As I argue above, Roughton decontextualizes this process of transformation in North America and Australia and thus, while he honors their production elsewhere, recontextualizes these versions as instantiations of an English tradition.
31. While the magazine's international inclusionary tendency in its creative contributions needs to be acknowledged, the strongest claims are made on its intellectual and creative position as an "English Surrealist Group." Issue 4–5 (August–September 1936) opened by declaring that "the foundation of an English surrealist group, and the publication of its bulletin, are matters of some importance to revolutionary culture" (74). The "Declaration on Spain" on behalf of the United Front in Spain (in the seventh issue) was signed by the "Surrealist Group in England." Beginning with this double issue (4–5), the back matter of every subsequent issue contained a declaration of support for the "people of Spain" against Fascism, and issue 7 contained the abovementioned Declaration. The "Surrealist Group in England" signatories were Hugh Sykes Davies, David Gascoyne, Humphrey Jennings, Diana Brinton Lee, Rupert Lee, Henry Moore, Paul Nash, Ronald Penrose, Valentine Penrose, Herbert Read, and Roger Roughton. Despite the magazine's international focus, its concerns were always framed along nationalist lines, and the only significant editorial claim it ever made (the Declaration) reinforces the perception that it was a domestically minded affair. In other words, it appears that its audience was never more than a coterie of leftist writers hanging around Parton Street.

## CHAPTER 3

1. Jeremy MacClancy makes the strongest case for the link in his article "Brief Encounter: The Meeting, in Mass-Observation, of British Surrealism and Popular Anthropology." Paul Ray, in his *The Surrealist Movement in England*, is more cautious in claiming this link (see 177–78). My contention here is that while M-O and English Surrealism shared personnel and ideas, the link is too often framed as causal, and as a result, other literary influences or ideas are ignored.
2. Hubble, citing a list from the Dorothy Sheridan et al.–edited *Writing Ourselves: Mass-Observation and Literacy Practices*, notes that it "has been characterized variously as a documentary or

photographic project (Laing 1980), as a deeply flawed social survey (Abrams 1951), as a middle-class adventure at the expense of the working class (Gurney 1997), as Salvationist (Hynes 1982), as a people's history (Calder 1985), and as a life history project which was a precursor to, for example, present-day oral history (Sheridan 1996)" (Sheridan et al. qtd. in Hubble 1).
3. My objection to the treatments of this book generally is that scholars tend to uncritically adopt Madge and Harrisson's self-rebuke as reason enough to think of it as a failure or glorious mess. The ongoing mistake has been to read the book back through its reception first and not treat it on its own terms. Furthermore, while the book's formal uniqueness has often been noted, no one seems to think of the book as a poetic production, preferring instead to treat it as a naive and unwieldy piece of field research.
4. Marc Manganaro, in his *Culture, 1922: The Emergence of a Concept*, makes a detailed and provocative claim about the relation of Richards's and Malinowski's ideas on language and culture based on the evidence of an edition of *Meaning of Meaning* (which Richards coauthored with C. K. Ogden) that contains an essay by Malinowski as an appendix. As Manganaro argues, "For Malinowski, reading language contextually, situationally, means reading language in, as a species of, the larger 'cultural context.'" "Culture," as it is understood by Malinowski, is a "'reality sui generis' [and] is the origin and base of meaning; itself refers to nothing beyond itself; is itself, in this respect, the meaning of meaning" (95). See especially Manganaro, 89–104. As this book attempts to emphasize the previously underestimated influence of Richards on M-O, as well as the centrality of poetic discourse in M-O's early articulation, I will not attend to the movement's clear debt to Malinowski at any length. For more on Malinowski's relation to M-O, see Nick Hubble, who brings in Malinowski's role at several important points in his *Mass-Observation and Everyday Life*.
5. James Buzard argues that M-O's claim of an "anthropology of ourselves" could be reconciled with its "temporary occupation of, or half-inside-half-outside relation to the space of the other . . . as doing so only from a perspective for which the claims of the more embracing imagined community of the nation *overrode* the relativistic claims made on behalf of the local or class-specific (working-class) culture, even at the cost of self-contradiction" (106).
6. Indeed, when Bronisław Malinowski was invited to contribute to M-O's *First Year's Work* (1938), one of his core critiques centered

on M-O's inability to elicit "answers with a real documentary significance"—a failure that could, he suggested, be corrected by an experienced ethnological field-worker (106). This failure resides in M-O's treatment of linguistic expression as undifferentiated: "Ask your informant questions which do not affect him, and you will receive rambling, irrelevant divagations; as you receive answers to which all the criticisms leveled against Mass-Observation relevantly apply" (107).

7. Humphrey Jennings and Charles Madge studied at Cambridge at different times, and both attended lectures by I. A. Richards. Jennings's postgraduate work in the late 1920s on Thomas Gray was under the supervision of Richards, and Madge attended Richards's college (Magdalene) in the early 1930s (Hubble 41, 43). Nick Hubble, using Madge's autobiographical manuscript as a guide, points out that Madge's self-designed reading list prior to attending Cambridge included Richards, Empson, Eliot, Pound, Sir James Frazer, and Malinowski (46).

8. In an earlier chapter, Richards defines the poem as "a class of experiences which do not differ in any character more than a certain amount, varying for each character, from a standard experience" (212).

9. Richards, in a letter to Eliot, regrets his use of the prefix "pseudo," as it carries a "derogatory smack." Earlier in the same letter, he further develops the above definition: "A Pseudo-Statement for me, is something utterly different in function, powers, status, nature, order of being, etc., from any scientific or other verifiable statement, true or false. One way of bringing out the differences might be to say that a statement has ideally one ascertainable limited meaning, and is, for science, defective if it is ambiguous; while a Pseudo-Statement normally has inexhaustible meanings" (Richards qtd. in Constable xlviii–xlix).

10. The contradistinction between poetry/emotive and science/intellectual in regard to belief holds the subject in direct relation to the society that he or she inhabits. The poem, read correctly, does not verify fact or reality but rather points to the shared values of the poet and the public. A poem, in this understanding, is a touchstone for all the intangibles that make up a community of readers. That that community was assumed to be specifically English is less obvious. There are some small clues within *Practical Criticism*: in Appendix C, where he lists the authors and titles of the poems, Poem 13 is "In the Churchyard at Cambridge:

By Henry Wadsworth Longfellow—Cambridge, *Massachusetts*, of course" (original emphasis) (350). Earlier, when reviewing a student's comments on Poem 1, Richards comments, "A Transatlantic smack now makes itself unmistakably felt," and he later notes the end of this student's comments by glibly stating that "we go back now to English speech-rhythm" (26–27). Richards's comments are petty, to be sure, but they illuminate another aspect of his long-running defense of poetry: that poetry, as a cultural agent, represents certain uncontaminated portions of the society in which it is produced (i.e., as he asserted earlier about poetry being conversant with "universal truths"). The above comment is the only time "rhythm" is modified by "English," and the idea of a return ("go back now") reinforces the fact that the geographical speaking point is England. That Richards assumes all that is normal, ordinary, and factual to be contained within his own experience, and further that that experience is universal, is one of the most potent aspects of English identity at this time—it is taken for granted.
11. See Hubble (40–41).
12. Michael North has emphasized the study of the functional over the semantic relevance of language that Malinowski expresses in this supplement: "[For Malinowski,] language . . . does not . . . serve the rather specialized function of conveying ideas or communicating thought. Its more prominent role in most societies is simply to maintain society, since it is the one indispensable instrument for creating the ties of the moment without which unified social action is impossible" (49).
13. North also notes that Malinowski often refers to "language" in the supplement as a "mode of action and not an instrument of reflection" (Malinowski qtd. in North 49).
14. His book proceeds to show "the ways in which the pastoral process of putting the complex into the simple (in itself a great help to the concentration needed for poetry) and the resulting social ideas have been used in English literature" (22).
15. A phrase Hubble takes from Terry Eagleton in *Literary Theory: An Introduction* (53).
16. As was noted earlier, Nick Hubble points out that in one of Madge's notebooks he initially toyed with the idea of calling Mass-Observation "Popular Poetry." This was a phrase that Madge got from Michael Roberts (the editor of the two anthologies that solidified the identity of the "Auden Group")—*New Signatures*

and *New Country*: "[It may be] possible to write 'popular' poetry again: not by a deliberate patronizing use of, say, music-hall material, but because the poet will find that he can best express his newly found attitude in terms of a symbolism which happens to be of exceptionally wide validity" (qtd. in Hubble 69).
17. The rhyme scheme: ababcc deefdf ghighi (often in near rhyme).
18. The editors do not elaborate on how they are using this term; however, without a central thesis, it is difficult to see how the national evidence can be "tested" against international data, unless, of course, the implied thesis is that precisely what is being examined assumes the character of a national expression.
19. As evidenced by his later films, like *Spare Time* (1939) and *Listen to Britain* (1942), in both of which he creates a montage of scenes of everyday life without a narrative or commentary. As Nick Hubble characterizes *Spare Time*, the film's "metaphoric images are imbued with an ambiguity . . . [that] invite audiences to identify with a sense of the possibilities of social transformation rather than with the reassuring comfort of an everyday plentitude" (86). By showing people performing everyday activities such as putting on makeup or cheering at a football match, *Spare Time* encourages the notion of shared identity, as opposed to the other tendency in documentaries, which is to invite the division of the observer and the observed.
20. The links are mainly found in the second chapter, with occasional references to the first: paragraphs 11, 16, and 21 (pages 96–97, 100–101, 104); 24 and 62 (106–7, 131); 18 and 36 (102, 115–16); 41 and 68 (118–19, 135); 42 and 58 (119, 128–29); 45, 57, and 82 (121, 128–29, 146–47); and 48, 50, 69, 74, and 79 (122–23, 124, 135–36, 139–40, 144–45), and paragraph 75 refers to Chapter 1, paragraph 9.
21. This is one possible way to read Anderson's suggestion that the newspaper connects the individual to a shared "imagined community."
22. David Cannadine, referring to Eric Hobsbawm, argues that "invented traditions" seek an illusory continuity with earlier phases in history, and "while the materials out which [invented traditions] were forged may have been on occasions genuinely venerable, their 'meaning' was specifically related to the social, political, economic, and cultural circumstances of the time" ("British Monarchy" 161). In the case of George VI's coronation

in 1937, it was an "extravagant, imperial re-affirmation of the stability of monarchy after the interruption of the abdication" (152). Cannadine also points to domestic manufacturers' zealous protection of their own Coronation-related souvenir production: "A 100 percent import duty was imposed on all foreign, imported souvenirs" (154). In essence, even the market envisioned the Coronation as a national, not imperial, event. The Coronation, in short, provided the opportunity for the British to proclaim themselves a nation in the face of external and internal instability.

23. Pound, as has been well established, was inspired by Ernest Fenollosa's writings on the ideogram. Fenollosa, in *The Chinese Written Character as a Medium for Poetry*, argued that "the more concretely and vividly we express the interactions of things the better the poetry," and this can be accomplished by "crowding maximum meaning into the single phrase" (28).

24. Marjorie Perloff defines montage and collage slightly differently from Bernstein. In *The Futurist Moment*, she acknowledges the distinction is "problematic": "It is customary to distinguish between montage and collage: the former refers, of course, to spatial relationships, the latter to temporal; the former to static objects, originally a film term, to things in motion. Accordingly, *collage* is generally used when referring to the visual arts; *montage*, to the verbal" (fn. 5 246). Perloff's visual-verbal distinction adds another level of complexity to these two terms that Highmore does not acknowledge. The significance of this complexity means that "montage" cannot be reduced simply to "Surrealist." Montage's particular use of parataxis can be compared to the broad use of intercutting texts and images that can be found across several modernist groups (Dada, Futurism, et al.) engaged in textual and visual experimentation. It is therefore reductive to draw too strong an equivalence between montage and Surrealism.

25. There were a few reviews that preceded *May the Twelfth*'s release and focused its comments on a pamphlet that had been released in June, simply entitled *Mass-Observation*. Derek Kahn, whom Nick Hubble identifies as one of the Observers at the Coronation, and also a possible contributor to the "Oxford Collective Poem" (136), commented in the July 1937 issue of *Left Review* that Mass-Observation is "right in choosing anthropology as their model" over Surrealism (373). D. W. Harding, in the September 1937 issue of *Scrutiny*, generally receives M-O positively and

states that one of its advantages over other social sciences "lies in the greater sense it gives of co-operative undertaking by the observers and their directors, and the resulting tendency for the observers' part in it to give them extra interest in the features of their daily life that they are reporting on" (201). As will be demonstrated below, Madge's and Jennings's poetic claims are never picked up on by M-O's reviewers, and the movement's turn away from poetry gave subsequent reviewers no reason to return to those early proclamations.

26. The negative reviews: G. W. Stonier, "Review of *May the Twelfth*" (*New Statesman* [October 9, 1937]); T. H. Marshall, "Is Mass-Observation Moonshine?" (*The Highway* [December 30, 1937]); Maria Jahoda, "Review of *May the Twelfth*" (*The Sociological Review* [April 2, 1938]).

27. Apropos of an earlier claim that Madge assumed the ubiquity of Richards's ideas when writing about "poetry," the above review in *New English Weekly* is followed by another reviewer criticizing a book that challenges *The Principles of Literary Criticism.*

28. Harrisson could be accused, as well, of pandering to his audience, since *The Highway* was published by the Worker's Educational Association (WEA), and Harrisson's stated goal in writing this article is to recruit WEA members into M-O, and thus his attempt to reject the literary is a coded move to reassure his readers of M-O's proletarian credentials.

29. Charles Bernstein performed a nearly identical reading of water imagery in *The New Yorker*—from January 30 to May 15, 1989—noting that 86 percent of the poems published contained water images. He, interestingly for the conversation in this chapter, characterizes his approach as "social scientific" ("Water Images" 175–77).

30. Moreover, he assumes that all poetry operates similarly and that its work can be summarized by quoting fragments of a few selected poets. Geoffrey Grigson's unsigned response to this article in *New Verse*—"Science and Mass-Observation: Poets and Poor Tom"—identifies this problem clearly. Grigson declares that Harrisson's selections for quotation are "selected by fancy and made serviceable by mutilation" (no. 29 16). After pointing to a few examples of selective quotation that alter the sampled lines' meanings, Grigson charges Harrisson with trying "to bully or to persuade, not to reason" (18).

31. No doubt a reference to the "Oxford Collective Poem."

32. Harrisson took no direct part in the compilation of *May the Twelfth*, and as he wrote to Geoffrey Gorer, "it was a crazy idea to have it edited by a whole bunch of intellectual poets" (qtd. in *May the Twelfth* 418).

33. Perhaps the most spirited attack on Harrisson's article was made in an unsigned editorial in *New Verse* 29 (it is likely that it was by Grigson himself, as the tone of the piece seems in keeping with the nickname he earned for his biting criticisms—"Billhook"). The writer stresses that they care for M-O but not Tom Harrisson and accuses him of selective reading and of lacking demonstration of a scientific approach (16, 18). The article concludes with an unflattering comparison and an alarming wish:

> Your language, Mr. Harrisson, is podgier and more ridiculous than Ezra Pound's. In your article there is very little science or true knowledge, and your method is altogether unscientific in a way that discredits Mass-Observation.
>
> What we should like to do is to bury you in a bag with Houston Stewart Chamberlain, Alfred Rosenberg, and Major Yeats-Brown. (18)

34. M-O, according to Kushner, "was not able to get beyond the idea of ethnic homogeneity or able to confront the full significance of racial exclusivity" (73). Nick Hubble quotes this passage to quibble with the idea that M-O was racially exclusionist and defends M-O as a project more concerned with "combat[ing] the very real threat of a British form of Fascism under the ruling Conservative Government with popular forms of anti-fascist resistance," ultimately characterizing the lack of attention to the very fact of racial heterogeneity in interwar Britain as "a very minor crime of omission" (249). It seems that Hubble fails to appreciate that an acknowledgment of an inclusionary British identity (one that would incorporate multiple racial and ethnic identities) would indeed be a useful exercise to "combat" one of the basic platforms of Fascism: racial hierarchization. Hubble, as my frequent citations of him in this chapter make evident, has written to date the most thoroughgoing analysis of M-O. However, I differ with him on many of his conclusions, and as this response to Kushner illustrates, Hubble has failed to appreciate broader social and cultural trends in interwar Britain, particularly the structural shift I address here and will elaborate on in

the following chapter: namely, an increasing tendency among the British intelligentsia to reclaim Englishness as the core identity of the British nation.

## CHAPTER 4

1. Juliet Gardiner points to a moment in 1942 when the Ministry of Supply "agreed to release an additional 250 tons of paper for books 'of national importance'" (417). She also notes that the general degradation of the quality of paper, primarily made of homegrown straw, "meant that publishers could probably manage to produce 60 per cent of the books they had produced before the war, despite having only 37.5 per cent of the paper" (418). A. T. Tolley adds that "before the war 80% of pulp for paper came to Britain from Sweden—a source of supply effectively cut off after the German invasion of Denmark and Norway in 1940" (*British Literary Periodicals* 2).
2. While Tambimuttu never directly identifies Mass-Observation with this type of poetry in any of his Letters, much of his characterization of "objective reporter" poetry could be applied to the movement. However, David Gascoyne, himself briefly involved in Mass-Observation, provocatively argued that "though they would not have expressed it thus, two of the co-founders of Mass-Observation, Charles Madge and Humphrey Jennings, undoubtedly at one time shared something like Tambi's belief [i.e., in the democratic openness of poetry]" ("Tambimuttu" 239).
3. The phrase "Welsh writing in English" is a more recent scholarly solution to the problematic hyphenated term "Anglo-Welsh." The change appears to be motivated by the problem of the cultural confusion that this term suggests when it was originally used simply (and one could argue, naively) as a linguistic marker. Historically, the Welsh poets covered in this chapter referred to themselves as Anglo-Welsh, and some of the pre-1990s scholarship also uses this terminology. To further complicate matters, the best anthology of Welsh poetry in English is entitled *Anglo-Welsh Poetry, 1480–1990*, and the two best books of criticism are entitled *The Dragon Has Two Tongues: Essays on Anglo-Welsh Writers and Writing* and *Frontiers in Anglo-Welsh Poetry*. I have decided to retain the term "Anglo-Welsh" in quotation marks, but I will henceforth refer to the poets in question with the more recently accepted phrase.

4. The intended audience for this broadcast is important to keep in mind: several million English-speaking Indians, and as George Orwell points out regarding the marker of class in speaking English, "the people who speak English are also the people likeliest to have access to short-wave radio sets" (7). The point of the broadcasts were to persuade the intelligentsia of an increasingly nationalist-driven Indian population to cooperate in the British war effort by presenting aspects of British life and culture in a positive light (Ranasinha 35).
5. Ruvani Ranasinha tracked the origin of these claims to a family myth: "Tambimuttu even fabricated a royal ancestry that was accepted by his new milieu. The BBC addressed its correspondence to Prince Tambimuttu . . . Tambimuttu's family tree makes an unsubstantiated claim for his being descended from the last king of Jaffna, baptized Don Constantino . . . Tambimuttu's claims were mocked in the Sri Lankan English press" (110, 110n.21).
6. The first issue of *Poetry (London)* was unpaginated. All subsequent issues contain page numbers.
7. Richards's influence is perhaps more covertly present in Tambimuttu's writings. He never mentions Richards or his works, but more so than with Eliot, he appears to be indebted to Richards's thinking on poetry and belief. Early on in the "First Letter," Tambimuttu argues that "by the reception of many different expressions of poets, a mind that has not already *felt* the whole truth is educated to feel it," and further that "one of the uses of written poetry [is] to educate every man into this consciousness." How the poem affects the reader finds similar expression in *Principles of Literary Criticism*: Richards, in his chapter entitled "The Analysis of a Poem," states that "feelings" is "a more subtle way of referring [than symbolically or scientifically]," and furthermore that the "arts are the most powerful [form of experience, as it is] in these experiences that the mind most easily and with least interference organizes itself" (120–21). Tambimuttu also alludes to Richards's distinction between intellectual and emotional beliefs when he states that "poetry is an altogether bigger thing than the intellect, . . . [and the] intellect is a very inefficient medium between life and its expression, . . . [as it] removes us further from life." Furthermore, he references Richards's and Eliot's debate on belief when he claims that "the trouble with the modern world is that it has no *real* beliefs or religions. Poetry is religion. Poetry

makes the world tangible to us and enables us to preserve order in it." John Constable, in his "Editorial Introduction" to the 10th volume of *I. A. Richards: Selected Works 1919–1938*, summarizes the debate as follows: "The debate has two distinct concerns, the first being the question of whether a poet need believe the thought or philosophy he employs in his poetry, and the second, dependent on the answer to the first of these, is whether a reader need share the beliefs of the poet to appreciate the poems" (xix). Constable goes on to note that the debate originated in Eliot's reviewing of Richards's *Science and Poetry* and *Principles of Literary Criticism* and continued in various essays published in periodicals as well as in personal correspondence until the mid-1930s (xxiv).

8. Keidrych Rhys was published in nos. 1, 6, 7, 9, and 11; Lynette Roberts in nos. 6, 7, 14, and 15; and Dylan Thomas in nos. 1, 2, 4, 6, and 9.

9. Kenneth O. Morgan points out that in 1931 nearly twice as many people over the age of 45 could speak Welsh compared to those under the age of 14 (245).

10. Tambimuttu arrived in London in November 1938, and by mid-December it is clear he had already contacted Thomas, based on the evidence of a letter the latter wrote to Vernon Watkins dated December 29, 1938: "There's a new periodical, *Poetry (London)* which promises to be, if nothing else, well produced. A monthly. Edited by man or woman called Tambimuttu. Contributors, God bless them, to the first number will have their names engraved on the special souvenir cover" (51).

11. "Poem in the Ninth Month" was later dropped as the title in the *Collected Poems*. Technically untitled, it appears in the table of contents with its first line—"A saint about to fall."

12. For the notion that Thomas is referring to Laugharne, see Lycett (167).

13. The 7th issue contains writing by both Roberts and Rhys: two poems and a prose piece by Roberts—"The New World," "River Plate," and "Time Was"—and Rhys's poem "Sheep: Gwynfe." All three of Roberts's pieces, much like "Poem from Llanybri," are full of references to local flora, products, and geography, the difference being the setting is in South America: ombu tree, maté, pampas, etc. Wilkinson argues that Roberts's poems display a "localized modernism [in that they are] intent on reanimating bodies of tradition to resist a planned and administered world"

(190). In both issues, Roberts's uniqueness was accentuated to support Tambimuttu's thesis in the 6th issue that poetry is "the incarnation of . . . the living principle, that is immanent in human activity" (163). Roberts's highly particularized attention to place in her poems suits the requirement of the "immanent" for the vitality of poetry. Rhys's poem largely involves the description of the roughness and violence of farming life. Lines such as "fingertips shrunken; nails blue. Mankind's / Shriek at crusted Stockholm backs at maggot cheats. / Long tails sheared; highland blood easy in red paint pools" and "The butting dog linked in the barn, old veteran [. . .] / the yard's a little / Smeared with fluid; last scalloped ear, near mad, the mottled face / Stood up on vetted feet" blend imagery of the farm and allusions to the war (36). Furthermore, akin to Wilkinson's claim that Roberts's poetry was most definitely not a brand of "warmed-over Georgianism," Rhys seems to be performing a full assault on the idyll of pastoral poetry by choosing to highlight the difficulty and strife of working on a farm: "the healthy cheviots / [. . .] great gangs wedged in there / [. . .] Legs well gripped in, then, only them lifted on haunches. / How the parings flew away from my penknife! / I had to get down on one knee for the front lot" (35).

14. While the rest of this issue is paginated, Rhys's manifesto contains no page number. It is located in the back of the issue, with a "Prologue" by Dylan Thomas opening the magazine.

15. Kenneth O. Morgan offers a thorough description of the history of eisteddfod and its historical role in Welsh life (*Rebirth* 97–99). It is further worth mentioning that Rhys dubbed both the August 1937 (no. 2) and the August 1938 (nos. 8–9) issues as "eisteddfod numbers."

16. This passage is a near quote of Williams's note on odes by Dafydd ap Gwilym: "A fairly strict system of alliteration and assonance is followed, known as *cynghanedd*, the chief feature of which is that instead of one consonant being repeated, as in English verse, a series of different consonants is repeated in varying order . . . Cynghanedd, slackly or strictly handled, is still the basis of Welsh versification" (119–20). Once again, Tambimuttu's use of another writer's words to make his argument illustrates the "weaving" approach in his Letters that he inherited from his grandfather.

17. Eliot (1933 136–37), in his "The Modern Mind" section of *The Use of Poetry—The Use of Criticism*, writes, in reference to Trotsky's *Literature and Revolution* and Soviet Russia, that "even

as things are, in the present chaos of opinion and belief, we may expect to find quite different literatures existing in the same language and the same country." Tambimuttu, throughout his Letters, demonstrated an ability to write near-to-exact quotations as if they were vague recollections or allusions. Once again, this instance illustrates Tambimuttu's "weaving" strategy when writing his Letters.

18. Chris Beckett's article "Tambimuttu and the Poetry London Papers at the British Library: Reputation and Evidence" is the best overview of Tambimuttu's publishing career to date. As the title suggests, he uses almost exclusively the recent acquisition by the British Library of various documents relating to Tambimuttu and his magazine. For a detailed overview of the financial dealings and eventual ousting of Tambimuttu, see 8–13.

19. A gesture that Chris Beckett quite rightly criticizes as "add[ing] further insult to injury" (11n.72).

20. Enright is here expressing a basic Leavisite division between the minority gatekeepers of culture, whose names would be known, and the masses, where Enright reads "anonymous" as "masses." Enright's reference to Tambimuttu's "anonymous tradition" comes from the latter's "Ninth Letter": "I edit this magazine since I feel that (1) poetry is more important than individual great poets, (2) the writing of important verse is only possible when the audience for it has been found, (3) the best work is anonymous in character in the sense that it expresses the feelings of a group of people; a magazine like this which is catholic in viewpoint helps to create a modern anonymous tradition from which the important work of the future may be derived" (3). Enright either missed or deliberately obscured the adjective "modern" preceding the "anonymous tradition," which would make Tambimuttu more in keeping with Eliot's notion of how the tradition operates on the individual. Enright, though, is too concerned with leveling *Poetry (London)*'s reputation to allow it any legitimate stand.

21. Enright cannot resist one closing jab at the "anonymous tradition": "What little criticism is permitted has to remember that we are all poets, and poets ought to be one happy family, living together in a kind of pre-fabricated barn called an 'anonymous tradition'" (10).

22. Indeed, Williams allows that "we were very anxious to see what Leavis would say about *us*, . . . [and] what he said . . . was that

we would succeed if we lived up to a series of objectives that amounted to a description of *Scrutiny*" (69).

## Conclusion

1. T. S. Eliot, in his *Notes Towards a Definition of Culture*, itself a seminal text in the formation of Cultural Studies in Britain, complained about the corrupting of the respective national cultures of the colonizer and colonized, which Esty interprets as "if colonization erodes traditional life, national culture kept inside its 'natural' or conventional boundaries, can guarantee . . . a certain degree of authenticity and continuity" (130). Indeed, Esty interprets Eliot's discussion of Scotland, Wales, and Ireland as "satellite cultures" that "enrich the life of the otherwise philistine modernity of the major power" to be an assumption of English superiority, but it also "relativizes England as one national culture among others" (133). Tambimuttu, as an imaginary test case for Eliot, would fall into the category of the partially westernized, and despite Tambimuttu's abovementioned declaration of acculturation—"I was shedding part of what England had given me in Ceylon"—he is not part of English culture in Eliot's framing.
2. "To raise the prickly and green-coated gourd / So grateful to the palate, and when rare / So coveted, else base and disesteemed,— / Food for the vulgar merely,—is an art / That toiling ages have but just matured, / And at this moment unessayed in song. / Yet gnats have had, and frogs and mice long since / Their eulogy; those sang the Mantuan bard, / And these the Grecian in ennobling strains; / And in thy numbers, Phillips, shines for aye / The solitary shilling. Pardon then, / Ye sage dispensers of poetic fame, / The ambition of one meaner far, whose powers / Presuming an attempt not less sublime, / Pant for the praise of dressing to the taste / Of critic appetite, no sordid fare, / A cucumber, while costly yet and scarce" (49–50).
3. Tambimuttu reviewed the anthology in the third issue of his *Poetry (London)* reboot—*Poetry London-New York*—and is, not surprisingly, critical of Conquest's claims. The review's impact must have been limited, as there is no evidence that it was countenanced by anyone in Britain.
4. The poets in *New Lines* (1956): Elizabeth Jennings, John Holloway, Philip Larkin, Thom Gunn, Kingsley Amis, D. J. Enright, Donald Davie, John Wain, and Robert Conquest.

5. Jeremy Braddock makes the argument for the anthology's ability to establish more cultural weight and permanence: "It differed ... from the institution of the little magazine, which played a decisive role in the promotion of modernist art and literature, but which (like individual exhibitions of art) played a comparatively weaker role in arguing for the terms and meaning of its long-term reception. Whereas the distinctions among these forms of literary collections are not absolute,. . . it was the unique capability of the interventionist anthology not merely to *identify* but perhaps more accurately to *interpellate* collective formations in the service of the volume's social reason for being" (16).
6. See Perry Anderson's "Origin of the Present Crisis" quoted above (Chapter One). One might take issue with Anderson's totalizing categorization of England as a conservative society. However, his analysis certainly applies to the Movement, with the distinction being that whereas Anderson reads Englishness as a structural issue of the society at large, the rhetoric of Conquest on behalf of the Movement worries about its abridgement.
7. Perhaps the best study of this period (albeit in a different country) and the central effects of the anthologization and institutionalization of certain kinds of poetry is performed by Jed Rasula in his *The American Poetry Wax Museum: Reality Effects, 1940–1990*. Tuma's book considers British-based anthologies more extensively, but like Rasula, Tuma is strictly concerned with an American audience and American reception. A fuller study of the educational effects of such anthologies would be most welcome (i.e., something that builds on Brian Doyle's *English and Englishness*, but in the vein of Rasula's book).
8. To be fair to Tuma, his book considers a broad range of publications in addressing the shifting fortunes of British poetry's reception in America. However, using the explanation that the Movement was able "to circumvent small literary quarterlies and gain access to the larger audiences of the BBC's Third Programme, the *Spectator*, and the *Times Literary Supplement*," he attends primarily to how anthologies are used as pedagogical propaganda, as it were (95). See especially his chapter "England in America, America in England: Rereading *New Poets of England and America* and British and American Fifties Poetry" (80–103).
9. Such poets are pejoratively referred to as "neglectorinos." The origin of this word is unclear, but it seems to have sprouted up

in late 2005/early 2006 in discussions on Ron Silliman's blog (ronsilliman.blogspot.com).

10. For full details of these events, see Peter Barry's *The Poetry Wars: British Poetry of the 1970's and the Battle of Earls Court*.

11. In 2012, Neil Pattison, Reitha Pattison, and Luke Roberts edited and published prose selections from the periodical through Mountain Press, entitled *Certain Prose of the "English Intelligencer"* (a revised edition was published in 2014). While its publication is absolutely most welcome, it works more as an interpretation of the periodical (i.e., framing the periodical's prime locus as both literary critical and theoretical) and less as a critical edition of its full run.

# Bibliography

## Periodicals

*Contemporary Poetry and Prose*
*Left Review*
*New Verse*
*Poetry (London)*
*Scrutiny*
*The Calendar of Modern Letters*
*transition*
*Wales*

Althusser, Louis. "Ideology and Ideological State Apparatuses." Ben Brewster, trans. *Lenin and Philosophy and Other Essays.* New York: Monthly Review Press, 1971. 127–86. Print.
Anand, Mulk Raj. "Talking of Tambi: The Dilemma of the Asian Intellectual." Jane Williams, ed. *Tambimuttu: Bridge between Two Worlds.* London: Peter Owen, 1989. 191–201. Print.
Anderson, Benedict. 1983. *Imagined Communities: Reflections on the Origin and Spread of Nationalism.* London: Verso, 1991. Print.
Anderson, Perry. "Origins of the Present Crisis." *English Questions.* London: Verso, 1992. 15–47. Print.
———. "Components of the National Culture." *English Questions.* London: Verso, 1992. 48–104. Print.
Arnold, Matthew. "The Study of Poetry." J. Keating, ed. *Selected Prose.* Harmondsworth, UK: Penguin Books, 1982. 340–66. Print.
Asad, Talal. "The Concept of Cultural Translation in British Social Anthropology." James Clifford and G. E. Marcus, eds. *Writing Culture: The Poetics and Politics of Ethnography.* Berkeley: U of California Press, 1986. 141–64. Print.
Attridge, Derek. *The Singularity of Literature.* London: Routledge, 2004. Print.

Baldick, Chris. *The Social Mission of English Criticism, 1848–1932*. Oxford: Clarendon Press, 1983. Print.

Barry, Peter. *The Poetry Wars: British Poetry of the 1970's and the Battle of Earls Court*. Cambridge, UK: Salt Publishing, 2006. Print.

Baucom, Ian. *Out of Place: Englishness, Empire, and the Locations of Identity*. Princeton, NJ: Princeton UP, 1999. Print.

Beckett, Chris. "Tambimuttu and the *Poetry London* Papers at the British Library: Reputation and Evidence." *Electronic British Library Journal*. British Library. 2009. Web. May 15, 2011.

Bergonzi, Bernard. *Wartime and Aftermath: English Literature and Its Background, 1939–60*. Oxford: Oxford UP, 1993. Print.

Bernstein, Charles. "Jackson at Home." *Contents Dream: Essays 1975–1984*. Los Angeles: Sun and Moon Press, 1986. 252–58. Print.

———. "Pound and the Poetry of Today." *My Way: Speeches and Poems*. Chicago: U of Chicago Press, 1999. 155–65. Print.

———. "Water Images of *The New Yorker*." *My Way: Speeches and Poems*. Chicago: U of Chicago Press, 1999. 175–77. Print.

Blunt, Anthony. "Rationalist and Anti-Rationalist Art." *Left Review* 2:10 (July 1936): iv–vi. Print.

Bradbrook, H. L. "Tuesday's Hash." *Scrutiny* 6:2 (September 1937): 226–28. Print.

Braddock, Jeremy. *Collecting as Modernist Practice*. Baltimore, MD: Johns Hopkins UP, 2012. Print.

Breton, Andre. *What Is Surrealism?* Franklin Rosemont, ed. London: Pluto Press, 1978. Print.

———. "Manifesto of Surrealism (1924)." *Manifestoes of Surrealism*. Richard Seaver and Helen R. Lane, trans. Ann Arbor, MI: U of Michigan Press, 2000. 1–48. Print.

———. "Second Manifesto of Surrealism (1930)." *Manifestoes of Surrealism*. Richard Seaver and Helen R. Lane, trans. Ann Arbor, MI: U of Michigan Press, 2000. 117–194. Print.

Bronowski, Jacob. "Experiment." *transition* 19–20 (Spring–Summer 1930): 107–12. Print.

Brooker, Peter, and Andrew Thacker. "General Introduction." Peter Brooker and Andrew Thacker, eds. *The Oxford Critical and Cultural History of Modernist Magazines*, vol. 1: *Britain and Ireland, 1880–1950*. Oxford: Oxford UP, 2009. 1–26. Print.

Buzard, James. "Mass-Observation, Modernism, and Auto-Ethnography." *Modernism/Modernity* 4:3 (1997): 93–122. Print.

Bylansen, Stephen. "Poetics and Poetry." *New English Weekly* 12:12 (December 30, 1937): 233. Print.

Caesar, Adrian. *Dividing Lines: Poetry, Class, and Ideology in the 1930's*. Manchester, UK: Manchester UP, 1991. Print.
Calder, Angus. *The People's War: Britain, 1939–1945*. New York: Pantheon Books, 1969. Print.
Cannadine, David. "The Context, Performance and Meaning of Ritual: The British Monarchy and the 'Invention of Tradition.'" Eric Hobsbawm and Terence Ranger, eds. *The Invention of Tradition*. Cambridge, UK: Cambridge UP, 1994. 101–64. Print.
Chinitz, David. "T. S. Eliot and the Cultural Divide." *PMLA* 110:2 (March 1995): 236–47. Print.
Clifford, James. *The Predicament of Culture: Twentieth-Century Ethnography, Literature, and Art*. Cambridge, MA: Harvard UP, 1999. Print.
Conquest, Robert, ed. *New Lines: An Anthology*. London: Macmillan and Co. Ltd., 1956. Print.
———. *New Lines-II: An Anthology*. London: Macmillan and Co. Ltd., 1963. Print.
Conran, Tony. *Frontiers in Anglo-Welsh Poetry*. Cardiff: U of Wales Press, 1997. Print.
Constable, John. "Editorial Introduction." John Constable, ed. *I. A. Richards and His Critics: Selected Reviews and Critical Articles*. London: Routledge, 2001. ix–lxx. Print.
Corbett, David Peters, and Andrew Thacker. "Raymond Williams and Cultural Formations: Movements and Magazines." *Prose Studies* 16:2 (August 1993): 84–106. Print.
Crozier, Andrew. "Thrills and Frills: Poetry as Figures of Empirical Lyricism." Alan Sinfield, ed. *Society and Literature, 1945–1970*. London: Methuen, 1983. 199–233. Print.
Cunningham, Valentine. *British Writers of the Thirties*. Oxford: Oxford UP, 1988. Print.
Davie, Donald. *Purity of Diction in English Verse and Articulate Energy*. New York: Penguin Books, 1992. Print.
Davies, Hugh Sykes. "Localism." *transition* 19–20 (Spring–Summer 1930): 114–16. Print.
Doyle, Brian. *English and Englishness*. London: Routledge, 1989. Print.
Dudman, George, and Patrick Terry. *Challenge to Tom Harrisson*. Oxford: Hall the Printer Ltd., 1938. Print.
Eagleton, Terry. *Literary Theory: An Introduction*. Minneapolis, MN: U of Minnesota Press, 1985. Print.
Easthope, Antony. "Donald Davie and the Failure of Englishness." James Acheson and Romana Huk, eds. *Contemporary British*

*Poetry: Essays in Theory and Criticism.* Albany: SUNY Press, 1996. 17–34. Print.

Eliot, T. S. "The Idea of a Literary Review." *New Criterion* 4:1 (January 1926): 1–6. Print.

———. "The Function of Criticism." Frank Kermode, ed. *Selected Prose of T. S. Eliot.* New York: Farrar, Straus, and Giroux, 1975. 68–76. Print.

———. "Tradition and the Individual Talent." Frank Kermode, ed. *Selected Prose of T. S. Eliot.* New York: Farrar, Straus, and Giroux, 1975. 37–44. Print.

———. *The Use of Poetry—The Use of Criticism: Studies in the Relation of Criticism to Poetry in England.* London: Faber and Faber Ltd., 1933. Print.

———. "What is Minor Poetry?" *Welsh Review* 3:4 (December 1944): 256–67. Print.

Empson, William. "[Review] Auden's *Paid on Both Sides.*" *Experiment* 7 (1931): 60–61. Print.

———. *Some Versions of Pastoral.* New York: New Directions, 1974. Print.

Enright, D. J. "The Significance of *Poetry London.*" *The Critic* 1:1 (Spring 1947): 3–10. Print.

Esty, Jed. *A Shrinking Island: Modernism and National Culture in England.* Princeton, NJ: Princeton UP, 2004. Print.

———. *Unseasonable Youth: Modernism, Colonialism, and the Fiction of Development.* Oxford: Oxford UP, 2011. Print.

———. "[Review] *Late Modernism: Politics, Fiction, and the Arts between the World Wars. Modernism/Modernity* 7:1 (2000): 172–73. Print.

Fenollosa, Ernest. *The Chinese Written Character as a Medium for Poetry.* Ezra Pound, ed. San Francisco, CA: City Lights, 1936. Print.

Fowler, H. K. *A Dictionary of Modern English Usage.* Oxford: Oxford UP, 1926. Print.

Friedman, Susan Stanford. "Planetarity: Musing Modernist Studies." *Modernism/Modernity* 17:3 (September 2010): 471–99. Print.

Gardiner, Juliet. *Wartime, 1939–1945.* London: Headline Book Publishing, 2004. Print.

Garlick, Raymond, and Roland Mathias, eds. *Anglo-Welsh Poetry 1480–1990.* Bridgend, Wales: Seren Press, 1982. Print.

Gascoyne, David. *A Short Survey of Surrealism.* London: Enitharmon Press, 2000. Print.

———. "Tambimuttu." Roger Scott, ed. *Selected Prose, 1934–1996.* London: Enitharmon Press, 1998. 239. Print.

# BIBLIOGRAPHY

Gervais, David. *Literary Englands: Versions of "Englishness" in Modern Writing.* Cambridge, UK: Cambridge UP, 1993. Print.

Gikandi, Simon. *Maps of Englishness: Writing Identity in the Culture of Colonialism.* New York: Columbia UP, 1997. Print.

Gilroy, Paul. *"There Ain't No Black in the Union Jack": The Cultural Politics of Race and Nation.* Chicago: U of Chicago Press, 1987. Print.

Goldie, David. *Critical Difference: T. S. Eliot and John Middleton Murry in English Literary Criticism, 1918–1929.* Oxford: Clarendon Press, 1998. Print.

Grigson, Geoffrey. "Science and Mass-Observation: Poets and Poor Tom." *New Verse* 29 (March 1938): 16–18. Print.

———. "On a Present Kind of Poem." *Polemic: A Magazine of Philosophy, Psychology, and Aesthetics* 7 (March 1947): 52–64. Print.

———. "Correspondence." *Poetry (London)* 4:13 (June–July 1948): 46. Print.

Haffenden, John. *William Empson*, vol. 1: *Among the Mandarins.* Oxford: Oxford UP, 2005. Print.

Harding, D. W. "[Review] *Mass Observation.*" *Scrutiny* 6:2 (September 1937): 200–201. Print.

Harding, Jason. "*Experiment* in Cambridge: 'A Manifesto of Young England.'" *Cambridge Quarterly* 27:4 (1998): 287–309. Print.

———. *Criterion: Cultural Politics and Periodical Networks in Inter-War Britain.* Oxford: Oxford UP, 2002. Print.

———. "Modernist Poetry and the Canon." *The Cambridge Companion to Modernist Poetry.* Cambridge, UK: Cambridge UP, 2007. 225–43. Print.

Harrisson, Tom. "Mass Observation and the W.E.A." *The Highway* 30 (December 1937): 46–48. Print.

———. "Mass-Opposition and Tom Harrisson." *Light and Dark* 2:3 (February 1938): 8–15. Print.

———. "Mass Observation: A Reply." *New Statesman and Nation* 15:368 New Series (March 12, 1938): 409–10. Print.

Heinemann, Margot. "*Left Review, New Writing* and the Broad Alliance against Fascism." Edward Timms and Peter Collier, eds. *Visions and Blueprints: Avant-Garde Culture and Radical Politics in Early Twentieth-Century Europe.* Manchester, UK: Manchester UP, 1988. 113–36. Print.

Hewison, Robert. *Under Siege: Literary Life in London, 1939–1945.* New York: Oxford UP, 1977. Print.

Highmore, Ben. *Everyday Life and Cultural Theory: An Introduction.* London: Routledge, 2002. Print.

Hobday, Charles. *Edgell Rickword: A Poet at War*. Manchester, UK: Carcanet Press, 1989. Print.

Hopkins, Chris. "*Wales* (1937–39), *Welsh Review* (1939–40)." Peter Brooker and Andrew Thacker, eds. *The Oxford Critical and Cultural History of Modernist Magazines*, vol. 1: *Britain and Ireland, 1880–1950*. Oxford: Oxford UP, 2009. 714–34. Print.

Hubble, Nick. *Mass-Observation and Everyday Life: Culture, History, Theory*. New York: Palgrave Macmillan, 2010. Print.

Huyssen, Andreas. "Geographies of Modernism in a Globalising World." Peter Brooker and Andrew Thacker, eds. *Geographies of Modernism: Literatures, Cultures, Spaces*. New York: Routledge, 2005. 6–18. Print.

Hynes, Samuel. *The Auden Generation: Literature and Politics in England in the 1930's*. New York: Viking Press, 1976. Print.

"Ille Ego." "Readers and Writers." *New English Weekly* (January 5, 1933): 282–83. Print.

Innes, C. L. *A History of Black and Asian Writing in Britain, 1700–2000*. Cambridge, UK: Cambridge UP, 2002. Print.

Jennings, Humphrey. "[Review] *Surrealism*." *Contemporary Poetry and Prose* 8 (December 1936): 167–68. Print.

Jones, Glyn. *The Dragon Has Two Tongues: Essays on Anglo-Welsh Writers and Writing*. Tony Brown, ed. Cardiff: University of Wales Press, 2001. Print.

Kahn, Derek. "Anthropology Begins at Home." *Left Review* 3:6 (July 1937): 373. Print.

Keery, James. "The Apocalyptic Poets, 'New Modernism,' and 'The Progressive View of Art': *Poetry London* (1939–51) and *Indian Writing* (1940–42)." Peter Brooker and Andrew Thacker, eds. *The Oxford Critical and Cultural History of Modernist Magazines*, vol. 1: *Britain and Ireland, 1880–1950*. Oxford: Oxford UP, 2009. 874–97. Print.

Kenner, Hugh. "The Making of the Modernist Canon." Robert von Hallberg, ed. *Canons*. Chicago: U of Chicago Press, 1984. 363–75. Print.

Knights, L. C. "Remembering *Scrutiny*." *Sewanee Review* 89:4 (Fall 1981): 560–85. Print.

Kumar, Krishan. *The Making of English National Identity*. Cambridge, UK: Cambridge UP, 2003. Print.

Kushner, Tony. *We Europeans?: Mass-Observation, "Race" and British Identity in the Twentieth Century*. Hampshire, UK: Ashgate, 2004. Print.

Large, E. C. "The Coronation Mass-Observed." *New English Weekly* 12:12 (December 30, 1937): 232–33. Print.
Latham, Sean. "Cyril Connolly's *Horizon* (1940–50) and the End of Modernism." Peter Brooker and Andrew Thacker, eds. *The Oxford Critical and Cultural History of Modernist Magazines*, vol. 1: *Britain and Ireland, 1880–1950*. Oxford: Oxford UP, 2009. 856–73. Print.
Leavis, F. R. "The Standards of Criticism." Eric Bentley, ed. *The Importance of "Scrutiny."* New York: New York UP, 1964. 393–406. Print.
———. *New Bearings in English Poetry*. 1932. Middlesex, UK: Penguin Books Ltd., 1967. Print.
———. *Mass Civilization and Minority Culture*. Reprinted in *For Continuity*. Cambridge, UK: Minority Press, 1933. 13–46. Print.
———. "Restatement for Critics." *Scrutiny* 1:4 (March 1933): 315–23. Print.
———. "This Poetical Renascence." *Scrutiny* 2:1 (June 1933): 65–76. Print.
———. "Auden, Bottrall and Others." *Scrutiny* 3:1 (June 1934): 70–83. Print.
———. "Marianne Moore." *Scrutiny* 3:2 (June 1935): 87–90. Print.
———. "Hugh MacDiarmid." *Scrutiny* 4:3 (December 1935): 305. Print.
———. *Revaluation: Tradition and Development in English Poetry*. London: Chatto and Windus, 1967. Print.
Leavis, F. R., et al. "Scrutiny: A Manifesto." *Scrutiny* 1:1 (May 1932): 2–7. Print.
Lehmann, John. *I Am My Brother*. New York: Reynal and Company, 1960. Print.
Levenson, Michael. *The Genealogy of Modernism: A Study of English Literary Doctrine, 1908–1922*. Cambridge, UK: Cambridge UP, 1984. Print.
Lindsay, Jack. "Not English." *Left Review* 2:8 (May 1936): 353–57. Print.
———. "The May-Day Tradition." *Left Review* 3:16 (May 1938): 963–66. Print.
Lindsay, Maurice. "Editorial Letter." *Poetry Scotland* 1 (1943): 3–4. Print.
Lloyd, A. L. "Surrealism and Revolutions." David Margolies, ed. *Writing the Revolution: Cultural Criticism from "Left Review."* London: Pluto Press, 1998. 145–49. Print.

Lucas, John. "Standards of Criticism: *The Calendar of Modern Letters* (1925–27)." Peter Brooker and Andrew Thacker, eds. *The Oxford Critical and Cultural History of Modernist Magazines*, vol. 1: *Britain and Ireland, 1880–1950*. Oxford: Oxford UP, 2009. 389–404. Print.

Lycett, Andrew. *Dylan Thomas: A New Life*. New York: Overlook Press, 2003. Print.

MacClancy, Jeremy. "Brief Encounter: The Meeting, in Mass-Observation, of British Surrealism and Popular Anthropology." *Journal of the Royal Anthropological Institute* 1:3 (September 1995): 495–512. Print.

MacKillop, Ian. *F. R. Leavis: A Life in Criticism*. London: Allen Lane, Penguin Press, 1995. Print.

Maclaren-Ross, Julian. *Memoirs of the Forties*. London: Sphere Books Ltd., 1984. Print.

MacNeice, Louis. *Autumn Journal*. 1939. London: Faber and Faber Ltd., 1998. Print.

McCaffery, Steve. *Prior to Meaning: The Protosemantic and Poetics*. Evanston, IL: Northwestern UP, 2001. Print.

McGuinness, Patrick. "Introduction to Lynette Roberts' *Collected Poems*." Patrick McGuinness, ed. *Collected Poems*. Manchester, UK: Carcanet Press, 2005. Print.

Madge, Charles. "Surrealism for the English." *New Verse* 6 (December 1933): 14–18. Print.

———. "The Meaning of Surrealism." *New Verse* 10 (August 1934): 13–15. Print.

———. "[Review] *A Short Survey of Surrealism*." *New Verse* 18 (December 1935): 20–21. Print.

———. "Magic and Materialism." *Left Review* 3:1 (February 1937): 31–35. Print.

———. "The Press and Social Consciousness." *Left Review* 3:5 (June 1937): 279–86. Print.

———. "A Note on Images." Mary-Lou Jennings, ed. *Humphrey Jennings: Film-maker, Painter, Poet*. London: BFI, 1982. 47–49. Print.

Madge, Charles, and Humphrey Jennings. "They Speak for Themselves: Mass Observation and Social Narrative." *Life and Letters To-day* 17:9 (Autumn 1937): 37–42. Print.

———. "Anthropology at Home." *New Statesman and Nation*. 13:306 New Series (January 2, 1937): 12. Print.

———. "Poetic Description and Mass-Observation." *New Verse* 24 (February–March 1937): 1–6. Print.

———. "Oxford Collective Poem." *New Verse* 25 (May 1937): 16–19. Print.

Madge, Charles, and Tom Harrisson, eds. *First Year's Work, 1937–1938*. 1938. London: Faber and Faber Ltd., 2009. Print.

Madge, Charles, Humphrey Jennings, et al. *May the Twelfth: Mass-Observation Day Surveys 1937*. 1937. London: Faber and Faber Ltd., 2009. Print.

Madge, Charles, Tom Harrisson, and Humphrey Jennings. "Anthropology at Home." *New Statesman and Nation* 13:310 New Series (January 30, 1937): 155. Print.

Malinowski, Bronisław. "Supplement I: The Problem of Meaning in Primitive Languages." I. A. Richards and C. K. Ogden, eds. *The Meaning of Meaning*. 1923. New York: Harcourt Brace Jovanovich, 1989. 296–336. Print.

Manganaro, Marc. *Culture, 1922: The Emergence of a Concept*. Princeton, NJ: Princeton UP, 2002. Print.

March, Richard. "Questions in the Silly Season." *Poetry (London)* 4:16 (September 1949): 1–2. Print.

Margolies, David, ed. *Writing the Revolution: Cultural Criticism from "Left Review."* London: Pluto Press, 1998. Print.

Mason, H. A. "[Review] *ABC of Reading*." *Scrutiny* 3:2 (September 1934): 192. Print.

———. "Yeats and the English Tradition." *Scrutiny* 5:4 (March 1937): 449–51. Print.

———. "Poetry in 1936." *Scrutiny* 6:1 (June 1937): 77–82. Print.

Mathias, Roland. *A Ride through the Wood: Essays on Anglo-Welsh Literature*. Bridgend, Wales: Poetry Wales Press, 1985. Print.

Matless, David. *Landscape and Englishness*. London: Reaktion Books Ltd., 1998. Print.

Matthews, Sean. "'Say Not the Struggle Naught Availeth . . .': *Scrutiny* (1932–53)." Peter Brooker and Andrew Thacker, eds. *The Oxford Critical and Cultural History of Modernist Magazines*, vol. 1: *Britain and Ireland, 1880–1950*. Oxford: Oxford UP, 2009. 833–55. Print.

Mengham, Rod. "'Nationalist Papers Please Reprint': Surrealist Magazines in Britain." Peter Brooker and Andrew Thacker, eds. *The Oxford Critical and Cultural History of Modernist Magazines*, vol. 1: *Britain and Ireland, 1880–1950*. Oxford: Oxford UP, 2009. 688–703. Print.

Miller, David, and Richard Price, eds. *British Poetry Magazines, 1914–2000: A History and Bibliography of "Little Magazines."* London: The British Library and Oak Knoll Press, 2006. Print.

Miller, Tyrus. *Late Modernism: Politics, Fiction, and the Arts between the Wars.* Berkeley: U of California Press, 1999. Print.

Milne, Drew. "Charles Madge: Political Perception and the Persistence of Poetry." *New Formations: Mass-Observation as Poetics and Science* 44 (Autumn 2001): 63–75. Print.

Morgan, Kenneth. *Rebirth of a Nation: Wales, 1880–1980.* New York: Oxford UP, 1981. Print.

Muir, Edwin. "The Zeit Geist." *Calendar of Modern Letters* 2:8 (October 1925): 112–18. Print.

———. "The Present State of Poetry." *Calendar of Modern Letters* 2:11 (January 1926): 322–31. Print.

Mulhern, Francis. *The Moment of "Scrutiny."* London: New Left Books, 1979. Print.

———. "English Reading." *The Present Lasts a Long Time: Essays in Cultural Politics.* Notre Dame, IN: U of Notre Dame Press, 1998. 133–46. Print.

Nasta, Sushelia. *Home Truths: Fictions of the South Asian Diaspora in Britain.* Houndmills, UK: Palgrave, 2002. Print.

Naylor, Paul. *Poetic Investigations: Singing the Holes in History.* Evanston, IL: Northwestern UP, 1999. Print.

Nicholls, Peter. *Modernisms: A Literary Guide.* Berkeley: U of California Press, 1995. Print.

———. "Surrealism in England." Laura Marcus and Peter Nicholls, eds. *The Cambridge History of Twentieth-Century English Literature.* Cambridge, UK: Cambridge UP, 2004. 396–416. Print.

North, Michael. *Reading 1922: A Return to the Scene of the Modern.* Oxford: Oxford UP, 1999. Print.

Orwell, George. "T. S. Eliot." *Poetry (London)* 2:7 (October–November 1942): 56–59. Print.

Pattison, Neil, Reitha Pattison, and Luke Roberts, eds. *Certain Prose of the "English Intelligencer."* Introduction by Neil Pattison. Cambridge, UK: Mountain Press, 2012. Print.

Perloff, Marjorie. *The Futurist Moment: Avant-Garde, Avant Guerre, and the Language of Rupture.* Chicago: U of Chicago Press, 2003. Print.

Pound, Ezra. "A Retrospect." *Literary Essays.* New York: New Directions, 1968. 3–14. Print.

———. "The Serious Artist." *Literary Essays.* New York: New Directions, 1968. 41–57. Print.

---. "Small Magazines." *The English Journal* 19:9 (November 1930): 689–704. Print.

---. *Guide to Kulchur*. New York: New Directions, 1970. Print.

Preminger, Alex, and T. V. F. Brogan. "Lyric." Alex Preminger and T. V. F. Brogan, eds. *The New Princeton Encyclopedia of Poetry and Poetics*. New York: MJF Books, 1993. 713–27. Print.

Rabaté, Jean-Michel. "Tradition and T. S. Eliot." David Moody, ed. *The Cambridge Companion to T. S. Eliot*. Cambridge, UK: Cambridge UP, 1994. 210–22. Print.

Raine, Kathleen. "Humphrey Jennings." Mary-Lou Jennings, ed. *Humphrey Jennings: Film-maker, Painter, Poet*. London: BFI, 1982. 50–52. Print.

---. *Defending Ancient Springs*. Ipswich, UK: Golgonooza Press, 1985. Print.

---. "[Untitled]." Jane Williams, ed. *Tambimuttu: Bridge between Two Worlds*. London: Peter Owen, 1989. 66–69. Print.

Rajan, Balachandra. "Bloomsbury and the Academies: The Literary Situation in England." *Hudson Review* 2:3 (Autumn 1949): 451–57. Print.

---. "Reviews: *Looking for Poetic Character, Young Commonwealth Poets '65*." *Journal of Commonwealth Literature* 2 (March 1967): 153–57. Print.

Ramazani, Jahan. *A Transnational Poetics*. Chicago: U of Chicago Press, 2009. Print.

Ranasinha, Ruvani. *South Asian Writers in Twentieth-Century Britain: Culture in Translation*. Oxford: Oxford UP, 2007. Print.

Rasula, Jed. *The American Poetry Wax Museum: Reality Effects, 1940–1990*. Urbana, IL: National Council of Teachers of English, 1996. Print.

Ray, Paul. *The Surrealist Movement in England*. Ithaca, NY: Cornell UP, 1971. Print.

Read, Herbert. "Views and Reviews." *New English Weekly* 8:10 (December 19, 1935): 191–92. Print.

---. *Surrealism*. London: Faber and Faber Ltd., 1971. Print.

---. *Form in Modern Poetry*. 1932. Plymouth, UK: Vision Press Ltd., 1989. Print.

Read, Herbert, and Hugh Sykes Davies. "Reply to A. L. Lloyd." 1937. David Margolies, ed. *Writing the Revolution: Cultural Criticism from "Left Review."* London: Pluto Press, 1998. 149–51. Print.

Remy, Michael. *Surrealism in Britain*. Aldershot, UK: Ashgate Publishing Ltd., 1999. Print.

Rhys, Keidrych. "[Untitled]." *Wales* 1 (Summer 1937): n. pag. Print.

———. "As You Know." *Wales* 2 (August 1937): 35–37. Print.
———. "Homage to a Split Man." *Poetry (London)* 1 (February 1939): n. pag. Print.
———. "Sheep: Gwynfe." *Poetry (London)* 2:7 (October–November 1942): 35–36. Print.
Richards, I. A. *Principles of Literary Criticism.* London: Routledge, 2001. Print.
———. *Science and Poetry.* London: Kegan Paul, Trench, Trubner and Co. Ltd., 1926. Print.
———. *Practical Criticism.* New York: Harcourt, Brace, and World, Inc., 1962. Print.
———. "Notes on the Practice of Interpretation." (1931). John Paul Russo, ed. *Complementarities: Uncollected Essays.* Manchester, UK: Carcanet Press, 1976. Print.
Richardson, Maurice. "Mass Observation." *Left Review* 3:10 (November 1937): 625–26. Print.
Rickword, Edgell. "A Fragmentary Poem." *Times Literary Supplement* (September 20, 1923). Reprinted in Michael Grant, ed. *T. S. Eliot: The Critical Heritage*, vol. 1. London: Routledge, 1982. 178–80. Print.
———. "Scrutinies (I): Sir James Barrie." *Calendar of Modern Letters* 1:1 (March 1925): 38–43. Print.
———. "Comments and Reviews." *Calendar of Modern Letters* 1:1 (March 1925): 70–71. Print.
———. "Among New Books." *Calendar of Modern Letters* 1:1 (March 1925): 87–88. Print.
———. "[Review] *Principles of Literary Criticism.*" *Calendar of Modern Letters* 1:2 (April 1925): 162–64. Print.
———. "The Returning Hero." *Calendar of Modern Letters* 1:6 (August 1925): 472–74. Print.
———. "Some Aspects of Yahoo Religion." *Calendar of Modern Letters* 3:3 (October 1926): 236–42. Print.
———. "A Valediction Forbidding Mourning." *Calendar of Modern Letters* 4:2 (July 1927): 175–76. Print.
———. "A Conversation with Edgell Rickword." Interview by John Lucas. *Poetry Nation* 1 (1973): n. pag. Poetrymagazines.org.uk. Web. August 18, 2010.
Riley, Peter. "Thomas and Apocalypse." *Poetry Wales* 44:3 (Winter 2008–09): 12–16. Print.
Roach, Joseph. *Cities of the Dead: Circum-Atlantic Performance.* New York: Columbia UP, 1996. Print.

Roberts, Lynette. "Poem from Llanybri." *Poetry (London)* 1:6 (May–June 1941): 180. Print.
———. "The New World," "River Plate," and "Time Was." *Poetry (London)* 2:7 (October–November 1942): 38–40, 49–50. Print.
———. *Collected Poems*. Patrick McGuinness, ed. Manchester, UK: Carcanet Press, 2005. Print.
Roughton, Roger. "Misunderstood." *Contemporary Poetry and Prose* 2 (June 1936): 46. Print.
Scarfe, Francis. *Auden and After: The Liberation of Poetry, 1930–1941*. London: George Routledge and Sons Ltd., 1942. Print.
———. "Seventh Letter." *Poetry (London)* 2:7 (October–November 1942): 52–55. Print.
Scholes, Robert, and Clifford Wulfman. *Modernism in the Magazines: An Introduction*. New Haven, CT: Yale UP, 2010. Print.
Schwartz, Sanford. *The Matrix of Modernism: Pound, Eliot, and Early Twentieth-Century Thought*. Princeton, NJ: Princeton UP, 1988. Print.
Sheppard, Robert. *Poetry of Saying: British Poetry and Its Discontents, 1950–2000*. Liverpool, UK: Liverpool UP, 2005. Print.
Sheppard, Robert, and Scott Thurston. "Editorial." *Journal of British and Irish Innovative Poetry* 1:1 (September 2009): 3–9. Print.
Sinfield, Alan. *Literature, Politics, and Culture in Postwar Britain*. Berkeley: U of California Press, 1989. Print.
Smith, Peter Macdonald. "A Tale of Two Literatures: The Periodicals and the Anglo-Welsh Tradition (Part 2)." *New Welsh Review* 1:2 (Autumn 1988): 68–70. Print.
Smith, Stan. "Poetry Then: Geoffrey Grigson and *New Verse* (1933–39), Julian Symons and *Twentieth Century Verse* (1937–39)." Peter Brooker and Andrew Thacker, eds. *The Oxford Critical and Cultural History of Modernist Magazines*, vol. 1: *Britain and Ireland, 1880–1950*. Oxford: Oxford UP, 2009. 647–68. Print.
Spender, Stephen. "MacNeice." *Poetry (London)* 1:3 (November 15, 1940): 86–87. Print.
Stanford, Derek. *Inside the Forties: Literary Memoirs, 1937–1957*. London: Sidgwick and Jackson Ltd., 1977. Print.
Stonier, G. W. "Mass Observation and Literature." *New Statesman and Nation* 16:366 New Series (February 26, 1938): 326–27. Print.
"Surrealist Group in England." "Declaration on Spain." *Contemporary Poetry and Prose* 7 (November 1936): n. pag. Print.
Symons, Julian. *Notes from Another Country*. London: London Magazine Editions, 1972. Print.

Tambimuttu, Meary James. "First Letter." *Poetry (London)* 1 (February 1939): n. pag. Print.
———. "Second Letter." *Poetry (London)* 2 (April 1939): n. pag. Print.
———. "Third Letter." *Poetry (London)* 1:3 (November 15. 1940): 65–66. Print.
———. "Sixth Letter." *Poetry (London)* 1:6 (May–June 1941): 161–64, 195. Print.
———. "Ninth Letter." *Poetry (London)* 2:9 (January 1943): 3. Print.
———. "Eleventh Letter." *Poetry (London)* 3:11 (September–October 1947): 5–8. Print.
———. "Correspondence." *Poetry (London)* 4:13 (June–July 1948): 46–47. Print.
———. *Natarajah: A Poem for Mr. T. S. Eliot's Sixtieth Birthday*. London: Editions Poetry London, 1949. Print.
———. "First Letter." *Poetry London-New York* 1:1 (March–April 1956): 1–2. Print.
———. "Third Letter." *Poetry London-New York* 1:3 (Winter 1957): 1–4, 44–47. Print.
Thomas, Dylan. "Poem in the Ninth Month." *Poetry (London)* 1 (February 1939): n. pag. Print.
———. "To Vernon Watkins." December 29, 1938. Vernon Watkins, ed. *Letters to Vernon Watkins*. London: J. M. Dent and Sons Ltd., 1957. 50–52. Print.
Thompson, E. P. *The Making of the English Working Class*. New York: Vintage Books, 1963. Print.
Thorpe, Andrew. *Britain in the 1930's: The Deceptive Decade*. Oxford: Blackwell, 1992. Print.
Tolley, A. J. *The Poetry of the Thirties*. New York: St. Martin's Press, 1975. Print.
———. *The Poetry of the Forties*. Manchester, UK: Manchester UP, 1985. Print.
———. *British Literary Periodicals of World War II and Aftermath: A Critical History*. Kemptville, Ontario: Golden Dog Press, 2007. Print.
Tuma, Keith. *Fishing by Obstinate Isles: Modern and Postmodern British Poetry and American Readers*. Evanston, IL: Northwestern UP, 1998. Print.
[Unsigned]. "Editorial." *Life and Letters To-day* 16:8 (Summer 1937): 1–2. Print.

[Unsigned]. "Experiment: A Manifesto." *transition* 19–20 (Spring–Summer 1930): 106. Print.
[Unsigned]. "The Reading Public and the Critical Reader." *Critic* 1:2 (Autumn 1947): 5–6. Print.
Viswanathan, Gauri. "Raymond Williams and British Colonialism." Dennis L. Dworkin and Leslie G. Roman, eds. *Views Beyond the Border Country: Raymond Williams and Cultural Politics.* New York: Routledge, 1993. 217–30. Print.
White, Eric. *Transatlantic Avant-Gardes: Little Magazines and Localist Modernism.* Edinburgh: Edinburgh UP, 2013. Print.
Wilkinson, John. "The Water-Rail of Tides." *The Lyric Touch: Essays on the Poetry of Excess.* Cambridge, UK: Salt Publishing, 2007. 189–94. Print.
Williams, Gwyn, ed. *The Rent That's Due to Love: A Selection of Welsh Poems Translated by Gwyn Williams.* London: Editions Poetry London, 1950. Print.
Williams, Raymond. *The Long Revolution.* 1961. Peterborough, Ontario: Broadview Press, 2001. Print.
———. *Culture.* London: Fontana, 1981. Print.
———. *Politics of Modernism: Against the New Conformists.* London: Verso Press, 2007. Print.
———. *The Country and the City.* New York: Oxford UP, 1973. Print.
———. *Marxism and Literature.* Oxford: Oxford UP, 1978. Print.
———. "The Bloomsbury Fraction." 1980. *Culture and Materialism: Selected Essays.* London: Verso, 2005. Print.
———. *Politics and Letters: Interviews with "New Left Review."* London: Verso, 1981. Print.
Young, Alan. *Dada and After: Extremist Modernism and English Literature.* Manchester, UK: Manchester UP, 1981. Print.
Ziegler, Philip. *London at War, 1939–1945.* New York: Alfred A. Knopf, 1995. Print.

# Index

"A. E." George Russell, 151
Abrams, Mark, 165n2
Abse, Dannie, 142
*Adelphi*, 147n1
aesthetic, 4, 5, 6, 10, 15, 16, 17, 21, 24, 31, 49, 59, 61, 64, 69, 70, 74, 79, 80, 101, 103, 107, 121, 132, 134, 135, 137, 142, 146, 147n2, 157n10
Alcock, R. S., 155n2
Alfred, Lord Tennyson, 73
Alighieri, Dante, 40, 51
Allott, Kenneth, 105
Althusser, Louis, 27, 150n8
Alvarez, A., 142
Amis, Kingsley, 177n4
Anabaptists, 71
Anderson, Benedict, 100
Anderson, Perry, 43, 60, 81, 157n11, 168n21, 178n6
Anglo-Welsh, 119, 120, 121, 124, 125, 172n 3. *See also* Welsh writing in English
anthology, 13, 51, 95, 127, 140, 141, 142, 143, 172n3, 177n3, 178n 5
anthropological, 4, 17, 38, 44, 45, 48, 49, 60, 81, 82, 91, 95, 97, 104, 107, 153n21, 157n9
anthropology, 16, 48, 49, 53, 58, 73, 78, 79, 81, 88, 89, 104, 107, 146, 153n21, 164n1, 165n5, 169n25
anti-Fascist, 16, 70, 74, 162n24, 171n34
Aragon, Louis, 72
Archer, William, 156n2
Aristotle, 13
Arnold, Matthew, 12, 13, 56, 138, 148n10, 149n11, 151n13
*Arson: an ardent review*, 64
Arts Café, The, 74
Asad, Talal, 82, 101
Attridge, Derek, 99
Auden, W. H., 4, 10, 16, 42, 46, 48, 64, 87, 105, 109, 117, 140, 155n28, 156n5, 158n14, 162n22, 167n16
Augustan, 43
autoethnography, 16, 79
avant-garde, 2, 6, 55, 58, 59, 70, 123, 147n3, 157n8

Baldick, Chris, 45
Ball, John, 71
ballad, 75, 92, 163n29
Barrie, James, 149n1
BBC Eastern Service, 111
BBC Third Programme, 178n8
Beachcroft, T. O., 97
Beckett, Chris, 176n18, 176n19
Beddoes, Thomas Lovell, 66

# Index

Bedlamites, 71
Belgion, Montgomery, 149n11
belief, 4, 55, 56, 58, 84, 85, 89, 90, 92, 107, 153n21, 156n3, 166n10, 173n7
Bennett, Arnold, 149n1
Bernstein, Charles, 96, 102, 169n24, 170n29
Bildje, Jasper. *See* Edgell Rickword
Binckes, Faith, 6, 147n3
Binyon, Laurence, 151n9
Blackburn, Julian, 97
Blake, William, 66
Blunt, Anthony, 72
Bottrall, Ronald, 42, 46, 48, 49
Bradbrook, H. L., 155n30
Braddock, Jeremy, 141, 178n5
Brathwaite, Kamau, 113
Breton, Andre, 15, 60, 61–3, 65, 66, 68, 69, 156n4, 162n23, 163n28
Breton, Louis le, 157n8
bricolage, 112, 113, 116
British Poetry Revival, 142, 144
British Popular Front, 15, 70
Bronowski, Jacob, 56, 155n2, 156n4, 157n8
Brooker, Peter, 2, 9–10
Browning, Robert, 73
buchedd, 120, 122
Bunting, Basil, 144
Burns, Robert, 51, 154n26
Buzard, James, 79, 165n5
Byron, George Gordon, 115

Cade, Jack, 71
Caesar, Adrian, 158n14, 162n27
Cage, John, 96, 100
Calder, Angus, 86, 165n2
*Calendar of Modern Letters*, 7, 11, 14, 21–36, 40, 41, 70, 145, 149n1, 150nn2–3, 151nn9–13
Cambridge Experiment, 56, 57, 157n8
Cambridge School, 10
Cannadine, David, 168n22
canon, 3, 6, 7, 18, 19, 43, 51, 75, 144, 154n23, 154n26
Carroll, Lewis, 66
Cartier-Bresson, Henri, 157n8
catholicity, 21, 118, 128, 129, 132, 133
Ceylon (Sri Lanka), 17, 18, 108, 109, 110, 113, 114, 115, 177n1
Chamberlain, Brenda, 120
Chamberlain, Houston Stewart, 171n33
Char, Rene, 66, 163n28
Chesterton, G. K., 115
Chinitz, David, 49
Churchill, Suzanne W., 6, 147n3
Clark Lectures, 37
Classicism, 4, 77, 147n1
Clifford, James, 78, 79
coincidences, 77–8, 80, 88, 99, 102
Coleridge, Samuel Taylor, 66, 69, 79–80, 83–4, 85, 90
collage, 80, 95, 102, 169n24
collective image, 16, 79
colonial, 4, 108, 113, 114, 118, 120, 126, 127, 139, 157n9, 163n29
Connolly, Cyril, 109, 131
Conquest, Robert, 140, 141, 142, 177nn3–4, 178n6
Conran, Tony, 120, 122
Constable, John, 166n9, 174n7
*Contemporary Poetry and Prose*, 7, 10, 16, 64, 74–5, 77, 162n26, 163n29

Corbett, David Peters, 10
Coronation Day, 86, 97–101, 103, 105, 168n22, 169n25
Cowper, William, 138
*Criterion*, 2–5, 9, 14, 16, 21–2, 39, 40, 63, 86, 111, 130, 147nn1–2, 149n11, 151n9, 154n22, 156n3, 161n19
critic, 12, 13, 14, 24, 30–1, 33–6, 38–41, 43–8, 50, 51, 53, 116, 127, 129
*Critic, The*, 131, 133
*Critical Quarterly*, 134
Cromwell, Oliver, 71
Crosby, Harry, 48
Cross, Charles, 162n26, 163n28
Crozier, Andrew, 140–1, 142–3, 145
Cullen, J. D., 156n2
cultural formations, 9–10, 13
Cultural Studies, 11, 134, 137, 154n21, 177n1
Culver, Donald, 149n1
Cunard, Nancy, 144
Cunningham, Valentine, 95
cynghanedd, 127–8, 175n16

Dada, 148n7, 155n1, 158n13, 159n16, 160n18, 169n24
*Daily Express*, 87
*Daily Herald*, 87
Dali, Salvador, 65, 161n20, 162n26, 163n28
Danielewski, Mark Z., 99
Davenport, John, 156n2
David Archer Bookshop, 74
Davie, Donald, 138–9, 177n4
Davies, Hugh Sykes, 57–9, 68, 69–70, 73–4, 75, 76, 77–8, 156n2, 156n5, 162n23, 164n31
Davies, Idris, 120

*Dial, The*, 153n19, 154n25
Donne, John, 40, 154n26
Douglas, Keith, 118
Doyle, Brian, 130–1, 134, 178n7
Dryden, John, 154n26
Dudman, George, 106
Dyment, Clifford, 120

Easthope, Anthony, 141
Eberhart, Richard, 46, 156n2
Eisenstein, Sergei, 102
Eliot, T. S., 1–5, 9, 11, 14, 16, 21, 23, 27–9, 32, 37–9, 41, 42, 48–52, 58, 71, 86, 110–14, 116, 118, 128, 130–1, 134, 137, 147nn1–2, 153nn20–1, 154n22, 155n28, 156n3, 166n7, 166n9, 173n7, 175n 17, 176n20, 177n1
Elizabethan, 42
Eluard, Paul, 65, 66, 69, 162n23, 162n26, 163n28
Empson, William, 42, 56, 79, 84, 85, 92, 97, 105, 114, 140, 155n2, 156n5, 166n7
Engels, Friedrich, 65
*English Intelligencer*, 145, 179n11
English Surrealism, 13, 15, 55, 57, 58, 59, 60, 63, 156n2, 157n10, 164n1
Englishness, 4, 13, 14, 19, 22, 36, 43, 67, 75, 107, 110, 119, 125, 126, 134, 139, 141, 145, 146, 154n23, 172n34, 178nn6–7
Enright, D. J., 131–3, 142, 176n20–1, 177n4
Ernst, Max, 64
Esty, Jed, 4–5, 22, 49, 60, 67, 79, 107, 137, 138, 147n2, 152n21, 177n1

ethnographic surrealism, 16, 78, 79, 80
*Experiment*, 55, 57, 63, 156n5, 157n8

Faber and Faber, 111, 112, 113
Fenollosa, Ernest, 169n23
Feuerbach, 65
*First Year's Work*, 17, 81, 87, 165n6
Fitzrovia, 114–15
Fraser, G. S., 118
Frazer, Sir James, 166n7
Freud, Sigmund, 15, 60, 62, 84, 156n6, 160n19
Friedman, Susan Stanford, 6
Futurism, 169n24

Garbo, Greta, 115
Gardiner, Juliet, 109, 172n1
Gardiner, Wrey, 130
Garman, Douglas, 150n3, 151n9, 151n13
Gascoyne, David, 15, 60, 64, 65–8, 72, 76, 79, 158n14, 159n17, 160nn18–19, 161n21, 164n31, 172n2
Georgian poetry, 112, 123, 175n13
Gervais, David, 36, 40–1, 154n23
Gikandi, Simon, 139
Gilroy, Paul, 11, 137–8, 139–140
Goldie, David, 147n1
Goldsmith, Oliver, 138
Gorer, Geoffrey, 171n32
Gray, Thomas, 43, 166n7
Griggs, Malcolm, 156n2
Grigson, Geoffrey, 13, 18, 64, 86, 109, 117, 118, 127–9, 131–2, 158nn14–15, 161n21, 170n30, 171n33

Gunn, Thom, 177n4
Gurney, Peter, 165n2

Hall, John, 118
Harding, D. W., 169n25
Harding, Jason, 2–3, 6–7, 9, 10, 142, 147nn1–2, 156n3, 157n8
Harrisson, Tom, 17, 79, 87–8, 95, 104–6, 165n3, 170n28, 170n30, 171nn32–3
Hegel, G. W. F., 65, 84
Heinemann, Margot, 71–2
Hendry, J. F., 118
Henry, Maurice, 163n28
Herrick, Robert, 43
Higgins, Bertram, 151n9
high modernism, 4–6
Highmore, Ben, 62, 78, 79, 81, 87, 89, 101, 103, 169n24
*Highway, The*, 104, 170n26, 170n28
Hobday, Charles, 150n3, 163n25
Hobsbawm, Eric, 168n22
*Hogarth Living Poets*, 47
Hogarth Press, 109
Holloway, John, 177n4
Hopkins, Chris, 120–1, 126
Hopkins, Gerard Manley, 42, 51, 52, 153n19
*Horizon*, 109, 131
Hubble, Nick, 58, 79, 82–3, 84, 92, 95–96, 103–4, 156n5, 156n7, 164n2, 165n4, 166n7, 167n11, 167nn15–16, 168n19, 169n25, 171n34
*Hudson Review*, 130
Hugnet, Georges, 66, 69, 163n28
Huyssen, Andreas, 157n9

# Index

hybridity, 79, 113, 116
Hynes, Samuel, 95–96, 162n22, 165n2

ideogrammic method, 81, 101–2
imagination, 80, 83–5, 95, 101, 102, 154n22
Imagist, 83, 112
Innes, C. L., 114
International Surrealist Exhibition, 58–9, 68–9, 160n19, 162n22
*Ireland To-Day*, 107
*Irish Statesman, The*, 107

Jahoda, Maria, 170n26
James, John, 145
Jameson, Fredric, 63
Jarry, Alfred, 163n28
Jennings, Elizabeth, 177n4
Jennings, Humphrey, 13, 68, 77–80, 82–4, 87, 88, 89, 91–3, 97–100, 102, 156n2, 156n5, 157n8, 164n31, 166n7, 170n25, 172n2
John, Augustus, 120
Jolas, Eugene, 55
Jones, David, 144
Jones, Glyn, 120, 121, 122, 124–5
Jones, Gwyn, 120
Jones, Sally Roberts, 121
Joyce, James, 5, 22, 96, 151n9

Kafka, Franz, 151n10
Kahn, Derek, 169n25
Keats, John, 43
Kenner, Hugh, 7
Knights, L. C., 149n1
Kumar, Krishan, 4
Kushner, Tony, 82, 107, 171n34

Laing, Stuart, 165n2
Large, E. C., 104
Larkin, Philip, 140, 177n4
late modernism, 4–5, 60
late modernist, 1, 5–6, 11, 15, 19, 59, 60, 63, 82, 107, 147n2
Latham, Sean, 7–8, 109
Lear, Edward, 66
Leavis, F. R., 7, 12, 14, 21, 22, 23, 25, 27, 28, 33–53, 57, 71, 86, 111, 130, 131, 134, 137, 144, 145, 149n1, 151n9, 152nn17–19, 153n21, 154nn22–3, 154nn25–6, 155n28, 158n15, 176n20, 176n22
Lee, Diana Brinton, 164n31
Lee, Rupert, 164n31
*Left Review*, 3, 16, 17, 64, 70–4, 80, 87, 88, 89, 97, 104, 161n19, 169n25
Legg, Stuart, 97
Lehmann, John, 109
Levellers, 71
Levenson, Michael, 2–3
Lewis, Alun, 120, 122
Lewis, C. Day, 48, 105, 158n14
Lewis, Wyndham, 5, 8, 22
*Life and Letters To-day*, 17, 87, 88, 91–2, 97, 120
*Light and Dark*, 87, 104–6
Lindsay, Jack, 70–2
Lindsay, Maurice, 119
*Listen to Britain*, 168n19
literary criticism, 11, 14–15, 22, 23, 24, 27, 33, 35, 38, 39, 43, 45, 58
literary review, 7, 14, 32, 33, 40, 43
little magazine, 6–7, 8, 108, 131, 178n5
Llanybri, 122–3, 174n13

Lloyd, A. L., 72–3, 162n26
Lollards, 71
*London Bulletin*, 64
*London Mercury*, 161n19
Longfellow, Henry Wadsworth, 167n10
Loy, Mina, 144
Lucas, John, 149n1, 152n14
Luddites, 71
Lycett, Andrew, 162n22, 174n12

Mac Low, Jackson, 96, 100
MacClancy, Jeremy, 164n1
MacDiarmid, Hugh, 50–1, 125, 144
MacKillop, Ian, 37–8, 152nn18–19
Macleod, Joseph Gordon, 144
MacNeice, Louis, 117–18, 155n30
McCaffery, Steve, 96
McGuinness, Patrick, 123
McKible, Adam, 6, 147n3
Madge, Charles, 17, 64–5, 67–8, 78–9, 82–4, 86–100, 104–5, 114, 155n30, 156n5, 159n17, 161n21, 165n3, 166n7, 167n16, 170n5, 170n27, 172n2
Malinowski, Bronisław, 17, 81, 90–1, 165n4, 165n6, 166n7, 167nn12–13
Manganaro, Marc, 165n4
March, Richard, 129
Mare, Walter de la, 149n1
Margolies, David, 70–1
Marlowe, Christopher, 66
Marshall, T. H., 170n26
Marx, Karl, 15, 45, 60, 62–3, 65, 84, 156n6, 160n19
Masefield, John, 149n1
Mason, H. A., 50, 51–2

Mass-Observation, 13, 16–17, 53, 76, 77–108, 146, 149n12, 156n2, 156n5, 156n7, 164nn1–2, 165nn4–6, 167n16, 169n25, 170n26, 170n28, 170n30, 171nn33–4, 172n2
Mathias, Roland, 120, 124
Matless, David, 67
Matthews, Sean, 44–5
*May the Twelfth*, 80–1, 86–7, 97–104, 107, 169n25, 170n26, 171n32
Mengham, Rod, 74–5, 162n27, 163n29
Mesens, E. L. T., 163n28
meter, 12, 14, 25–7, 148n8
Miller, David, 2, 143, 148n5
Miller, Tyrus, 5, 11, 60
Milne, Drew, 17
Milton, John, 43
minority culture, 12, 33
Miro, Joan, 64, 65
*Modern Scot, The*, 107
montage, 101–3, 169n19, 169n24
Moore, Henry, 164n31
Moore, Marianne, 50, 87
Moore, Nicholas, 118
Moore, Reginald, 130
Morgan, Kenneth O., 174n9, 175n15
Morris, William, 71
Morrisson, Mark, 6, 147n3
Mottram, Eric, 144
Movement, The, 13, 18, 135, 137, 140–4, 178n6, 178n8
Muggletonians, 71
Muir, Edwin, 29–30, 48, 140, 151nn9–10
Mulhern, Francis, 12, 39, 44, 155n27
Murry, John Middleton, 147n1

Nash, Paul, 164n31
*Nation and Athenaeum*, 87, 154n25
nationalist, 4, 58, 59, 65–6, 81, 107, 127, 138, 158n13, 164n31, 173n4
neglectorino, 178n9
networks, 3, 9, 10, 147n2
New Apocalypse, 10, 18, 87
*New Country*, 47, 168n16
*New English Weekly*, 39, 80, 104, 154n24, 161n19, 170n27
New Romanticism, 118
*New Signatures*, 47, 167n16
*New Statesman*, 17, 87, 88, 89–90, 97, 106, 154n25, 170n26
*New Verse*, 3, 7, 10, 16, 17, 18, 47, 53, 63–5, 67–8, 78, 86, 87, 88, 92–4, 99, 100, 105, 109, 156n5, 158nn14–15, 159n17, 161n21, 170n30, 171n33
*New Writing and Daylight*, 17, 109
Newbolt Report, 126–7, 134
*News Chronicle*, 87
Nicholls, Peter, 5–6, 61, 70, 162n22, 162n27
North, Michael, 92, 167nn12–13
Noxon, G. F., 156n2
Noyes, Alfred, 151n9

O'Connor, Philip, 118
objective reporter, 18, 109–10, 117, 118, 120, 126, 128, 172n2
Ogden, C. K., 90–1, 165n4
orature, 75, 163n30
organic community, 35
Orwell, George, 118, 173n4
"Oxford Collective Poem," 94–7, 169n25, 170n31

Parton Street, 74, 164n31
pastoral, 66, 92, 105, 121, 167n14, 175n13
Pattison, Neil, 179n11
Pattison, Reitha, 179n11
Penrose, Ronald, 164n31
Penrose, Valentine, 164n31
Peret, Benjamin, 66–7, 163n28
periodical formations, 2, 10, 11, 17, 19, 59, 145–6
periodical networks, 3, 147n2, 156n3
Perloff, Marjorie, 169n24
Picasso, Pablo, 65
*Poetry (Chicago)*, 161n19
*Poetry (London)*, 4, 10, 17–18, 108, 109, 115–23, 127–34, 141, 146, 173n6, 174n10, 176n20, 177n3
*Poetry Review*, 144–5
*Poetry Scotland*, 119
Poetry Wars, 144–5, 179n10
*Polemic*, 127–8, 131
Pope, Alexander, 43
Popular Poetry, 16, 79, 93, 167n16
Porteus, Hugh Gordon, 118
Pound, Ezra, 5, 41, 42, 48, 50, 51, 52, 81, 83, 96, 101–3, 148n6, 155n30, 166n7, 169n23, 171n33
Preminger, Alex, 73
Price, Richard, 2, 143–4, 148n5
Prynne, J. H., 145
pseudo-statements, 85, 166n9

racism, 137–8, 139–40
Raine, Kathleen, 79, 82, 97, 105
Rajan, Balachandra, 129–30
Ramazani, Jahan, 11, 112–14, 116

Ranasinha, Ruvani, 114, 116–17, 118, 173nn4–5
Ray, Paul, 68, 155n1, 158n13, 161n19, 161n22, 164n1
Read, Herbert, 60, 68–70, 72–4, 75, 76, 77–8, 161n19, 162n23, 162n26, 164n31
Reavey, George, 48, 156n2, 157n8
Reeves, J. M., 155n2
Remy, Michael, 155n1, 157n10, 158n13
retrenchment, 4, 6, 49–50, 63, 112
Rhys, Keidrych, 109, 119–22, 123–7, 174n8, 174nn13–15
rhythm, 12, 14, 25–6, 36, 37, 38, 148n8, 150n7, 152n19, 153n20, 167n10
Richards, I. A., 11–14, 21–7, 32, 36–8, 41, 42, 55–6, 58, 79–80, 81, 82, 83–6, 89–93, 99, 101, 150nn6–7, 151n9, 151n13, 152nn18–19, 153n20, 156n3, 165n4, 166nn7–10, 170n27, 173n7
Richardson, Maurice, 104
Rickword, Edgell, 1, 13, 14, 22, 23–31, 33, 38, 70, 145, 149n1, 150n3, 150n6, 151n9, 152n16, 162n25
Ridler, Anne, 118
Riley, Peter, 110, 145
Roach, Joseph, 75, 163n30
Roberts, Luke, 179n11
Roberts, Lynette, 109, 120, 122–3, 126, 174n8, 174n13
Roberts, Michael, 167n16
Romanticism, 4, 18, 59, 63, 69–70, 73, 77, 101, 147n1
Rosenberg, Alfred, 171n33
Rosenberg, Isaac, 46

Rosey, Gui, 163n28
Roughton, Roger, 74–5, 163n27, 163nn29–30, 164n31
Savage, D. S., 118
Scholes, Robert, 7–8, 148n6
Schwartz, Sanford, 102
*Scrutiny*, 7, 8, 10, 11, 12–14, 21–3, 25, 27, 33, 35, 39, 40, 43, 44–53, 57, 86, 109, 130, 145, 149n1, 155n27, 155n30, 158n15, 169n25, 177n22
second-order universalism, 22, 123
Sergeant, Howard, 142
Shakespeare, William, 40, 66
Shaw, Bernard, 149n1
Shelley, Percy, 43
Sheppard, Robert, 141, 142, 144, 145
Sheridan, Dorothy, 164n2
Sinfield, Alan, 134
Smith, Peter Macdonald, 124
Smith, Stan, 158n15
Smith, Stevie, 87
*Sociological Review, The*, 170n26
Södergran, Edith, 163n28
*Spare Time*, 168n19
*Spectator*, 178n8
Spender, Stephen, 48, 105, 114, 118, 158n14
Spenser, Edmund, 155n26
standards of criticism, 14, 21, 28, 31, 145
Stephens, James, 151n9
Stonier, G. W., 106, 170n26
Subramaniam, Alagu, 115
Surrealism, 10, 13, 15–17, 53, 55–79, 80, 81, 83, 101, 106, 145, 155n1, 156n2, 156nn4–5, 157n10, 158nn13–14, 159nn16–17, 160nn18–19,

161n21, 162nn22–3, 162n26,
  163n27, 164n1, 169nn24–5
Swift, Jonathan, 30, 66
Synge, J. M., 138

Tambimuttu, Meary James, 13,
  17–18, 108, 109–39, 141,
  146, 172n2, 173n5, 173n7,
  174n10, 175n13, 175n16,
  176nn17–18, 176n20, 177n1,
  177n3
Terry, Patrick, 106
Thacker, Andrew, 2, 9–10
Thiong'o, Ngugi wa, 163n30
Thomas, Dylan, 18, 87, 109,
  118, 119, 120, 121–2, 124,
  126, 127–8, 131, 140–1,
  158n14, 162n22, 174n8,
  174n10, 174n12, 175n14
Thomas, R. S., 109, 120
Thompson, E. P., 7, 147n4
*Times Literary Supplement*, 1,
  154n25, 161n19, 178n8
Tolley, A. J., 87, 95, 162n22,
  172n1
transcultural, 112–13, 116, 118,
  128, 137, 139
translocalism, 114
Treece, Henry, 118
Trevelyan, Julian, 155n2, 157n8
Tuma, Keith, 143, 144,
  178nn7–8
*Twentieth Century Verse*, 64
Tzara, Tristan, 65, 67

*Use of English, The*, 134

Victorian, 31, 152n16
Viswanathan, Gauri, 126

Wain, John, 177n4
Walcott, Derek, 113
*Wales*, 18, 120, 121, 123–6
Warner, Rex, 155n30
*Waste Land, The*, 1–3, 4, 13, 14,
  21, 28, 38, 48–9, 112–14,
  116, 153n21, 154n22
Watkins, Vernon, 120, 124,
  174n10
Webb, Beatrice, 87
Webb, Harri, 124
Webb, Sidney, 87
Wells, H. G., 149n1
*Welsh Review*, 18, 120, 121,
  130–1
Welsh writing in English, 110,
  119–20, 172n3
West, Alick, 72
White, Eric, 6, 147n3
Wilkinson, John, 123, 174n13
Williams, Gwyn, 127
Williams, Raymond, 9–11, 59,
  131, 134, 137–8, 154n21,
  175n16, 176n22
Wishart & Co., 74, 150n3
Wishart, Ernest, 150n3
Woolf, Leonard, 109
Woolf, Virginia, 5, 109
Wordsworth, William, 43, 73
Wright, Basil, 155n2
Wulfman, Clifford, 7–9, 148n6
Wycliffe, John, 71

Yeats-Brown, Major Francis,
  171n33
Yeats, W. B., 51–2, 140
Young, Alan, 69–70, 155n1,
  158n13, 159n16, 162n22
Young, Edward, 66

PGMO 08/24/2018